AF334410

JAPANESE HISTORY: A GUIDE TO SURVEY HISTORIES

Part II   Literature

日本文学史文献解題

JAPANESE HISTORY: A GUIDE TO SURVEY HISTORIES

Part II   Literature

日本文学史文献解題

Edited by
Naomi Fukuda

Ann Arbor

Center for Japanese Studies, University of Michigan
1986

Library of Congress Cataloging in Publication Data
(Revised for part 2)

Fukuda, Naomi
Japanese history.

In English.
Vol. 1 has parallel title in Japanese.
Includes indexes.
Contents: pt. 1. By period—pt. 2.
Literature.
1. Japan—Bibliography. I. Nihon shi bunken
kaidai. II. Title.
Z3306,F83   1984   [DS806]   016.952   84-1807
ISBN 0-939512-19-X (v. 1)
ISBN 0-939512-25-4 (v. 2)
ISBN 0-939512-26-2 (pbk. : v. 2)

Typeset by Typographic Insight, Ltd. and Kyōdō Ōbun Center, Tokyo
Printed in the United States of America

Contents

A   GENERAL HISTORY

D   MEDIEVAL PERIOD

AUTHOR/TITLE INDEX

FOREWORD

When in the spring of 1984 Miss Fukuda completed the manuscript of her *Japanese History: A Guide to Survey Histories*, she promised an additional volume covering the field of literature and the arts. True to her word, she has now compiled her second volume, and this in less than a year and a half.

Miss Fukuda's first volume was conceived as an updating of the volume on Japanese history in the University of Michigan Bibliographical Series published in 1954. So greatly had the field of history grown in the thirty years that had elapsed since the earlier work that Miss Fukuda was obliged to limit her coverage to the field of survey histories alone. And even with that limitation, she found it necessary to leave to a second volume works on Japanese literature and the arts. Those who are familiar with the 1954 *Guide* will realize that Miss Fukuda has done much much more than simply update the sections on literary history in that work. She has, in fact, provided a new and full coverage of the area of Japanese literary and cultural studies in a way never before attempted.

Dr. Rimer has written an appreciation of this remarkable effort from the point of view of the student of Japanese literature. It remains for me to acknowledge the importance of what Miss Fukuda has done for the general cultural historian. Here for the first time we find the work of Japanese scholars of literature, language, performing arts, life and culture, laid out systematically for the use of the analytical scholar. Admittedly the 1954 *Guide* had been heavily weighted towards political, social and economic history. With this volume, that bias has been remedied. This certainly is a major contribution for which all historians of Japan should be grateful.

John Whitney Hall
Yale University
September, 1985

FOREWORD

Research in the area of Japanese literary studies began modestly in this country during the early postwar years, yet has by now reached a level of sophistication that would have been difficult to imagine even a decade or so ago. One of the reasons for such an important advance in this area lies in the fact that there is now available in this country's libraries an ever greater quantity of useful and meticulous research materials, written in Japanese, which can guide and stimulate readers and scholars to broaden the base of their own enthusiasm and concerns. The first consistent attempt to document this body of scholarship in bibliographic form was the pioneering effort of Joseph K. Yamagiwa, *Japanese Literature of the Showa Period*, published by the University of Michigan Press in 1959. This volume, of course, only touched on the later modern period, although in a very useful fashion. Despite other occasional efforts since that time to deal with works in the Japanese language on the history of Japanese literature, however, no volume on a scale sufficient to encompass in an organized form the whole field of historical literary studies has been undertaken until the appearance of this authoritative volume by Naomi Fukuda, which now provides a guide to materials on the whole history of Japanese literature, and, implicitly as well, a sketch of the history of the development of modern Japanese scholarship.

Readers at any level of expertise in the Japanese language will find much to learn from this bibliography. To give one example, Miss Fukuda has chosen to introduce her readers to the ways in which the field of Japanese literary history has been conceptualized by scholars in that country. She has wisely retained Japanese categories of chronology and genre, so that the user will quickly become familiar with the mechanisms of literary scholarship as practiced in Japan. Miss Fukuda also supplies annotations where needed on the wide range of volumes she has chosen to include; although these are descriptive, rather than analytical, they serve their purpose well, as they identify for readers those monographs and other materials that have been viewed as valuable in the Japanese academic field. Indeed, there are few scholars in either this country or Japan who could attempt to provide an informed critical judgment on the vast array of items included. Miss Fukuda has travelled to visit a number of important collections in North America in order to compile her bibliography. Since no single library possesses all the items included, the bibliography can be used as a comprehensive checklist to identify items which can be then sought to augment a given collection.

Students, readers, and researchers in the field of Japanese literature will find themselves both grateful and excited by the opportunities that a book like this can provide. A look through its pages suggests new connections, new topics of interest. Many scholars who work in communities with smaller or more restricted collections in the Japanese language can now have access, and for the first time, to a conscientious and large-scale compilation of our national resources in this field. Because of the descriptive annotations and the indexes provided, researchers will now be able to locate materials that up until now have escaped certain bibliographic control, particularly as multi-volume sets are broken down to indicate the contents of each section, and books with evocative but ambiguous titles now have their contents plainly delineated.

This project of compilation has been an arduous one that has occupied the indefatigable Miss Fukuda for several years. I can only hope that the gratitude that all of us in the field of Japanese literary studies will feel for her efforts can help compensate her for her knowledge, time, energy, and enthusiasm.

J. Thomas Rimer
Library of Congress
October, 1985

PREFACE

It is now two years since we published volume 1 of *Japanese History: A Guide to Survey Histories*. It was well received by scholars and has become a standard reference guide in the field. We are pleased to complete this work by bringing forth the second volume, which casts a wider net over Japanese history.

Several institutions generously provided the financial support that made the project possible. We are grateful to the U.S.-Japan Foundation, particularly Richard Petree and Ronald Aqua; and to the Japan-U.S. Friendship Commission, particularly its former director, Richard Ericson. The Japan Foundation helped defray publication costs. Travel funds were received from the Northeast Asia Council of the Association for Asian Studies, and the Council on International Educational Exchange. We thank all these organizations, and those who helped us raise funds, including Professor John W. Hall and Shigeharu Matsumoto, Chairman of International House of Japan.

The faculty and staff of the Center for Japanese Studies would like to take this opportunity to express our regards and appreciation for Naomi Fukuda's many years of dedicated and skillful work as librarian and then as our research associate. The entire field has benefitted, but we have the pleasure of watching her operate.

John Creighton Campbell
Center for Japanese Studies
October, 1985

ACKNOWLEDGEMENT

I wish to record my heartfelt gratitude to Professor John W. Hall. It was his continuing interest in the bibliography that gave me the courage to see it through.

J. Thomas Rimer of the Library of Congress and Robert H. Brower of the University of Michigan gave valuable suggestions on selecting books and translating titles. My thanks also to the following scholars: Donald Keene, Robert E. Morrell, and Warren Tsuneishi; and to many librarians: Hisao Matsumoto and his staff at the Library of Congress, Hideo Kaneko, Ryoko Toyama, Eiji Yutani, Masaei Saito and the staff at the University of Michigan's Asia Library.

I am indebted to the Japanese scholars who contributed to this bibliography: Professor Shin'ichi Watanabe on education and Professor Toshio Iwasaru on book selection. Yuri Chiyo of the National Diet Library, Ikuko Horiuchi of the Keio University Library, and Mrs. Takagi of the Tokyo University Library verified the bibliographic particulars of each book and provided capsule descriptions.

Special mention is due to Masaei Saito, curator of the Japanese collection at the University of Michigan's Asia Library. His professional expertise was an irreplaceable asset in the compilation of this work. I am grateful to him also for his contribution of titles and annotations on book publishing.

University of Michigan graduate students who worked on this bibliography include Robert Rann, who edited the English annotations, Sharalyn Orbaugh who helped in general, and Rebecca Hubbert and Sachiko Nagai who helped in Heian period. Gregory Benadom read the entire manuscript and offered much appreciated advice on editorial matters.

Rebecca Hubbert and Elizabeth Murray typed the manuscript into the computer.

Finally, many thanks to Dr. John Campbell, Director of the Center for Japanese Studies at the University of Michigan, to Elsie Orb, Administrative Associate of the Center, and to Bruce Willoughby, Associate Editor, for bearing with me and the problems that arose in the course of completing this project.

Naomi Fukuda
October, 1985

INTRODUCTION

In the two years since the publication of Part I of this series, there has been a sizeable increase in the number of Japanese books held by libraries in the United States. The average increase in the larger university collections now stands at some 4,000 volumes per year. The introduction in 1983 of the CJK (Chinese, Japanese, Korean language) computer has made these books more accessible. When this computer reaches full operation it will lead to a national network of information on cataloging and locating books.

The CJK computer and the accessibility it affords does not eliminate the need for a select bibliography, however. Hence Part II- a bibliography of survey histories of Japanese literature, prepared as a guide and teaching aid for the student and the interested layman. It lists specific titles, gives a brief summary of their contents, and indicates trends in research followed by Japanese scholars over the past several decades.

There is a difference in the listing of pre-Meiji and post-Meiji materials. The pre-Meiji materials include specific titles of books and works on individual authors, grouped under the title heading or the author's name, e.g., Genji monogatari of the Heian period, or Chikamatsu Monzaemon of the early modern period. The post-Meiji materials are grouped under survey history topics, which include authors and their works.

Selection of titles: Reference works used in the selection of titles are as follows:

Kokubungaku kenkyū shomoku kaidai, by Ichiko Teiji. Tokyo Daigaku Shuppankai, 1982. 739p.

Kokubungaku nenkan, ed. by Kokubungaku Kenkyū Shiryōkan, 1977-

Kodansha Encyclopedia of Japan. Kōdansha, 1983. 9v.

and other survey histories.

EXPLANATORY NOTES

Scope: This bibliography lists books published between 1955 and 1982.

Arrangement: Entries are by historical period with subject subdivisions, and are listed in order of publication date.

Entries: Each entry is preceded by characters for author and title, followed by a romanized reading. No English translations of the titles are given in the entry headings. When a work is by one author, his or her name is the main entry word; all other works are listed by title. When a volume is part of a publisher's series, the name of the series is given in parenthesis at the end of the entry citation. In listing the contents of a multiple set of works or a collection of essays, the names of authors or editors are given for scholarly works, while only the English translations of titles are given for other works.

Place of publication: All works are published in Tokyo unless otherwise indicated.

Pagination: Total pagination is given.

Names of persons: Family name precedes given name.

Annotations: Titles and contents are described as concisely as possible.

Index: Authors and titles are indexed in alphabetical order with entry numbers.

Japanese terms: Those listed in *Webster's seventh new collegiate dictionary*, 1972, are used as they are. Common terms not in Webster's appear with brief explanations wherever necessary.

References used for the English translation of Japanese terms: For pre-modern terms, various English works on Japanese literature, *Kodansha encyclopedia*, *Kenkyusha's Japanese-English dictionary*, and *Japanese literature, character and culture*, by Robert E. Morrell. A comprehensive work on Japanese literature, with an extensive glossary-index, is to be published in December 1985, titled *Princeton companion to classical Japanese literature*, by Earl Miner, Hiroko Odagiri, and Robert Morrell (Princeton University Press, 1985). For modern terms and translations of titles: *Dawn to the West, Japanese literature in the modern era*, by Donald Keene (Holt, Rhinehart and Winston, 1984. 2v.).

Macrons: Geographical names: macrons are used for obscure place names, but not for well-known regional and metropolitan city names. Macrons are omitted in corporate names that begin with place names, such as Tokyo Daigaku, etc. Era names: macrons are used for pre-Meiji era names, but not for post-Meiji era names, e.g., Taisho, Showa. Macrons are omitted in corporate names that begin with post-Meiji era names.

Festschrift: Kinen ronbunshū (A collection of essays by students and colleagues) are published to honor a Professor on his 60th, 77th, and 88th year. The essays gathered for the celebration of the 60th year are often edited in the name of the Professor himself, and are treated as a festschrift.

Ⓐ GENERAL HISTORY

This section contains works of general history - i.e., histories of several period or literary genres. It does not contain reference works such as encyclopedias or dictionaries. For these the reader should see *Bibliography of reference works*, published by the Center for Japanese Studies in 1979.

GENERAL

A1 久松潜一　日本文学研究史
Hisamatsu Sen'ichi. *Nihon bungaku kenkyūshi*. Yamada Shoin, 1957. 365p.

History of the study of Japanese literature, arranged by period and subject.

V.1 Classical literature.
V.2 Medieval poetry (waka).
V.3 National Japanese literature. Index.

A2 風巻景次郎　日本文学史の研究
Kazamaki Keijirō. *Nihon bungakushi no kenkyū*. Kadokawa Shoten, 1961. 2v.

A collection of essays on the study of Japanese literary history. Essays selected by Saigō Nobutsuna, et. al.

V.1 Focuses on Heian narrative literature and aesthetics.
V.2 Contains essays on waka and zuihitsu (essays) as well as sections on Saigyō, Ki no Tsurayuki, and others. A short bio-bibliography is appended.

A3 日 本 女 流 文 学 史
Nihon joryū bungakushi. Dōbun Shoin, 1969. 2v.

A history of literary works by women.

V.1 The ancient and medieval periods, ed. by Hisamatsu Sen'ichi.

V.2 The Edo and modern periods, ed. by Yoshida Seiichi.

A4 古 典 と そ の 時 代
Koten to sono jidai. New ed. San'ichi Shobō, 1971. 8v.

A series on the literary classics.

V.1 *Kojiki, Nihon shoki*, by Umezawa Iseji.
V.2 *Man'yōshū*, by Yoshinaga Noboru.
V.3 Fiction, by Nanba Hiroshi.
V.4 *Heike monogatari*, by Tani Hiroshi.
V.5 Setsuwa (legendary tales) literature and picture scrolls, by Masuda Osamu.
V.6 Chikamatsu Monzaemon, by Mori Osamu.
V.7 Bashō, by Asada Zenjirō, and Yayoshi Kan'ichi.
V.8 Saikaku, by Noda Hisao.

A5 久徳高文　国文学草径
Kyūtoku Takafumi. *Kokubungaku sōkei*. Ōfūsha, 1974. 392p.

Essays and lectures on topics in literature from ancient to modern times with emphasis on medieval waka and modern tanka. Includes verification of botanical names used in classical literature. Contains numerous excerpts from literary texts.

A6 日 本 文 学 史　久松潜一 等編
Nihon bungakushi, ed. by Hisamatsu Sen'ichi, et al. New, enlarged ed. Shibundō, 1975. 7v.

History of Japanese literature. Each volume includes a list of reference materials.

V.1 Ancient period.
V.2 Heian period.
V.3 Medieval period.
V.4 Early modern period.
V.5 Modern period, 1 (Meiji).
V.6 Modern period, 2 (Taisho and Showa).

V.7 General introduction and chronology. General index.

A7　日本古典文学史の基礎知識　秋山虔 等編
Nihon koten bungakushi no kiso chishiki, ed. by Akiyama Ken, et al. Yūhikaku, 1975. 533p.

Basics of Japanese literary history; toward an understanding of literary tradition. Consists of short, signed articles, with an index to works, topics and personal names.

A8　実方　清　日本文芸学
Sanekata Kiyoshi. *Nihon bungeigaku.* Ōfūsha, 1976. 333p.

Essays on selected topics in the history of Japanese literature. Discusses methodology of the field, with emphasis on language, thought and aesthetic background.

A9　久松潜一　日本文学評論史
Hisamatsu Sen'ichi. *Nihon bungaku hyōronshi.* Enlarged ed. Shibundō, 1976. 5v.

History of Japanese criticism.

V.1 The ancient and modern periods.
V.2 The early modern and modern periods.
V.3 General criticism, poetics, style.
V.4 Poetry and waka.
V.5 Thought and expression. Reference bibliography.

A10　日 本 文 学 史　木下正俊 等編
Nihon bungakushi, ed. by Kinoshita Masatoshi, et al. Yūhikaku, 1976. 5v.

Consists of signed essays by specialists on the history of literature, arranged chronologically.

A11　資 料　日 本 文 学 史　山崎正之 等編
Shiryō Nihon bungakushi. ed. by Yamazaki Masayuki, et al. Ōfūsha, 1976. 2v.

A college textbook. Provides a general introduction to the history of Japanese literature through excerpts from various literary works. Includes lesser known works and anthologies. Contains a chronology and a list of sources.

A12　近藤忠義　日本文学原論
Kondō Tadayoshi. *Nihon bungaku genron.* Shin Nihon Shuppansha, 1977. 352p. (Kondō Tadayoshi. Nihon bungakuron. V.1)

The pioneer work on the theory of Japanese literature, based on a historical and social analysis of authors and their works. 1st ed. in 1937.

A13　日本文学全史　市古貞次 等編
Nihon bungaku zenshi, ed. by Ichiko Teiji, et al. Gakutōsha, 1978. 6v.

Complete history of Japanese literature. Each volume includes a reference bibliography.

V.1 Antiquity.
V.2 Heian.
V.3 Medieval period.
V.4 Edo.
V.5 Modern.
V.6 Contemporary.

A14　加藤周一　日本文学史序説
Katō Shūichi. *Nihon bungakushi josetsu.* Revised and enlarged ed. Chikuma Shobō, 1980-83. 2v.

An introduction to the history of Japanese literary thought. Compares the Japanese view of the role of literature with that of other cultures by placing emphasis on four periods of change.

The first change was brought about by the influx of culture from mainland China, the age of Man'yōshū, and the institutionalization of literature in the age of *Genji monogatari* and *Konjaku monogatari.*

The second change came with the political situation of the two imperial governments and cultural influences in the reformation of Buddhism: the age when the Nō and kyōgen flourished under feudalism.

The third change came in the Edo period when Confucian and national learning (kokugaku) scholars prospered.

The fourth change came in the Meiji period when Japan started modernizing all phases of the arts and sciences.

The modern period is analyzed by grouping scholars and literary men by the age in which they lived, e.g. 1830's, 1860's, 1880's, and 1900's. Each volume is indexed. V.1 was translated by David Chibbett in 1979, titled: A history of Japanese literature: the first thousand years; V.2, The years of isolation, and V.3, The modern years, translated by Don Sanders, cover V.2 of Katō Shūichi's work.

Thought

A15　宮西一積　日本文学の思想史
Miyanishi Kazumi. *Nihon bungaku no shisōshi.* Fukumura Shoten, 1958. 331p.

Introduction to the thought, both Japanese and foreign, that shaped Japanese literature. Includes a list of reference works, a chronology, and an index to works cited.

A16　永井義憲　日本佛教文学
Nagai Yoshinori. *Nihon bukkyō bungaku*. Hanawa Shobō, 1963. 282p.

An introduction to Buddhism in Japanese literature in 3 sections:

1) A survey of the influence of Buddhist literature; 2) a history of Buddhist chant; 3) a bibliography of reference works.

A17　津田左右吉　文学に現はれたる我が国民思想の研究
Tsuda Sōkichi. *Bungaku ni arawaretaru waga kokumin shisō no kenkyū*. Rev. ed. Iwanami Shoten, 1965-69. 5v. (His complete works, v.4-8)

Japanese National thought as manifested in the literature.

V.1　From the period of aristocratic literature to the Kamakura period.
V.2　From the period of warrior literature to the early Edo period.
V.3-5 Literature of the common people.

8 volume edition in the Iwanami bunko series, 1977-78.

A18　永井義憲　日本佛教文学研究
Nagai Yoshinori. *Nihon bukkyō bungaku kenkyū*. Toshima Shobō, 1966. 2v.

V.1　Discusses methodology in the study of Buddhist literature.
V.2　On issues relating to court women's literature and Buddhism.

A19　和辻哲郎　日本精神史研究
Watsuji Tetsurō. *Nihon seishinshi kenkyū*. Rev. ed. Iwanami Shoten, 1970. 271p.

Intellectual history of Japan. Consists of a study of Japanese civilization; Buddhist influence on Japanese culture; Heian period literature, (794-1185); history and criticism of Kabuki theater, etc.

A20　唐木順三　日本人の心の歴史
Karaki Junzō. *Nihonjin no kokoro no rekishi*. Chikuma Shobō,1970-72. 2v. (Chikuma Sōgō Daigaku)

Traces the history of Japanese lyrical thought, especially the appreciation of seasonal changes, with reference to various literary works.

V.1　From the ancient to the medieval age.
V.2　From the early modern period to the present. Index.

A21　臼田甚五郎　神 道 と 文 学
Usuda Jingorō. *Shintō to bungaku*. Enlarged ed. Hakuteisha, 1973. 316p.

A study of the relationship between Shinto and literature.

A22　津田左右吉　日本文芸の研究
Tsuda Sōkichi. *Nihon bungei no kenkyū*. Iwanami Shoten, 1974. 425p. (Tsuda Sōkichi zenshū, v.10)

Studies in Japanese literature and the arts. Contains excerpts from thirteen original works published between 1911 and 1951. Includes a general index.

A23　斉藤正二　日本的自然観の研究
Saitō Shōji. *Nihonteki shizenkan no kenkyū*. Yasaka Shoten, 1978. 2v.

V.1　The Japanese view of nature as exemplified by institutions, e.g. the 'ritsu-ryō' state, and literary works such as *Makura no sōshi*, *Ōkagami*, *Konjaku monogatari*.

V.2　The development of Japanese aesthetics, and the view of things in nature, such as pine, bamboo, chrysanthemum, etc. Index to both volumes.

A23a　九鬼周造　文 芸 論
Kuki Shūzō. *Bungeiron*. Iwanami Shoten, 1981. 518p. (Kuki Shūzō zenshū, v.1)

Reprint of the 1941 edition. Consists of essays on aesthetic interpretation of literature, including essays on the philosophy of refinement in literature and an anaylsis of emotions expressed in tanka such as joy, love, sorrow, etc. These two essays were reprinted in 1979, titled: "Iki no kōzō". (Iwanami bunko)

A24　日 本 思 想 大 系
Nihon shisō taikei (Compendium of Japanese thought). Iwanami Shoten, 1970-82. 67v.

Basic set of works on Japanese thought, from antiquity to the end of the Edo period. Each volume contains original texts with annotations, readings for difficult words, and explanatory articles, bibliography, biography, maps, etc.

V. 1 *Kojiki*.
V. 2 Collected works of Prince Shōtoku.
V. 3 Ritsuryō (statutes).
V. 4 Saichō.

V. 5 Kūkai.

V. 6 Genshin.

V. 7 Ōjōden, etc.

V. 8 Ancient socio-political thought.

V. 9 Absolute truth of the Tendai sect.

V.10 Hōnen; Ippen.

V.11 Shinran.

V.12-13 Dōgen.

V.14 Nichiren.

V.15 Early Kamakura period Buddhism.

V.16 Medieval Zen thought.

V.17 Rennyo and Ikkō sect riots.

V.18 *Omorosōshi*.

V.19 Medieval Shinto.

V.20 Origins of temples and shrines.

V.21 Medieval socio-political thought.

V.22 Medieval socio-political thought.

V.23 Ancient and medieval treatises on the arts.

V.24 Zeami; Zenchiku.

V.25 Books on Christianity.

V.26 *Mikawa monogatari*; *Hagakure*.

V.27 Military thought of the early modern period.

V.28 Fujiwara Seika; Hayashi Razan.

V.29 Nakae Tōju.

V.30 Kumazawa Banzan.

V.31 Yamazaki Anzai school of thought.

V.32 Yamaga Sokō.

V.33 Itō Jinsai; Itō Tōgai.

V.34 Kaibara Ekiken; Muro Kyūsu.

V.35 Arai Hakuseki.

V.36 Ogyū Sorai.

V.37 Sorai school of thought.

V.38 Edo period political principles.

V.39 Edo period National learning (kokugaku) and Shinto.

V.40 Motoori Norinaga.

V.41 Miura Baien.

V.42 Sekimon shingaku.

V.43 Tominaga Nakamoto; Yamakata Bantō.

V.44 Honda Toshiaki; Kaiho Seiryō.

V.45 Andō Shōeki; Satō Shin'en.

V.46 Satō Issai; Ōshio Chūsai.

V.47 Late Edo period Confucian thought.

V.48 Edo period historiography.

V.49 Rai San'yō.

V.50 Hirata Atsutane; Ban Nobutomo; Ōkuni Takamasa.

V.51 The Kokugaku movement.

V.52 Ninomiya Sontoku; Ōhara Yūgaku.

V.53 Mitogaku (Mito school of thought).

V.54 Yoshida Shōin.

V.55 Watanabe Kazan; Takano Chōei; Sakuma Shōzan; Yokoi Shōnan; Hashimoto Sanai.

V.56 Political theory at the end of the Edo period.

V.57 Edo period Buddhist thought.

V.58 Popular movement.

V.59 Mercantile thought in the Edo period.

V.60 Eroticism in the Edo period.

V.61 Edo period artistic thought.

V.62 Edo period scientific thought 1.

V.63 Edo period scientific thought 2.

V.64 Western learning 1.

V.65 Western learning 2.

V.66 Encountering the West.

V.67 Popular religions.

Multiple Sets

A25 国 文 学 論 叢　慶應義塾大学国文学研究会 編
Kokubungaku ronsō, ed. by Keiō Gijuku Daigaku Kokubungaku Kenkyūkai. Shibundō, 1957-63. 6v.

A serial publication on literature.

No.1 Saikaku-research and materials. 1957.

No.2 Medieval period literature, research and materials. 1958.

No.3 Heian period literature, research and materials. 1959.

No.4 Ancient literature, research and materials. 1961.

No.5 Modern literature, research and materials. 1962.

No.6 Early modern period fiction, research and materials. 1963.

A26 国文学論叢新修　慶應義塾大学国文学研究会 編
Kokubungaku ronsō shinshū, ed. by Keiō Gijuku Daigaku Kokubungaku Kenkyūkai. Ōfūsha, 1980-83. 6v.

No.1 Poetry and narrative literature of the Heian period. 1980.

No.2 Literature and folklore in antiquity. 1980.

No.3 Modern verse. 1981.

No.4 Medieval and early modern literature. 1982.

No.5 Origuchi Shinobu and his work, published in commemoration of the 30th anniversary of his death. I. 1983.

No.6 Origuchi Shinobu and his work. II. 1983.

A27 日本文学の歴史　高木市之助 等編
Nihon bungaku no rekishi, ed. by Takagi Ichinosuke, et al. Kadokawa Shoten, 1967-68. 13v.

The historical and social background of literature. Bibliography and chronology in each volume. Readings are given for difficult names and book titles.

V.1　The gods and those who worshipped them, ed. by Kobayashi Yukio, et al.

V.2　The world of the *Man'yōshū*, ed. by Takagi Ichinosuke, et al.

V.3　The court salon and women of talent, ed. by Akiyama Ken, et al.

V.4　Restoration and reform, ed. by Satō Kenzō, et al.

V.5　The literature of love and impermanence, ed. by Kadokawa Motoyoshi, et al.

V.6　Power struggles in literature, ed. by Okami Masao, et al.

V.7　Enlightenment, ed. by Inomoto Noichi, et al.

V.8　The diffusion of culture, ed. by Nakamura Yukihiko, et al.

V.9　The modern awakening, ed. by Itō Sei, et al.

V.10　The Japanese spirit and Western learning, ed. by Yoshida Seiichi, et al.

V.11　Songs of praise for humanity, ed. by Inagaki Tatsurō, et al.

V.12　The contemporary standard bearers, ed. by Yoshida Seiichi, et al.

V.13　(Supplement) Japanese literary atlas, and index.

A28 日本文学研究資料叢書
Nihon bungaku kenkyū shiryō sōsho. Yūseido, 1967- .

To be completed in 100 volumes in 3 series. A collection of previously published studies of literary genres, periods, authors, and their works.

Series I. 1967-77. 50v.

Japanese mythology.
Kojiki, Nihon shoki 1,2.
Man'yōshū 1,2.
Heian period fiction 1,2.
Heian period diaries 1,2.
Kokin wakashū.
Makura no sōshi.
Genji monogatari.
Rekishi monogatari.

Konjaku monogatari-shū.
Setsuwa bungaku (legendary tales).
Heike monogatari.
Senki monogatari (military tales).
Hōjōki, Tsurezuregusa.
Bashō 1.
Saikaku.
Chikamatsu.
Akinari.
Buson, Issa.
Bakin.
Modern poetry.
Kitamura Tōkoku.
Mori Ōgai 1.
Shizenshugi bungaku (naturalist literature).
Shimazaki Tōson.
Natsume Sōseki 1.
Ishikawa Takuboku.
Nagai Kafū.
Tanizaki Jun'ichirō.
Shiga Naoya 1.
Shirakabaha bungaku (white birch school).
Takamura Kōtarō, Miyazawa Kenji.
Proletarian literature.
Akutagawa Ryūnosuke 1.
Hagiwara Sakutarō.
Hori Tatsuo.
Yanagida Kunio.
Origuchi Shinobu.
Kawabata Yasunari.
Dazai Osamu.
Mishima Yukio.
Abe Kōbō, Ōe Kenzaburō.
Methodology in researching Japanese classical literature.

Series II. 1977-80. 30v.

Japanese mythology 2.
Man'yōshū 3.
Heian period fiction 3,4.
Shin kokin wakashū.
Nō, Kyōgen.
Bashō 2.
Tsubouchi Shōyō, Futabatei Shimei.
Kōda Rohan, Higuchi Ichiyō.
Mori Ōgai 2.
Natsume Sōseki 2.

Izumi Kyōka.

Akutagawa Ryūnosuke 2.

Shiga Naoya 2.

Yokomitsu Riichi and the new sensationalists.

Kajii Motojirō, Nakajima Ton.

Kobayashi Hideo.

Japanese romanticists.

Nakano Shigeharu, Miyamoto Yuriko.

Ishikawa Jun, Sakaguchi Ango.

Ibuse Masuji, Fukuzawa Shichirō.

Ōoka Shōhei, Fukunaga Takehiko.

Yoshimoto Takaaki, Etō Jun.

Saito Mokichi.

Nakahara Chūya, Tachihara Michizō.

Children's literature.

Literature of the Meiji era.

Literature of the Taisho era.

Literature of the Showa era.

Bibliography of modern Japanese literature, Meiji era.

Series III. (20v.) In progress.

Ancient songs.

Genji monogatari 4.

Saigyō, Teika.

Otogi zōshi.

Jōruri.

Japanese classical literature and oral transmission.

Natsume Sōseki 3.

Arishima Takeo.

Shi shōsetsu (I novels).

Miyazawa Kenji 2.

Dazai Osamu 2.

Itō Sei, Takeda Taijun.

Noma Hiroshi, Shimao Toshio.

Yasuoka Shōtarō, Yoshiyuki Junnosuke.

Modern women's literature.

Modern poetry.

Modern haiku.

Comparative literature.

Research methodology—modern period.

Yōkyoku, kyōgen.

Yūseidō published a 29 page pamphlet in 1983, indexing all the essays included in *Nihon bungaku kenkyū shiryō sōsho*.

A29 叢書日本文学史研究

Sōsho Nihon bungakushi kenkyū. Hōsei Daigaku Shuppankyoku, 1971-(80)- . (11v.)
谷川徹三　宮沢賢治の世界
Tanikawa Tetsuzo. The world of Miyazawa Kenji. 1963.
西尾　實　つれづれ草文学の世界
Nishio Minoru. The literary world of the *Tsurezuregusa*. 1964.
今尾哲也　変身の思想
Imao Tetsuya. Metamorphosis: the principle of acting in Japanese drama. 1970.
西田　勝　近代文学の発掘
Nishida Masaru. The study of modern literature.
外間守善　沖縄の言語史
Hokama Shuzen. A history of the Okinawan language. 1971.
前田　愛　幕末・維新期の文学
Maeda Ai. Literature of the late Edo and early Meiji period. 1972.
松田　修　日本近世文学の成立
Matsuda Osamu. The development of Edo literature. 1972.
瀬沼茂樹　明治文学研究
Senuma Shigeki. Meiji literature. 1974.
松田　修　日本芸能史論考
Matsuda Osamu. A history of Japanese performing arts. 1974.
仲程昌徳　山之口　貘
Nakahodo Masanori. Yamanoguchi Baku and his works. 1975.
服部幸雄　江戸歌舞伎論
Hattori Yukio. Studies in Edo kabuki. 1980.

A30 シンポジウム日本文学

Shinpojūmu Nihon bungaku. Gakuseisha, 1975-78. 20v.

V.1 *Man'yōshū*.

V.2 *Kokinshū*,1.

V.3 *Kokinshū*,2.

V.4 *Kokinshū*,3.

V.5 *Heike monogatari*.

V.6 Hermit literature of the medieval period.

V.7 Chikamatsu.

V.8 Matsuo Bashō.

V.9 Saikaku.

V.10 Ueda Akinari.

V.11 Literature of the late Tokugawa period.

V.12 Establishment of modern literature.

V.13 Mori Ōgai.

V.14 Natsume Sōseki.

V.15 Shimazaki Tōson.

V.16 Tanizaki Jun'ichirō.

V.17 Taisho literature.

V.18 Politics and literature.

V.19 Postwar literature.

V.20 Modern poetry.

A31　国語国文学研究史大成
Kokugo kokubungaku kenkyūshi taisei. Enlarged ed.
Sanseidō, 1977. 15v.

V.1-2 *Man'yōshū*, by Takeda Yūkichi, et al.

V.3-4 *Genji monogatari*, by Abe Akio, et al.

V.5 Heian diaries, including the *Tosa nikki*, by Akiyama Ken, et al.

V.6 *Makura no sōshi*, *Tsurezuregusa*, by Saitō Kiyoe, et al.

V.7 *Kokinshū*, *Shinkokinshū*, by Nishishita Tsunekazu, et al.

V.8 *Yōkyoku*, kyōgen, by Nishio Minoru, et al.

V.9 *Heike monogatari*, by Takagi Ichinosuke et al.

V.10 Chikamatsu, by Shuzui Kenji, et al.

V.11 Saikaku, by Teruoka Yasutaka, et al.

V.12 Bashō, by Imoto Nōichi, et al.

V.13 Tōson, Katai, by Yoshida Seiichi, et al.

V.14 Ōgai, Sōseki, by Naruse Masakatsu, et al.

V.15 Kokugogaku, by Saeki Umetomo, et al.

Each volume contains important critical essays of a sort seldom found in other publications. These are reprinted with explanatory notes and bibliographies.

Lecture Series

A32　岩波講座　日本文学史
Iwanami kōza: Nihon bungakushi. Iwanami Shoten, 1958- 59. 16v.

Iwanami lecture series on the history of Japanese literature. Each volume contains several short monographs (several chapters each), on topics in Japanese literary history.

V.1 The ancient period.
-The sagas of heroes, by Takagi Ichinosuke.
-Kakinomoto no Hitomaro, by Saigō Nobutsuna.
-*Kokinshū*, by Kubota Toshio.
-The origins of monogatari literature, by Kazamaki Keijirō.
-*Genji monogatari*, by Imai Gen'e.
-Setsuwa literature of the ancient era, by Masuda Katsumi.
-Ancient court life and women, by Satō Kenzō.

V.2 The ancient period.
-The early *Man'yōshū* period, by Tanabe Sachio.
-Yamanoue no Okura and Ōtomo no Tabito, by Takagi Ichinosuke.
-The spirit of the ancient nobility, by Ienaga Saburō.
-The introduction of kana, by Ōno Susumu.
-The development of monogatari literature, by Nanba Hiroshi.
-A history of the arts, by Ikeda Yasaburō.

V.3 The ancient period
-Myth and history, by Kawasaki Tsuneyuki, and Ishimoda Shō.
-Fudoki, records of regional customs and land, by Yoshino Yutaka.
-Incantory literature (jubaku bungaku), by Kurano Kenji.
-Ancient ballads, by Tsuchihashi Yutaka.
-Yamabe no Akahito and Ōtomo no Yakamochi, by Gomi Tomohide.
-Ancient waka (Japanese poetry) and kanshi (poetry in Chinese), by Sayama Wataru.
-*Makura no sōshi*, by Akiyama Ken.
-Ancient diary and travel diary literature, by Imai Takuji.
-The intent and themes of ancient literature, by Takasaki Masahide.

V.4 The medieval period
-Medieval Buddhism and literature, by Saitō Kiyoe and Kikuchi Ryōichi.
-*Hōjōki* and *Tsurezuregusa*, by Nagatsumi Yasuaki.
-Medieval diaries and travel accounts, by Ishida Yoshisada.
-Medieval poetic criticism, Hisamatsu Sen'ichi.
-Medieval songs and ballads, by Agō Toranoshin.
-Zeami, by Nishio Minoru.
-Illustrated scrolls (emakimono) and literature, by Mushakōji Minoru.

V.5 The medieval period.
-Culture in medieval period cities and villages, by Hayashiya Tatsusaburō.
-The art of recited narrative (katarimono), by Tomikura Tokujirō.
-*Heike monogatari* and *Taiheiki*, by Tani Hiroshi.
-Saigyō and Minamoto no Sanetomo, by Kubota Shōichirō.
-The origins and development of renga (linked verse), by Kitō Saizō.
-Medieval drama, by Toida Michizō and Koyama Hiroshi.

-Christian literature, by Morita Takeshi.

V.6 The medieval period.

-The culmination of medieval literature, by Nagatsumi Yasuaki.

-Setsuwa literature in the medieval period, by Nishio Kōichi.

-The development of medieval monogatari (tales), by Ichiko Teiji.

-Historical tales and zuihitsu (essays), by Matsumoto Shinpachirō.

-The world of *Shinkokinshū*, by Saigō Nobutsuna.

-Shinkei and Sōgi, by Araki Yoshio.

-Gozan literature, by Yasuraoka Kōsaku.

-The literature of the late medieval period, by Araki Shigeru.

-The development of medieval aesthetics, by Nishio Minoru.

V.7 Edo period.

-Early haikai, by Itasaka Gen.

-Yosa Buson and Katō Gyōtai, by Kuriyama Riichi.

-The kanazōshi genre, by Teruoka Yasutaka.

-Early puppet theatre (jōruri), by Tsunoda Ichirō.

-The literature of the Edo townsman (chōnin), by Mizuno Minoru.

-The literary view of Edo Confucianists, by Nakamura Yukihiko.

V.8 Edo period.

-After Yosa Buson, by Nakamura Shunjō.

-The art of Chikamatsu, by Hirosue Tamotsu.

-Ueda Akinari, by Moriyama Shigeo.

-The last phase of Edo gesaku literature (popular novels), by Okitsu Kaname.

-Kabuki, by Gunji Masakatsu.

-Kokugaku (national learning), by Hirano Jinkei.

-Illustration and the Edo novel, by Shibui Kiyoshi.

V.9 Edo period.

-The yomihon genre, by Shigetomo Ki.

-The culmination of literati consciousness, by Nakamura Yukihiko.

-Comic waka (kyōka) and humorous verse (senryū), by Hamada Giichirō.

-Edo period songs and ballads, by Kikkawa Eishi.

-The history of Edo dramaturgy, by Iizuka Tomoichirō.

-Edo period poetry and poetics, by Ōkubo Tadashi.

V.10 Edo period.

-Literature under the Edo feudal system, by Teruoka Yasutaka.

-Ihara Saikaku and thereafter, by Noma Kōshin.

-Matsuo Bashō and his disciples, by Ogata Tsutomu.

-The history of haikai and haiku criticism, by Miyamoto Saburō.

-The golden age of jōruri and thereafter, by Ōkubo Tadakuni.

-Kawatake Mokuami, by Yamamoto Jirō.

V.11 Modern: Meiji era.

-Tsubouchi Shōyō and Futabatei Shimei, by Sakakibara Yoshifumi.

-The origin and development of Japanese Romanticism, by Yoshida Seiichi.

-Modern haiku, by Yamamoto Kenkichi.

-The literature of Naturalism, by Kawazoe Kunimoto and Ino Kenji.

-The literature of the Aesthetic School (Tanbiha), by Takada Mizuho.

-Modern drama, by Ozaki Hirotsugu.

V.12 Modern: Meiji/Taisho period.

-Ozaki Kōyō and Kōda Rohan, by Itō Sei.

-The development of Realism, by Miyoshi Yukio.

-The literature of the Shirakabaha group, by Usui Yoshimi.

-Shishōsetsu (the I novel) and the psychological novel, by Odagiri Hideo.

-Modern poetry, by Ishimaru Hisashi.

-The development of modern poetry, by Andō Tsuguo.

-The history of military tales as literature and its modern form, by Sugiwara Minpei.

-The literature of the Meiji Restoration period and the revolution in literature, by Takami Jun and Hanada Kiyoteru.

V.13 Modern period.

-The literature of the enlightenment period, by Yanagida Izumi.

-The literature of Socialism, by Inagaki Tatsurō.

-Proletarian literature, by Sofue Shōji and
Takeuchi Yoshimi.

-Ishikawa Takuboku, by Iwaki Yukinori.

-Modern tanka, by Kubokawa Tsurujirō.

-Pre-war and wartime literature, by Nakajima
Kenzō.

-Modern literature and the Japanese language,
by Terada Tōru.

V.14 Modern period.

-Japan's modernization and literature, by
Nakamura Mitsuo.

-The history of popular literature, by Ara
Masahito.

-The development of modern criticism, by
Hasegawa Izumi and Yoshimoto Takaaki.

-Post-war literature, by Ara Masahito and
Noma Hiroshi.

-Translated literature, by Ōta Saburō.

-The classics and post-Meiji literature, by
Shioda Ryōhei.

V.15 Modern period.

-Modern Japanese thought and literature, by
Maruyama Masao.

-Mori Ōgai, by Katō Shūichi.

-Natsume Sōseki, by Ino Kenji.

-The Humanist group and the Artistic group,
by Hirano Ken.

-Taisho democracy and literature, by Senuma
Shigeki.

-The New Sensationalist group (Shin-
kankakuha) and thereafter, by Sasaki Kiichi.

-The Japanese people and literature, by Kamei
Katsuichirō and Maruyama Shizuka.

V.16 General.

-Civilization and literature, by Doi Kōchi.

-The forms of Japanese literature, by Okazaki
Yoshie.

-Folklore and literature, by Yanagita Kunio.

-Changes in literary style and language, by
Ikegami Teizō.

-Japanese literature in Chinese, by Kanda
Kiichirō.

-A history of the study of the classics, by
Kazamaki Keijirō.

-The literature of the Ryūkyū Islands, by
Nakahara Zenchū.

-The literature of the Ainu, by Chiri Mashiho.

A33　講座　日本文学の争点　久松潜一　等編
Kōza Nihon bungaku no sōten, ed. by Hisamatsu
Sen'ichi, et al. Meiji Shoin, 1968-69. 6v.

Lecture series: issues in Japanese literature.

V.1 Antiquity.
V.2 Heian.
V.3 Medieval.
V.4 Edo.
V.5 Modern.
V.6 Contemporary.

A34　講座　日本文学　全国大学国語国文学会　編
Kōza Nihon bungaku, ed. by Zenkoku Daigaku
Kokugo Kokubun Gakkai. Sanseidō, 1968-71. 14v.

V.1 Antiquity.
-Ancient life
-Chinese characters and literature
-*Nihon shoki* and *Nihongi*
-Fudoki (Records of regional customs and land)
-Comparative mythology
-Ancient ballads

V.2 Antiquity.
-Various topics in the study of the *Man'yōshū*

V.3 Heian period.
-Early prose
-*Kokinshū* and Ki no Tsurayuki
-Monogatari
-Poems and monogatari
-Literature of the court women
-*Gosenshū* and *Shūishū*

V.4 Heian period.
-*Genji monogatari*
-Izumi Shikibu
-Historical stories
-Chinese classical writing
-Priest Saigyō

V.5 Medieval period.
-*Shinkokinshū* and Fujiwara no Teika
-*Shinchokusenshū*
-*Shokushūishū* and later anthologies
-*Heike monogatari*
-Medieval setsuwa (tales)
-*Hōjōki* and *Tsurezuregusa*
-Diaries and travel accounts
-Buddhism and Buddhist literature

V.6 Medieval period.

-Poetic criticism and historical stories
-Waka in the Northern and Southern dynasties and Muromachi periods
-Linked verse (renga)
-Stories for women and children (otogi zōshi)
-Military tales
-Zeami
-Medieval songs and ballads

V.7 Edo period.
   -Haikai
   -Story books written in kana
   -Matsuo Bashō
   -Stories of everyday life (ukiyo zōshi)
   -Ihara Saikaku
   -Puppet theater and Chikamatsu
   -Kabuki theater
   -Confucianism and the Japanese scholars of the classics
   -Waka (poetry)

V.8 Edo period.
   -Comic verse (kyōka)
   -Supernatural stories and Ueda Akinari
   -The novelettes of the gay quarter and love stories
   -Santō Kyōden and Kyokutei Bakin
   -Picture books and novels
   -Edo raconteurs
   -Kabuki

V.9 Meiji period.
   -Meiji politics and literature
   -Ozaki Kōyō
   -Kōda Rohan and Higuchi Ichiyō
   -Romanticism
   -Social novels
   -New colloquial style writing
   -Haikai
   -Dramatic poetry

V.10 Taisho period.
   -Naturalism
   -Natsume Sōseki and Mori Ōgai
   -Literary sketches
   -The aesthetic group
   -The Shirakaba group
   -Akutagawa Ryūnosuke
   -'Watakushi' shōsetsu ('I' novel)
   -Christianity and literature

-Modern literature and tanka (poetry)
-Translated literature

V.11 Modern period.
   -Proletarian literature
   -The new sensationalist group
   -Modern criticism
   -Romanticism
   -Wartime literature
   -Postwar literature
   -Takamura Kōtarō
   -Modern poetry
   -Drama
   -Children's literature
   -Modern haiku

V.12 Issues in the study of Japanese literature.

V.13 The background of Japanese literature. Includes essays on setsuwa literature, geography, political environment, and music.

V.14 (Supplement) Annotated bibliography of works related to the study of Japanese literature.

Collected Works of Individual Authors (select list)

A35 岡崎義恵 著作集
Okazaki Yoshie chosakushū. Hōbunkan, 1959-62. 10v.

   V.1 Essays on the study of the arts in Japan.
   V.2 The form and development of Japanese arts.
   V.3 Studies in the arts of antiquity.
   V.4 Investigation of *Man'yōshū* style.
   V.5 The aesthetics of *Genji monogatari*.
   V.6 The art of Bashō.
   V.7 The symbols and spirit of Japanese poetry: medieval and Edo periods.
   V.8 The symbols and spirit of Japanese poetry: modern period.
   V.9 The novel in modern Japan.
   V.10 Poetry in modern Japan.

   There is a new edition titled: Okazaki Yoshie chosakusen. 1970. 10v.

A36 窪田空穂 全集
Kubota Utsubo zenshū. Kadokawa Shoten, 1965-68. 29v.

   V.1-3 Studies of poetry collections.

V.4 Studies of tales.

V.5 Studies of tales and essay literature (zuihitsu).

V.6 Travel diaries and zuihitsu.

V.7-8 Studies in waka criticism.

V.9-10 Essays on ancient literature.

V.11 Essays on modern literature.

V.12 Essays on modern poetry.

V.13-19 *Man'yōshū* commentary.

V.20-21 *Kokinshū* commentary.

V.22-24 *Shinkokinshū* commentary.

V.25 Commentary on ancient prose.

V.26 Commentary on ancient poetry (Chinese and Japanese).

V.27-28 Translation of *Genji monogatari* into modern Japanese.

V.29 Bio-biliography of Kubota Utsubo.

A37 久松潜一 著作集
Hisamatsu Sen'ichi chosakushū. Shibundō, 1968-69. 13v.

V.1 Japanese literature: methodology and intent.

V.2 Trends in thought.

V.3 Critical history: ancient and medieval periods.

V.4 Critical history: early modern and modern periods.

V.5 Poetics and poetic style.

V.6 Critical study of poetry.

V.7 Philosophy as expressed in literature.

V.8 *Man'yōshū*, I.

V.9 *Man'yōshū*, II.

V.10 Ancient Japanese literature.

V.11 The study of Japanese literary history.

V.12 Biography of Keichū.

V.13 (supplement) Author's bio-biography.

A38 風巻景次郎 全集
Kazamaki Keijirō zenshū. Ōfūsha, 1969-71. 10v.

V.1 Method in Japanese literary history.

V.2 The conception of literary history.

V.3 The development of ancient literature.

V.4 The writing of *Genji monogatari*.

V.5 Traditions of waka poetry.

V.6 The *Shinkokinshū* period.

V.7 The world of medieval waka.

V.8 The people of medieval Japan.

V.9 Criticism and general essays.

V.10 Post-war diaries and letters.

A39 小田切秀雄 著作集
Odagiri Hideo chosakushū. Hōsei Daigaku Shuppankyoku, 1970-74. 7v.

Collected works of Odagiri Hideo:

V.1 Essays concerning trust in people.

V.2 Democracy and literature.

V.3 Universities, students and literature: a guide to the study of literature and an essay on the image of students described in literature of the Meiji, Taisho and Showa periods.

V.4 Modern Japanese society and literature.

V.5 Survey of Edo period literature including Saikaku, Bashō, etc. and essays on Natsume Sōseki's style of composition.

V.6 Contemporary history of Japanese literature with emphasis on 13 representative works.

V.7 Thought and social environment in modern Japanese literature.

A40 山岸徳平 著作集
Yamagishi Tokuhei chosakushū. Yūseido, 1971-71. 5v.

V.1 Japanese literature in the Chinese language.

V.2 Waka literature.

V.3 Monogatari (narrative literature) and zuihitsu (essay literature).

V.4 Monogatari on historical events and battles.

V.5 Setsuwa (legends, tales).

A41 高木市之助 全集
Takagi Ichinosuke zenshū. Kōdansha, 1976-77. 10v.

V.1 Pre-war essays on *Nihongi*, *Kojiki*, and *Man'yōshū*.

V.2 Post-war essays on *Nihongi*, *Kojiki*, and *Man'yōshū*.

V.3 Hitomaro, Okura and Tabito.

V.4 Essays on the *Man'yōshū* and ancient literature.

V.5 The *Heike monogatari* and medieval literature.

V.6 Essays on the ancient arts and the rebirth of literature.

V.5 The environment of Japanese literature.

V.8 Techniques in lyricism.

V.9 Fifty years of Japanese literary study.

V.10 Chronology, bibliography and index.

A42 能勢朝次 著作集
Nose Asaji chosakushū, ed. by the editorial committee. Shibunkaku, 1981-82. 10v.

V.1 A survey of Japanese literature.

V.2 Medieval literature.
V.3 Edo period waka.
V.4 Nōgaku 1.
V.5 Nōgaku 2.
V.6 Nōgaku 3.
V.7 Renga (linked verse).
V.8 Renga, Haikai.
V.9 Haikai, 1.
V.10 Haikai, 2.

Festschrifts (select list)

A43 日本文学叢攷　西尾光雄　先生
9 *Nihon bungaku sōko*, ed. by Nishio Mitsuo
Sensei Kanreki Kinenkai. Tōyō Hōki, 1968. 349p.

Collection of essays on Japanese literature in honor
of Professor Nishio Mitsuo.

A44 日本文学論考　塩田良平　先生
Nihon bungaku ronkō, ed. by Shioda Ryūhei Sensei
Koki Kinen Ronbunshū Kankōkai. Ōfūsha, 1970.
596p.

Collection of essays on classical and modern Japanese literature in honor of Professor Shioda
Ryōhei.

A45 近世近代のことばと文学　真下三郎　先生
Kinsei kindai no kotoba to bungaku, ed. by
Mashimo Saburō Sensei Taikan Kinen Ronbunshū
Kankōkai. Hiroshima, Daiichi Gakushūsha, 1972.
772p.

A festschrift in honor of Professor Mashimo
Saburō. Language and literature of the Edo and
modern periods. Emphasis is on the interaction
between linguistics and literature.

A46 国語国文学論集　武智雅一　先生
Kokugo kokubungaku ronshū, ed. by Takechi
Masakazu Sensei Taikan Kinen Kokugo
Kokubungaku Henshū Kankōkai. Matsuyama,
Ehime Daigaku, 1972. 422p.

Essays on Japanese language and literature in honor
of Professor Takechi Masakazu. Includes a bio-
bibliography.

A47 国語国文学論集　谷山　茂　教授
Kokugo kokubungaku ronshū, ed. by Taniyama
Shigeru Kyōju Taishoku Kinen Jigyō Jikkō Iinkai.
Hanawa Shobō, 1972. 562p.

Essays on Japanese language and literature in honor
of Professor Taniyama Shigeru.

A48 日本文学の研究　重友　毅　先生
Nihon bungaku no kenkyū, ed. by the Nihon Bungaku Kenkyūkai. Bunri Shoin, 1974. 479p.

Festschrift in honor of Professor Shigetomo Ki. 27
essays on various topics in Japanese literature.

A49 国文学論攷　鈴木知太郎　博士
Kokubungaku ronkō, Suzuki Tomotarō Hakushi
Koki Kinen, ed. by Suzuki Tomotarō Hakushi no
Koki o Iwau Kai. Ōfūsha, 1975. 903p.

Essays on Japanese literature in honor of Professor
Suzuki Tomotarō.

A50 日本文学の伝統と歴史　臼田甚五郎　博士
Nihon bungaku no dentō to rekishi, ed. by Usuda
Jingorō Hakushi Kanreki Kinen Ronbunshū Henshū
Iinkai. Ōfūsha, 1975. 826p.

Essays on Japanese literature: its history and tradition, in honor of Professor Usuda Jingorō.

A51 日本文学新見　野田寿雄　教授
Nihon bungaku shinken, Noda Kyōju taikan kinen,
ed. by the publishing committee, Kasama Shoin,
1976. 480p.

Essays on new perspectives on Japanese literature:
research and materials, in honor of Professor Noda
Hisao.

A52 日本文芸論叢　北住敏夫　教授
Nihon bungei ronsō, Kitazumi Toshio Kyōju taikan
kinen, ed. by Tōhoku Daigaku Bungakubu
Kokubungaku Kenkyūshitsu. Kasama Shoin, 1976.
640p.

A collection of essays on Japanese literature, in
honor of Professor Kitazumi Toshio.

A53 国語国文学論集　熊谷武至　教授
Kokugo kokubungaku ronshū, Kumagaya Takeshi
Kyōju koki kinen, ed. by Tōkai Gakuen Kokugo
Kokubun Gakkai. Kasama Shoin, 1977. 481p.

Essays on Japanese language and literature, in
honor of Professor Kumagaya Takeshi.

A54 日本文学―日本語　阪倉篤義　等編
Nihon bungaku Nihongo, ed. by Sakakura
Atsuyoshi and Hamada Keisuke, et al. Kadokawa
Shoten, 1977-78. 5v.

A festschrift in honor of Professor Sakakura
Atsuyoshi. Each volume consists of essays on Japanese language and literature.

V.1 Antiquity.
V.2 The Heian period.

V.3 The medieval period.
V.4 The Edo and modern periods.
V.5 The contemporary era.

A55 国語学国文学論考　岩佐　正　教授
Kokugogaku kokubungaku ronkō: Iwasa Tadashi Kyōju koki kinen, ed. by Hiroshima Bunkyō Joshi Daigaku Kokubun Gakkai. Keisuisha, 1978. 416p.

Essays on studies of Japanese literature and language, in honor of Professor Iwasa Tadashi.

A56 日本文学始源から現代へ　森山重雄　編
Nihon bungaku shigen kara gendai e, ed. by Moriyama Shigeo. Kasama Shoin, 1978. 572p.

Japanese literature from its origins to the modern era. Essays in honor of Professor Moriyama Shigeo.

A57 日本文芸の研究　実方　清　博士
Nihon bungei no kenkyū: koki kinen ronshū, ed. by Sanekata Hakushi Koki Kinen Ronshū Henshū Iinkai. Ōfūsha, 1978. 473p.

Essays in honor of Professor Sanekata Kiyoshi on Japanese arts and literature. Includes bibliographical references.

A58 国語国文学論集　松村博司　先生
Kokugo kokubungaku ronshū, ed. by Matsumura Hiroji. Sensei Koki Kinen Jikkō Iinkai. Kasama Shoin, 1979. 596p.

Essays on Japanese language and literature in honor of Professor Matsumura Hiroji. Includes a bio-bibliography.

A59 高崎正秀博士喜寿記念論文集
Takasaki Masahide Hakushi kiju kinen ronbunshū. Kokugakuin Daigaku Tochigi Tanki Daigaku Kokubungakkai, 1981. 491p. (Special issue of *Yashū Kokubungaku*)

27 essays on classical Japanese literature in honor of Professor Takasaki Masahide.

A60 文　学　論　叢　今井源衛　教授
Bungaku ronsō, Imai Gen'e Kyōju taikan kinen, ed. by the publishing committee. Kyushu Daigaku Bungakubu Kokugo Kokubungaku Kenkyūshitsu, 1982. 605p.

Studies in literature, a collection of essays in honor of Professor Imai Gen'e.

Collections of Texts

A61 未 刊 国 文 資 料　未刊資料刊行会　編
Mikan kokubun shiryō, ed. by Mikan Shiryō Kan-·kōkai. Hitaku Shobō.

Previously unpublished texts with commentary.

Series I, 1955-58. 10v.

V.1 Teika's jihitsubon (holograph) *Monogatari ni-hyakuban utaawase.*
V.2 Otogi zōshi, I.
V.3 Teika's *Hachidaishō*, I.
V.4 Imagawa Ryōshun's essays on poetry.
V.5 Otogi zōshi, II.
V.6 *Hachimonjiyabonshū* (collection of ukiyozōshi) published by Hachimonjiya.
V.7 *Yamato monogatari.*
V.8 Teika's *Hachidaishō*, II.
V.9 *Shinsen* (newly compiled) *Man'yōshū.*
V.10 *Zoku nanakuruma.*

Series II, 1959-63. 16v.

V.1 *Edoza haironshū.*
V.2 *Hōgen monogatari.*
V.3 *Kokinshū.*
V.4 Kana zōshi, I.
V.5 *Heiji monogatari.*
V.6 Otogi zōshi.
V.7 *Sagoromo monogatari*, I.
V.8 *Heike monogatari*, I.
V.9 *Heike monogatari*, II.
V.10 *Nara no ha wakashū.*
V.11 *Heike monogatari*, III.
V.12 *Heike monogatari*, IV.
V.13 *Haikai Tsuizenshū.*
V.14 *Genpei Tōsōroku.*
V.15 *Sagoromo monogatari*, II.
V.16 *Sagoromo monogatari*, III.

Series III, 1964-72. 18v.

V.1 *Kenchō hachinen* (1257) *hyakushu utaawase*, I.
V.2 *Soga monogatari*, I.
V.3 *Sumiyoshi monogatarishū.*
V.4 *Gikeiki*, I.
V.5 *Chūsei utaawaseshū*, I.
V.6 *Gikeiki*, II.
V.7 *Otogi zōshishū*, I.
V.8 *Soga monogatari*, II.
V.9 Ton'a's utaawase.
V.10 Early Genroku period, *Edo haishoshū.*
V.11 *Otogi zōshishū*, II.
V.12 *Gosen wakashū*, I.
V.13 *Gosen wakashū*, II.

V.14 *Chūsei utaawaseshū*, II.

V.15 *Atsutabon kaishi wakashū*.

V.16 *Chūsei utaawaseshū*, III.

V.17 *Kenchō hachinen* (1257) *hyakushu utaawase*, II.

V.18 *Okibon Shinkokinshū*.

Series IV, 1973-81. 10v. + supplement.

V.1 *Minobusanbon Hōbutsushū*.

V.2 *Soga monogatari*, I.

V.3 *Chūsei utaawaseshū*.

V.4 *Okazaki nikki*.

V.5 *Soga monogatari*, II.

V.6 *Beppon Wakan kensakushū*.

V.7 *Ihon Musashi abumi*.

V.8 *Renga yoriaishū*, I.

V.9 *Renga yoriaishū*, II.

V.10 *Otogi zōshi emakishū*, in West Berlin.

Supplement vol. Index to Edo publishers.

A62 日本古典文学大系
Nihon koten bungaku taikei. Iwanami Shoten, 1957-68. 100v.

Comprehensive series of major classical texts. Includes extensive headnotes and readings for kanji, as well as critical introductions to each work.

V.1 *Kojiki* and norito (Shinto prayers).

V.2 Collection of fudoki.

V.3 Ancient songs and ballads.

V.4-7 *Man'yōshū*.

V.8 *Kokinshū*.

V.9 *Taketori monogatari, Ise monotagari, Yamato monogatari*.

V.10-12 *Utsubo monogatari*.

V.13 *Ochikubo monogatari, Tsutsumi chūnagon monogatari*.

V.14-18 *Genji monogatari*.

V.19 *Makura no sōshi, Murasaki Shikibu nikki*.

V.20 *Tosa nikki, Kagerō nikki, Izumi Shikibu nikki, Sarashina nikki*.

V.21 *Ōkagami*.

V.22-26 *Konjaku monogatari*.

V.27 *Uji shūi monogatari*.

V.28 *Shinkokinshū*.

V.29 *Sankashū, Kinkai wakashū*.

V.30 *Hōjōki, Tsurezuregusa*.

V.31 *Hōgen monogatari, Heiji monogatari*.

V.32-33 *Heiki monogatari*.

V.34-36 *Taiheiki*.

V.37 *Gikeiki*.

V.38 Collection of otogizōshi.

V.39 Collection of renga (linked verse).

V.40-41 Nō.

V.42-43 Kyōgen (farce).

V.44 Medieval and Edo period songs and ballads.

V.45 Bashō's haiku.

V.46 Bashō's essays (zuihitsu).

V.47-48 Saikaku.

V.49-50 Chikamatsu.

V.51-52 Puppet theater.

V.53-54 Kabuki scripts.

V.55 Fūrai Sanjin (Hiraga Gennai).

V.56 Ueda Akinari.

V.57 Collection of senryū (humorous verse) and kyōka.

V.58 Buson and Issa.

V.59 Collection of kibyōshi and sharebon.

V.60-61 *Chinsetsu yumiharizuki*.

V.62 *Tōkaidōchū hizakurige*.

V.63 *Ukiyoburo*.

V.64 *Shunshoku umegoyomi*.

V.65 Critical essays on waka and Nō.

V.66 Critical essays on renga, haikai and haiku.

Added in 1964-68:

V.67-68 *Nihon shoki*.

V.69 *Kaifūsō, Bunka shūreishū, Honchōmonzui*.

V.70 *Nihon ryōiki*.

V.71 *Sangōshiki, Shōryōshū*.

V.72 *Kankebunshū* (Writings of Sugawara no Michizane).

V.73 *Wakan rōeishū*.

V.74 Collection of utaawase (poetry competition).

V.75-75 *Eiga monogatari*.

V.77 *Takamura monogatari, Heichū monogatari, Hamamatsu chūnagon monogatari*.

V.78 *Yo no nezame*.

V.79 *Sagoromo monogatari*.

V.80 Heian and Kamakura private poetry collections.

V.81 *Shōbō genzō, Shōbō genzō zuimonki*.

V.82 The writings of Shinran, the writings of Nichiren.

V.83 Collection of kana hōgo (Buddhist sermons in kana).

V.84 *Kokonchomonjū*.

V.85 *Shasekishū.*

V.86 *Gukanshō.*

V.87 *Shinnō shōtōki.*

V.88 *Soga monogatari.*

V.89 Gozan bungaku.

V.90 Collection of kanazōshi (storybook in kana).

V.91 Collection of ukiyozōshi (floating world fiction).

V.92 Edo haiku and criticism.

V.93 Edo waka.

V.94 Edo literary criticism.

V.95 *Taionki, Oritaku shiba no ki.*

V.96 Edo zuisō (essays).

V.97 Essays by Edo philosophers.

V.98 Kabuki jūhachibanshū (Collection of 18 Kabuki plays).

V.99 Puppet theater texts.

V.100 Edo waraibanashi (amusing stories) collection.

A63　古典日本文学全集
Koten Nihon bungaku zenshū. Chikuma Shobō, 1960-67. 37v.

Classical texts rendered into modern Japanese transliteration. Commentary and critical essays at the back of each volume. Vol. 37 consists of a series of essays by Kubota Shōichirō, et al., designed to give a comprehensive overview of Japanese literary history from antiquity to early Edo period.

A64　日本古典文学全集
Nihon koten bungaku zenshū. Shōgakkan, 1973-76. 51v.

Comprehensive collection of classical texts. Intended for student use, with extensive headnotes, modern paraphrase, readings for difficult kanji, and critical commentary.

V.1 *Kojiki*; ancient songs.

V.2-5 *Man'yōshū.*

V.6 *Nihon ryōiki.*

V.7 *Kokinshū.*

V.8 *Taketori monogatari, Ise monogatari, Yamato monogatari, Heichū monogatari.*

V.9 *Tosa nikki, Kagerō nikki.*

V.10 *Ochikubo monogatari, Tsutsumi chūnagon monogatari.*

V.11 *Makura no sōshi.*

V.12-17 *Genji monogatari.*

V.18 *Izumi shikibu nikki, Murasaki shikibu nikki Sarashina nikki, Sanuki no suke nikki.*

V.19 *Yo no nezame.*

V.20 *Ōkagami.*

V.21-24 *Konjaku monogatari.*

V.25 *Kagurauta, Saibara, Ryōjinhishō, Kanginshū.*

V.26 *Shinkokinshū.*

V.27 *Hōjōki, Tsurezuregusa, Shōbō Genzō zuimonki.*

V.28 *Uji shūi monogatari.*

V.29-30 *Heike monogatari.*

V.31 *Gikeiki.*

V.32 Collection of renga (linked verse) and haiku.

V.33-34 Nō texts.

V.35 Collection of kyōgen.

V.36 Otogizōshi collection (story books).

V.37 Collection of kanazōshi and ukiyozōshi.

V.38-40 Ihara Saikaku.

V.41 Matsuo Bashō.

V.42 Edo haiku and haiku criticism.

V.43-44 Chikamatsu Monzaemon.

V.45 Puppet theater.

V.46 Kibyōshi, senryū, and kyōka.

V.47 Sharebon, kokkeibon, ninjōbon.

V.48 *Hanabusa zōshi, Nishiyama monogatari Ugetsu monogatari, Harusame monogatari.*

V.49 *Tōkaidōchū hizakurige.*

V.50 Poetics.

V.51 Renga criticism, Nō criticism, haiku criticism.

A65　新撰日本古典文庫
Shinsen Nihon koten bunko. Gendai Shichōsha, 1974-76. 5v.

New collection of Japanese classics. Includes lesser known texts. V.1 *Jōkyūki, Jikaishū,* V.2 *Shōmonki (Masakadoki),* V.3 *Baishōron,* V.4 *Kogo shūi,* V.5 *Kyōunshū.*

A66　鑑賞　日本古典文学
Kanshō Nihon koten bungaku. Kadokawa Shoten, 1975-78. 36v.

Excerpts from classical literature with translations into modern Japanese, notes and commentary. Readings are given for difficult kanji.

A67　新潮　日本古典集成
Shinchō Nihon koten shūsei. Shinchōsha, 1976. 45v.

Shinchōsha collection of major pre-modern literary texts, including monogatari (narrative literature), poetry, etc.

POETRY

Waka (Japanese poetry)

A68　実方　清　日本文芸理論　風姿論
Sanekata Kiyoshi. *Nihon bungei riron: Fūshiron.*
Kōbundō, 1956. 424p. (Kansai Gakuin Daigaku
kenkyū sōsho v.1)

Systematic study of the development of waka, renga
and haikai from antiquity to the early modern
period.

A69　久松潜一　和　歌　史
Hisamatsu Sen'ichi. *Wakashi.* Tokyodō, 1969-70.
5v.

A history of waka poetry. Each volume is indexed.

V.1　General survey.

V.2　Ancient period.

V.3　Medieval period.

V.4　Early modern period.

V.5　Pre-modern and modern periods.

A70　女人和歌大系　長沢美津　編
Nyonin waka taikei, ed. by Nagasawa Mitsu. Kazama Shobō, 1962-78. 6v.

Collection of waka by women, from antiquity to
1945. Index to names of poets.

A71　日本歌人講座　久松潜一　等編
Nihon kajin kōza, ed. by Hisamatsu Sen'ichi and
Sanekata Kiyoshi. Kōbundō, 1968-69. 9v.

Signed essays on individual poets. Volumes are
divided by period: ancient, Heian, medieval and
early modern. V.9 (supplement) consists of a general list of poets and a general index. Gives
readings for difficult names.

A72　和歌文学講座　和歌文学会　編
Waka bungaku kōza, ed. by Waka Bungakkai.
Ōfūsha, 1969-70. 12v.

Lecture series on waka literature, signed essays.

V.1　The essence of waka and its expression.

V.2　A history of waka and its poetics.

V.3　Poet groups, utaawase (poetry competition),
renga (linked verse).

V.4　*Man'yōshū* and Imperial anthologies.

V.5　Man'yō poets.

V.6　Poets of Heian period.

V.7　Medieval and early modern poets.

V.8　Modern poets, 1.

V.9　Modern poets, 2.

V.10　Appreciation of famous waka, 1.

V.11　Appreciation of famous waka, 2.

V.12　A history of waka studies.

A73　和　歌　の　歴　史　藤田福夫　等編
Waka no rekishi, ed. by Fujita Fukuo and Abe
Masamichi. Ōfūsha, 1972. 294p.

Signed articles, chronologically and topically arranged, providing an introduction to the history of
waka.

A74　和歌文学の世界　和歌文学会　編
Waka bungaku no sekai, ed. by Waka Bungakkai.
Kasama Shoin, 1973-74. 7v.

An introduction to the world of waka literature
through signed essays on topical and historical
aspects of waka. V.7 includes a facsimile of *Kokin
wakashū jochū* (introduction and notes to the
Kokinshū), owned by the Yōmei Bunko.

A75　歌　論　集　橋本不美男　等編
Karonshū, ed. by Hashimoto Fumio, et al. Shōgakkan, 1975. 637p. (Nihon koten bungaku zenshū,
v.50)

A collection of important critical essays on poetry,
including *Meigetsushō* by Fujiwara no Teika and
Kokka hachiron, by Kada no Arimaro.

A76　阿部正路　和歌文学発生史論
Abe Masamichi. *Waka bungaku hasseishiron.*
Ōfūsha, 1977. 695p.

Topical essays on the origins and development of
waka. Includes an index and readings for difficult
kanji.

Kanshi (poetry in Chinese)

A77　日本詩人選　臼井吉見　等編
Nihon shijin sen, ed. by Usui Yoshimi and
Yamamoto Kenkichi. Chikuma Shobō, 1970-81.
30v.

Selected works of more than 30 poets, from antiquity to the Edo period. Each poem is given with
annotations and brief critical comments by specialists. Includes readings for difficult names. Index
in each volume.

Kayō (songs and ballads)

A78　志田延義　日本歌謡圏史
Shida Nobuyoshi. *Nihon kayōkenshi.* Isseidō, 1958,
1968. 2v.

A detailed history of songs and ballads from the period of the *Kojiki* and *Nihon shoki* through the medieval period. Index with readings for difficult names.

Continuation titled: *Zoku Nihon kayōkenshi*, 1968. Discusses songs and ballads of the Edo and modern periods, and the relationship between song and other literary forms.

A79 淺野健二　日本歌謡の研究
Asano Kenji. *Nihon kayō no kenkyū*. Tokyodō, 1961. 421p.

Study of Japanese songs and ballads, especially of the medieval and early modern periods. Traces the history of kouta (little songs) and lists collections of kouta from the medieval period. Also discusses dance songs and folk songs of the early modern period. Contains a bibliography of Kayō, p. 367-392. Indexes to subjects and songs.

A80 淺野健二　日本歌謡の発生と展開
Asano Kenji. *Nihon kayō no hassei to tenkai*. Meiji Shoin, 1972. 644p.

Origins and development of songs and ballads, in 5 sections: 1. Origins of kayō; 2. aspects of Heian period kayō; 3. characteristics of medieval kayō; 4. issues in early modern period kayō such as Okuni jōruri and early kabuki dance; 5. Japanese folk song. A collection of unpublished local dance songs, and a bibliography are appended. Index of first words of songs and a subject index.

A81 日本伝承童謡集成　北原白秋 編
Nihon denshō dōyō shūsei, ed. by Kitahara Hakushū. Sanseidō, 1974-76. 6v.

Collection of orally transmitted children's songs, organized by region, and covering the years between the early modern and end of the Meiji era. V.1 contains a reference bibliography; V.6 a general index.

A82 高野辰之　（改訂）日本歌謡史
Takano Tatsuyuki. *Kaitei Nihon kayōshi*. Revised ed. Satsuki Shobō, 1978. 1282p.

A scholarly history of Japanese vocal music. Traces the history of songs and ballads from antiquity to the Meiji period. Extensively documented, with source materials, illustrations, readings for difficult names and a detailed index.

The source materials collected for the above work were published under the title: *Nihon kayō shūsei*, revised edition, Tokyodō, 1942-61. 12v. This work was supplemented under the title: *Zoku Nihon kayō*

shūsei, ed. by Shima Shin'ichi. Tokyodō, 1961-64, in 5 vols. divided by historical period.

Haiku

A83 俳　句　講　座
Haiku kōza. Meiji Shoin, 1969. 10v.

Lecture series on Haiku:

V.1 History of haiku.
V.2-3 Biographies of haiku poets.
V.4 Commentaries on famous classical haiku.
V.5 Haiku poetics and prose haiku.
V.6 Commentaries on famous contemporary haiku.
V.7 History of modern haiku.
V.8 Modern haiku poets.
V.9 History of the study of haiku.
V.10 History of haiku of various regions. Bibliography. Index.

PROSE LITERATURE

Setsuwa (tales)

A84 日　本　の　説　話
Nihon no setsuwa. Tokyo Bijutsu Shuppan, 1973-76. 8v.

Each volume is a collection of signed essays on topics in the study of setsuwa. Readings are given for difficult names.

V.1 A general introduction to the origins and background of setsuwa in India, China and Japan.
V.2 The influence of setsuwa literature on other genre of literature from the ancient and Heian periods.
V.3 The relationship between medieval setsuwa and Buddhism, and between setsuwa and other medieval literary genres.
V.4 The origins of specific types of setsuwa and their relationship to medieval fiction and drama.
V.5 Setsuwa in the Edo period.
V.6 Setsuwa's influence on children's literature and on modern writers (including Mori Ōgai, Yamada Bimyō, Tanizaki Jun'ichirō, Akutagawa Ryūnosuke, etc.); the connection between setsuwa and European fairy tales.
V.7 The literary style and form of setsuwa.
V.8 A handbook and dictionary of setsuwa literature. Lists over 100 setsuwa collections,

providing information on author/compiler, contents and history of each compilation. Also lists over 80 modern translations, annotated editions, etc., of famous setsuwa collections, including critical commentary. Source material and index.

A85　論纂説話と説話文学　西尾光一 教授
Ronsan setsuwa to setsuwa bungaku, Nishio Kōichi Kyōju taikan kinen ronshū, ed. by Kubota Jun, et al. Chikuma Shobō, 1979. 580p.

Collection of essays by specialists on selected topics in setsuwa literature, a festschrift in honor of Professor Nishio Kōichi.

Nikki (diaries)

A86　キーン　ドナルド　百代の過客
Keene, Donald. *Hyakudai no kakaku,* translated by Kanaseki Hisao. Asahi Shinbunsha, 1985. 2v. (Asahi sensho)

One hundred generations of travellers: toward understanding the Japanese through diaries. A collection of critical reviews of 80 travel diaries, from Ennin's travels in T'ang China (838 AD) to the *Shimoda nikki* (1854) by Kawaji Toshiakira. (Not published in English) V.1 covers the Heian and Kamakura periods. V.2 the Muromachi and Tokugawa periods. Reference bibliography. Index.

Kanbungaku

A87　岡田正之　日本漢文学史
Okada Masayuki. *Nihon kanbungakushi.* Revised and supplemented by Yamagishi Tokuhei and Nagasawa Kikuya. Yoshikawa kōbunkan, 1960. 477p.

Traces the development of literature written by the Japanese in Chinese from the Nara to the Muromachi period. Index.

A88　和田利男　日本漢詩鑑賞のすゝめ
Wada Toshio. *Nihon kanshi kanshō no susume.* Aiiku Shuppansha, 1968. 216p.

Introduction to Chinese style poetry composed by representative Japanese poets, from Abe Nakamaro, 701-770 A.D., to Natsume Sōseki, 1867-1916.

A89　日本漢文学史論考　山岸徳平 編
Nihon kanbungakushi ronkō, ed. by Yamagishi Tokuhei. Iwanami Shoten, 1974. 624p.

Collection of essays by specialists on the history and study of Japanese literature in Chinese. A festschrift in honor of Professor Yamagishi Tokuhei.

PERFORMING ARTS

A90　須田敦夫　日本劇場史の研究
Suda Atsuo. *Nihon gekijōshi no kenkyū.* Sagami Shobō, 509p.

A history of the theater in Japan, from antiquity through the Edo period. Emphasis is on staging and the design of the theater itself. Chronology of Japanese theaters and troupes. Illustrations. Index.

A91　河竹繁俊　日本演劇全史
Kawatake Shigetoshi. *Nihon engeki zenshi.* Iwanami Shoten, 1959. 1490p.

Authoritative history of Japanese theater, covering court dance and music (bugaku), Nō, the rise and fall of kabuki, the diversification of kabuki in the Meiji, Taisho, Showa periods, and modern theatrical arts. Illustrations, detailed index.

A92　井浦芳信　日本演劇史
Inoura Yoshinobu. *Nihon engekishi.* Shibundō, 1963. 1578p.

History of Japanese theater from ancient court dance and music to contemporary theater, with emphasis on ancient and medieval arts and the development of Nō. Gives readings for difficult names. Index.

A93　河竹繁俊　日本戯曲史
Kawatake Shigetoshi. *Nihon gikyokushi.* Ōfūsha, 1964. 701p. (Nihon janru betsu bungakushi, v.9)

A history of Japanese drama from antiquity to modern times, tracing in detail the development of Nō, kabuki and jōruri (the puppet theater). Includes readings for special names. A detailed index.

A94　河竹繁俊　概説　日本演劇史
Kawatake Shigetoshi. *Gaisetsu Nihon engekishi.* Iwanami Shoten, 1966. 533p.

A survey history of Japanese drama intended for students and the general reader. Contains many illustrations and genealogies of famous theatrical families. Gives readings for special names. A detailed index.

A95　本田安次　日本の民俗芸能
Honda Yasuji. *Nihon no minzoku geinō.* Mokujisha, 1966- 70. 5v.

A study of the early forms of popular performing arts before they developed into the high art forms of Nō, kyōgen, etc. Each volume includes an index.

V.1 Kagura (sacred Shinto music and dance).

V.2 Dengaku and fūryū (ritual Shinto and Buddhist music and dance).

V.3 Ennen (dance performed by priests).

V.4 Katarimono (dramatic recitation) and fūryū, 2.

V.5 Performing arts of Okinawa and the southern islands.

A96 日本の古典芸能　芸能史研究会編
Nihon no koten geinō, ed. by Geinōshi Kenkyūkai. Heibonsha, 1969-71. 10v.

Japan's traditional performing arts. Each volume is edited by specialists, discussing the history and practice of the performing arts. Bibliography. Illustrated and indexed.

V.1 Kagura (Shinto music).

V.2 Gagaku (Court music).

V.3 Nō.

V.4 Kyōgen.

V.5 The tea ceremony, flower arranging, incense.

V.6 Dance

V.7 Jōruri (The puppet theater).

V.8 Kabuki.

V.9 Yose (variety hall).

V.10 Essays on comparative arts.

A97 折口信夫　日本芸能史ノート編
Origuchi Shinobu. *Nihon geinōshi nōtohen*, ed. by Origuchi Hakushi Kinen Kodai Kenkyūjo. Chūō Kōronsha, 1971. 516p. (Origuchi Shinobu zenshū, Nōtohen, v.5)

Notes on the performing arts, from the earliest, prototypical forms to the established forms such as Nō and kyōgen. Includes essays on the beliefs and cultural background that gave rise to the arts in ancient Japan. Index.

A98 日本庶民文化資料集成　芸能史研究会編
Nihon shomin bunka shiryō shūsei, ed. by Geinōshi Kenkyūkai. San'ichi Shobō, 1973-79. 16v.

A collection of texts concerning Japanese popular culture.

V.1 Kagura, Bugaku (court dance).

V.2 Dengaku (ritual Shinto and Buddhist music and dance), Sarugaku (antecedent of Nō).

V.3 Nō.

V.4 Kyōgen.

V.5 Kayō (songs and ballads).

V.6 Kabuki.

V.7 Ningyō jōruri (puppet theater).

V.8 Yose (variety hall and misemono).

V.9 Games.

V.10 Refined arts.

V.11 Performing arts of the Southern islands.

V.12-15 Records of performing arts.

V.16 (Supplement) Chronology of the performing arts.

A99 岩橋小弥太　芸能史叢説
Iwahashi Koyata. *Geinōshi sōsetsu*. Yoshikawa Kōbunkan, 1975. 446p.

Essays on the history of the performing arts from ancient times to the middle ages. Includes detailed commentary on specific ballads, dances, musical forms, Nō and kyōgen.

A100 三隅治雄　芸能史の民俗的研究
Misumi Haruo. *Geinōshi no minzokuteki kenkyū*. Tokyodō, 1976. 373p.

Folkloristic studies on the history of the performing arts. Covers Japan and Okinawa from antiquity to the early modern period.

A101 芸能論纂　本田安次博士
Geinō ronsan, ed. by Honda Yasuji Hakushi Koki Kinenkai. Kinseisha, 1976. 764p.

Festschrift in honor of Professor Honda Yasuji. Most of the 37 essays that make up the book concentrate on the folk or popular performing arts of Japan. Illustrations.

A102 芸能と文学　井浦芳信博士
Geinō to bungaku: Inoura Yoshinobu Hakushi kakō kinen ronbunshū. Kasama Shoin, 1977. 529p.

Festschrift in honor of Professor Inoura Yoshinobu. Essay subjects range from ancient music and dance, to Chikamatsu and the puppet theater.

A103 日本の芸談　尾崎秀樹等編
Nihon no geidan, ed. by Ozaki Hotsuki, et al. Kyūgei Shuppan, 1978-79. 8v.

Essays on the performing arts. Each volume is edited by a specialist in the subject. V.1-2 Kabuki; V.3 Nō, kyōgen, and jōruri; V.4 Dance and music; V.5 The new school of drama, comedy; V.6 Motion pictures; V.7-8 Dramatic arts.

A104　大衆芸能資料集成
Taishū geinō shiryō shūsei. San'ichi Shobō,
1980-81. 10v.

Collection of texts on the popular arts.

V.1　Sacred and festival arts, I: manzai (felicitous
recitation and dance).

V.2　Sacred and festival arts, II: kagura (Shinto
music).

V.3　Sacred and festival arts, III: zashikigei (performing arts at banquets), etc., daidōgei (street
arts).

V.4　Yose arts (variety hall), I: rakugo (comic
monologue).

V.5　Yose arts, II: Kōdan (storytelling).

V.6　Yose arts, III: rōkyoku (narration of historical
stories).

V.7　Yose arts, IV: manzai (comic dialogue).

V.8　Stage arts, I: niwaka (impromptu kyōgen),
mansaku (Kanto region folk dance), kagura
shibai (Shinto music and drama).

V.9　Stage arts, II: popular drama, I.

V.10　Stage arts, III: popular drama, II.

A105　日 本 芸 能 史　芸能史研究会 編
Nihon geinōshi, ed. by Geinōshi kenkyūkai. Hōsei
Daigaku, 1981-83. 7v.

History of Japanese performing arts:

V.1　The primitive and the ancient period.

V.2　From antiquity to the Kamakura period.

V.3　The medieval period: war period of the Northern and Southern courts and the Muromachi
period.

V.4　From the medieval period to the Kan'ei era of
the early modern period, 1532-1644.

V.5　1661-1801 of the early modern period.

V.6　From Bunka-Bunsei to the 20th year of Meiji,
1804/1830-1886.

V.7　From the 20th year of Meiji to the present,
1886-1975.

Each volume contains a reference bibliography.

Music

A106　吉川英史　日本音楽の歴史
Kikkawa Eishi. *Nihon ongaku no rekishi.* Sōgensha,
1965. 733p.

A history of traditional Japanese music, from antiquity to modern times, with emphasis on the music
of the Edo period.

A107　岸辺成雄　日 本 の 音 楽
Kishibe Shigeo. *Nihon no ongaku*: rekishi to riron.
Kokuritsu Gekijō Jigyōbu, 1974. 104p. (Kokuritsu
Gekijo geinō kanshō kōza)

The history and theory of Japanese music. A primer
of Japanese traditional music, part of a lecture
series of publications on the appreciation of the arts
sponsored by the National Theater of Japan. Includes a bibliography and a chronological table.

Narrative Arts

A108　角川源義　語り物文芸の発生
Kadokawa Gen'yoshi. *Katarimono bungei no
hassei.* Tokyodō, 1975. 621p.

The development of narrative arts. Traces the origin
and refinement of narrative arts from antiquity
through the Edo period, focusing on the relationship
between katarimono and other art forms. Also comments in detail on famous recited narratives such as
Heike Monogatari, Soga Monogatari, Gikeiki and
others.

A109　中山太郎　日 本 盲 人 史
Nakayama Tarō. *Nihon mōjinshi.* Yagi Shoten,
1976. 2v.

A reprint of the 1934 edition. A history of the blind
in Japan, from antiquity to Meiji 4 (1872), when
the Office for the Blind was terminated. Gives a
history of the role the blind played in the performing arts. Appended are a list of source materials and
an explanation of the specialized vocabulary used
by the blind.

A110　佐々木八郎　語 り 物 の 系 譜
Sasaki Hachirō. *Katarimono no keifu.* Enl. ed.
Chikuma Shobō, 1977. 289p.

The lineage of recited narrative, from antiquity
through the Edo period.

ORAL LITERATURE

A111　柳田国男　口 承 文 芸 史 考
Yanagita Kunio. "Kōshō bungei shikō," in *Teihon:
Yanagaita Kunio shū*, vol. 6. Chikuma Shobō,
1963. p.1-150.

Thoughts on the history of orally transmitted
literature.

A112　柳田国男　昔話と文学
Yanagita Kunio. "Mukashi banashi to bungaku," in
Teihon: Yanagita Kunio shū, vol. 6. Chikuma
Shobō, 1963. p.151-329.

Folktales and literature.

A113　柳田国男　女性と民間伝承
Yanagita Kunio. "Josei to minkan denshō," in
Teihon: Yanagita Kunio shū, vol. 8. Chikuma
Shobō, 1962. p. 315-451.

Women and the transmission of popular culture.

A114　口承文芸の綜合研究　臼田甚五郎 編
Kōshō bungei no sōgō kenkyū, ed. by Usuda Jingorō. Miyai Shoten, 1974. 314p.

Eighteen essays by specialists on issues in the study
of oral literature and the transmission of folk
culture.

A115　口承文芸の展開　臼田甚五郎 博士
Kōshō bungei no tenkai, ed. by Usuda Jingorō
Hakushi Kanreki Kinen. Kokugakuin Daigaku,
Bungaku Dai 2 Kenkyūshitsu, Kinen Ronbunshū
Iinkai. Ōfūsha, 1974-75. 2v.

A festschrift in honor of Professor Usuda Jingorō,
on the development of oral literature.

A116　関　敬吾　日本の昔話
Seki Keigo. *Nihon no mukashi banashi*: hikaku
kenkyū josetsu. Nippon Hōsō Shuppan Kyōkai,
1977. 424p.

Compares Japanese folktales with those of the West
and Asia.

A117　日本昔話大成　関　敬吾 編
Nihon mukashi banashi taisei, ed. by Seki Keigo.
Rev. and enlarged ed. Kadokawa Shoten, 1978-80.
12v.

Anthology of Japanese folktales. Grouped into three
types with more than 700 subdivisions. Also includes data on the distribution and variations of a
given story type.

A118　新編　柳田国男　全集
Shinpen Yanagita Kunio zenshū. Chikuma Shobō,
1978- 79. 12v.

Based on "Teihon Yanagita Kunio shū," 1963-71,
in 31v. A new complete collection of Yanagita
Kunio's works, rewritten in modern Japanese. Each
volume contains an explanatory essay by a specialist. V.12 contains a bibliographical essay, ed. by
Kamada Fusako.

LANGUAGE

A119　服部四郎　日本語の系統
Hattori Shirō. *Nihongo no keitō*. Iwanami Shoten,
1959. 421p.

The etymology of the Japanese language. Traces the
origins of Japanese using sources from Altaic,
Korean, Ryukyuan, and Ainu. Index.

A120　日本語の歴史　土井忠生 編
Nihongo no rekishi, ed. by Doi Tadao. Rev. ed.
Shibundō, 1959. 258p. (Kokubungaku kaishaku to
kanshō, special issue, 10/19/59)

Collection of essays which gives a sociological
interpretation of the history of the Japanese
language:
-The birth of the Japanese language, by Ōno
Susumu;
-The language of the Heian period, by Nakata
Norio;
-The language of the Edo period, by Yoshida
Sumio;
-The establishment and development of the modern
language, by Matsumura Akira.

A121　永山　勇　国語意識史の研究
Nagayama Isamu. *Kokugo ishikishi no kenkyū*. Kazama Shobō, 1963.

Studies in the history of the Japanese language from
antiquity through the medieval period. Based on
poetic criticism and other sources. Index.

A122　岩井良雄　日本語法史
Iwai Yoshio. *Nihon gohōshi*. Kasama Shoin,
1970-74. 4v.

Traces changes in idiom use, phraseology and syntax from antiquity through the Edo period. Each
volume includes readings for difficult characters,
and modern translations of ancient source materials.
Index.

V.1 Nara and Heian periods.

V.2 Kamakura period.

V.3 Muromachi period.

V.4 Edo period.

A123　講座　国語史
Kōza kokugoshi. Taishūkan Shoten, 1971-77. 7v.

Lecture series on the history of the Japanese
language.

V.1 A historical overview of Japanese, ed. by Matsumura Akira.

V.2 Phonology and writing systems, ed. by Nakata Norio.

V.3 Vocabulary, ed. by Sakakura Atsuyoshi, et al.

V.4 Grammar, ed. by Tsukijima Yutaka.

V.5 Honorifics, ed. by Tsujimura Toshiki.

V.6 Style and everyday words, ed. by Satō Kiyoji.

V.7 (Supplement) Contains source materials, chronology and a glossary.

A124　佐藤喜代治　国語語彙の歴史的研究
Satō Kiyoji. *Kokugo goi no rekishiteki kenkyū*. Meiji Shoin, 1971. 381p.

A historical study of the Japanese vocabulary, focusing on various geographical regions and various historical periods. Index.

A125　新村　出　全集
Shinmura Izuru zenshū. Chikuma Shobō, 1971-73. 15v.

V.1-7 contains essays and extensive works on topics in the study of the Japanese language.

A126　小松英雄　国語史学基礎論
Komatsu Hideo. *Kokugoshigaku kisoron*. Kasama Shoin, 1973. 538p. (Kasama sōsho)

Basic history of the Japanese language. Bibliography includes materials in English, French and German. Index.

A127　時枝誠記　博士論文集
Tokieda Motoki Hakushi ronbunshū. Iwanami Shoten, 1973- 76. 3v.

Collection of Professor Tokieda's essays on Japanese language study.

V.1 The essential nature of Japanese language.

V.2 Grammar and syntax.

V.3 Language in everyday life.

A128　シンポジューム　日本語　松村　明　等編
Shinpojūmu Nihongo, ed. by Matsumura Akira, et al. Gakuseisha, 1974-75. 5v.

Symposium: the Japanese language. Index in each volume.

V.1 The history of the Japanese language.

V.2 Japanese grammar.

V.3 Meaning and vocabulary.

V.4 Japanese writing system.

V.5 Dialects.

A129　新日本語講座
Shin Nihongo kōza. Chōbunsha, 1974-75. 10v.

New lectures on the Japanese language.

V.1 Modern Japanese words and writing systems.

V.2 Japanese grammar.

V.3 Dialects and pronunciation in modern Japanese.

V.4 The history of the Japanese language.

V.5 The Japanese language in everyday life.

V.6 The past, present and future of Japanese language education.

V.7 Writers and style.

V.8 The spoken language in modern Japan.

V.9 The people responsible for the shaping of modern Japanese.

V.10 Language in culture and society.

A130　岩波講座　日本語　大野　晋　等編
Iwanami kōza Nihongo, ed. by Ōno Susumu and Shibata Takeshi. Iwanami Shoten, 1976-78. 13v.

Lecture series: the Japanese language. Bibliography in each volume.

V.1 The Japanese language and language study.

V.2 Language in everyday life.

V.3 Topics in the study of the Japanese language and the classics.

V.4 Keigo (honorific language).

V.5 Phonetics.

V.6 Grammar.

V.7 Grammar.

V.8 Writing systems.

V.9 Vocabulary and meaning.

V.10 Written style.

V.11 Dialects.

V.12 The etymology and history of the Japanese language.

V.13 (Supplement) Issues in the study of the Japanese language. General index.

A131　土井忠生　国語史論考
Doi Tadao. *Kokugoshi ronkō*. Sanseidō, 1977. 386p. (Doi Tadao Hakushi On-Chosaku senshū v.3)

Nineteen previously published essays on the historical characteristics of the Japanese language. Divided into Christian literature, Heian literature and Kamakura-Muromachi literature.

A132　岩渕悦太郎　国語史論集
Iwabuchi Etsutarō. *Kokugoshi ronshū*. Chikuma Shobō, 1977. 550p.

Festschrift of previously published essays on the history of the Japanese language in honor of Professor Iwabuchi Etsutarō's 70th birthday.

A133　国語学と国語史　松村　明 敎授
Kokugogaku to kokugoshi, ed. by Matsumura Akira Kyōju Kanreki Kinenkai. Meiji Shoin, 1977. 1220p.

The Japanese language: its study and history. A festschrift.

A134　佐藤喜代治　日 本 の 漢 語
Satō Kiyoji. *Nihon no Kango*. Kadokawa Shoten, 1979. 466p.

Japanese words of Chinese origins.

A135　日 本 語 の 系 統　大 野　晋 編
Nihongo no keitō, ed. by Ōno Susumu. Shibundō. 1980. 273p. (Gendai no espuri, special issue)

Traces the origins of the Japanese language with reference to the languages of Tibet, Burma, the islands of Southeast Asia, etc.

A136　日 本 語 の 世 界
Nihongo no sekai. Chūō Kōronsha, 1980-(83) (16v.)

The world of the Japanese language.

V.1　Formation of the Japanese language, by Ōno Susumu.
V.2　Not yet published.
V.3　Chinese characters, ed. by Kaizuka Shigeki and Ogawa Tamaki.
V.4　Japanese characters.
V.5　Kana, by Tsukishima Hiroshi.
V.6　Grammar, by Kitahara Yasuo.
V.7　Phonemes, by Komatsu Hideo.
V.8　Words: East and West, by Tokugawa Munekata.
V.9　The language of Okinawa, by Hokama Shuzen.
V.10　Not yet published.
V.11　Poetry, by Ōoka Makoto.
V.12　Drama, by Kinoshita Junji.
V.13　The novel, by Noguchi Takehiko.
V.14　Prose, ed. by Sugimoto Hidetarō.
V.15　Translation, by Kawamura Jirō.

A137　講 座　日 本 語 学　森岡健二 等編
Kōza Nihongogaku, ed. by Morioka Kenji et al. Meiji Shoin, 1981-82. 13v.

Lectures on the Japanese language.

V.1　General introduction.
V.2　Historical changes in grammar.
V.3　Comparison of classical and modern grammar.
V.4　Historical changes in vocabulary.
V.5　Comparison of classical and modern vocabulary.
V.6　Comparison of classical and modern writing.
V.7　Sentence structure, history, 1.
V.8　Sentence structure, history, 2.
V.9　Honorifics, history.
V.10　Comparison of Japanese and other languages, 1.
V.11　Comparison of Japanese and other languages, 2.
V.12　Comparison of Japanese and other languages, 3.
V.13　Index.

A138　国 語 学 史 論 叢　竹岡正夫 編
Kokugogakushi ronsō, ed. by Takeoka Masao. Kasama Shoin, 1982. 459p.

Treatises on the history of the Japanese language. Contains 20 essays by specialists in honor of Professor Takeoka Masao.

LIFE AND CULTURE

Life and culture of the Japanese people who produced or appreciated the literature. Includes such subjects as ethnological and folklore studies, living conditions, arts, education, publishing and the reading public wherever related to literature.

A139　西岡虎之助　日本文学における生活史の研究
Nishioka Toranosuke. *Nihon bungaku ni okeru seikatsushi no kenkyū*. Tokyo Daigaku Shuppankai, 1954. 428p.

History of Japanese life and customs as manifested in literature. Examines the social environment that led to the development of literature in Japan from antiquity to the Edo period. Gives readings for difficult names. Index of topics, personal names and titles.

A140　国民生活史研究
Kokumin seikatsushi kenkyū, ed. by Itō Tasaburō. Yoshikawa Kōbunkan. 1957-62. 5v.

Collection of essays on everyday Japanese life.

V.1　Life and politics.
V.2　Life and socio-economics.
V.3　Life and education.
V.4　Life and religion.
V.5　Life and ethics, customs.

A141　日本民俗学大系
Nihon minzokugaku taikei. Heibonsha, 1958-60.
13v.

Systematic study of Japanese folklore: a collection
of essays:

V.1　The origins and development of ethnology.

V.2　Issues and history of Japanese ethnology.

V.3　Society and folklore, 1.

V.4　Society and folklore, 2.

V.5　Occupations and folklore.

V.6　Daily life and folklore, 1.

V.7　Daily life and folklore, 2.

V.8　Religious beliefs amd folklore.

V.9　Entertainment and recreation.

V.10　Oral traditions.

V.11　Folklore studies by geographical area.

V.12　Okinawan folklore.

V.13　Research methods in Japanese ethnology. Bibliography. General index.

A142　図説　日本庶民生活史　奈良本辰也 等編
Zusetsu Nihon shomin seikatsushi, ed. by Naramoto
Tatsuya, et al. Kawade Shobō Shinsha, 1961-62. 8v.

Illustrated history of the life of the Japanese people.
Divided by period, each volume describes living
conditions, including, food, clothing, shelter, occupations, religion and and the arts. Index.

A143　生　活　史　森末義彰 等編
Seikatsushi, ed. by Morisue Yoshiaki, et al.
Yamakawa Shuppansha, 1965-. 3v. (Taikei Nihonshi
sōsho, v.15-17)

Collection of essays on the history of living conditions in Japan. V.16 covers Sengoku through the
Edo period. V.17, from Meiji to World War II.
Bibliography. Index. (V.15, to be published in
1985)

A144　篠田　統　米　の　文　化　史
Shinoda Osamu. *Kome no bunkashi*. Shakai
Shisōsha, 1970. 326p.

History of eating habits in Japan, focusing on the
use and consumption of rice. Illustrations.

A145　日本生活文化史　坪井清足 等編
Nihon seikatsu bunkashi, ed. by Tsuboi Kiyotari, et
al. Kawade Shobō Shinsha, 1974-75. 10v.

Profusely illustrated cultural history of Japanese
life. Contains a chronological table. Index.

V.1　The fount of Japanese life. (Pre-history - Tu-
mulus age)

V.2　Life of the commoner and the nobleman.
(Asuka - Heian period)

V.3　Origins of the Japanese way of life. (Heian -
Kamakura period)

V.4　Rise of living standard of the commoners.
(Kamakura - Muromachi period)

V.5　From the chaos of war to an orderly life.
(Sengoku - Edo period)

V.6　Japanese way of life, established. (Edo period)

V.7　Impact of western civilization. (Edo - Meiji
period)

V.8　The nation in the life of the people. (Meiji
period)

V.9　Development of a citizenry. (Meiji - Showa
period)

V.10　From a warring nation to a democratic nation.
(Wartime - Postwar period)

A146　講座　日本の民俗　大藤時彦 等編
Kōza Nihon no minzoku, ed. by Ōtō Tokihiko, et al.
Yūseidō, 1978-82. 10v.

Lectures on Japanese folklore:

V.1　Introduction, ed. by Ōtō Tokihiko.

V.2　Structure of society, ed. by Mogami Takayoshi.

V.3　Etiquette, ed. by Inoguchi Shōji.

V.4　Food, clothing, shelter, ed. by Miyamoto
Kōtarō.

V.5　Occupations, ed. by Kawaoka.

V.6　Annual events, ed. by Ōshima Takehiko.

V.7　Religion, ed. by Sakurai Tokutarō.

V.8　Performing arts, ed. by Honda Yasuji.

V.9　Oral literature, ed. by Mitani Eiichi.

V.10　(Supplement) handbook for research in
folklore.

A147　日本民俗学文献總目録　日本民俗学会 編
Nihon minzokugaku bunken sōmokuroku, ed. by
Nihon Minzokugaku Gakkai. Kōbundō, 1980.
1474p.

A bibliography of Japanese studies in folklore,
covering such subjects as social structure, conven-
tional formalities, food and clothing, occupations,
annual events, religion, performing art and oral
literature. Also included are listings of folklore
magazines arranged by prefecture and the contents
of collected works of specialists in the field.

A148　年中行事の文芸学　山中　裕 等編
Nenjū gyōji no bungeigaku, ed. by Yamanaka Hiroshi and Imai Gen'e. Kōbundō, 1981. 456p.

Collection of essays on literature and the annual events of the Japanese religious and social calendar.

A149　和歌森太郎 著作集
Wakamori Tarō chosakushū, ed. by the Publishing Committee. Kōbundō, 1980-83. 16v.

V.1　Japanese communal society.

V.2　Shugendō (mountaineering aestheticism).

V.3　Shrines and festivals.

V.4　Ancient religion and society.

V.5　Social life and customs.

V.6　Japanese life.

V.7　Life of the common people.

V.8　The Japanese people.

V.9　Theory of folklore.

V.10　Historiography and ethnology.

V.11　Interpretation of history.

V.12　Society and etiquette.

V.13　Teaching history.

V.14　History, legends and climate.

V.15　Sumō and folklore.

V.16　(Supplement) Essays on books.

B ANCIENT PERIOD

This section covers the years between the beginnings of recorded history and end of the 8th century. *Nihon shoki*, *Kojiki*, and *Man'yōshū* are the major works of this period, important to students of literature and history alike.

Special terms:

> waka (Japanese poetry)
> kayō (songs and ballads)
> setsuwa (tales, legends, fables)

GENERAL

B1   三谷栄一　日本文学の民俗学的研究
Mitani Eiichi. *Nihon bungaku no minzokugakuteki kenkyū*. Yūseidō, 1960. 672p.

A study of the origins of Japanese literature in folklore and religion, continuing the scholarly tradition of Origuchi Shinobu and Yanagita Kunio. Contains chapters on the foundations and characteristics of oral literature, the transmission of folklore by occupational groups such as fishermen and bamboo gatherers, etc.

B2   上代文学　研　究　と　資　料
Jōdai bungaku: kenkyū to shiryō, ed. by Keiō Gijuku Daigaku Kokubungaku Kenkyūkai. Shibundō, 1961. 280 p. (Kokubungaku ronsō, no.4)

A collection of essays on the *Man'yōshū* and Chinese literature. Pt.1 discusses the poetic description of nature. Pt.2 contains a documented study of *Nihon shoki*, citing sources in chronicles such as *Kojiki*, *Sendai kujiki* (legends of antiquity), and *Kogoshūi* (Gleanings from ancient stories).

B3   太田善麿　古代日本文学思潮論
Ōta Yoshimaro. *Kodai Nihon bungaku shichōron*. Ōfūsha, 1961-66. 6v. (4 parts)

Essays on ancient Japanese literary trends, discussing the origins of *Kojiki*, *Nihon shoki*, ancient poems, etc.

B4   小島憲之　上代日本文学と中国文学
Kojima Noriyuki. *Jōdai Nihon bungaku to Chūgoku bungaku*. Hanawa Shobō, 1962-65. 3v.

Study of the Chinese influence on early Japanese literature as seen in the *Kojiki*, *Nihon shoki*, Fudoki, *Manyōshū* and Chinese books introduced to Japan in the ancient period.

B5   大久保　正　　上代日本文学概説
Ōkubo Tadashi. *Jōdai Nihon bungaku gaisetsu*. Shūei Shuppan, 1963. 271p.

A survey of ancient Japanese literature, from ritual chants, ballads and songs to lyrical literature, *Man'yōshū*, and *Kaifūsō* (Fond recollection of poetry). Contains a bibliography and a chronology. Index.

B6   西郷信綱　日本古代文学史
Saigō Nobutsuna. *Nihon kodai bungakushi*. Revised ed. Iwanami Shoten, 1963. 318p. (Iwanami zensho)

History of Japanese literature in antiquity, divided by period and genre: mythology and descriptive poetry, lyric poetry, and monogatari (narrative) literature. Chronology. Index.

B7   大久間喜一郎　古代文学の源流
Ōkuma Kiichirō. *Kodai bungaku no genryū*. Ōfūsha, 1966. 263p.

Collection of essays on the intellectual life of the ancient Japanese as revealed in literature.

B8   平野仁啓　古代日本人の精神構造
Hirano Jinkei. *Kodai Nihonjin no seishin kōzō*. Miraisha, 1966. 355p.

Spirituality of the ancient Japanese as reflected in incantation, religion, literature, mythology, and the arts. Coverage is from the pre-historic period to the Nara period.

B9　平野仁啓　続　古代日本人の精神構造
Hirano Jinkei. *Zoku Kodai Nihonjin no seishin kōzō*. Miraisha, 1976. 499p.

Continuation of the above entry. Discusses the ancient Japanese view of religion, humanity, nature, literature, and time.

B10　倉野憲司　上代日本古典文学の研究
Kurano Kenji. *Jōdai Nihon koten bungaku no kenkyū*. Ōfūsha, 1968. 336p.

A study of the classical literature of ancient Japan. In 3 sections: ritual chants, *Kojiki*, and *Man'yōshū*.

B11　三谷栄一　古典文学と民俗
Mitani Eiichi. *Koten bungaku to minzoku*. Iwasaki Bijutsusha, 1968. 443p. (Minzoku mingei sōsho)

A collection of essays on classical literature and folklore. Discusses the methodology of the combined study of folklore and literature. Indexes for names, subjects, waka, haiku, kayō.

B12　尾畑喜一郎　古代文学序説
Obata Kiichirō. *Kodai bungaku josetsu*: Kiki to kodai. Ōfūsha, 1968. 446p.

An introduction to the *Nihon shoki*, *Kojiki*, and ancient drama. The author focuses on antiquity, a period about which very little is known, and proposes a new genre that combines poetry, prose and drama. The development of this genre is traced. Index, p.427-46.

B13　大久間喜一郎　古代文学の構想
Ōkuma Kiichirō. *Kodai bungaku no kōsō*: Man'yō shū no sekai. Musashino Shoin, 1971. 280p.

Continuation of *Kodai bungaku no genryū* (B7). On the world of the *Man'yōshū*.

B14　大久間喜一郎　古代文学の伝統
Ōkuma Kiichirō. *Kodai bungaku no dentō*. Kasama Shoin, 1978. 445p.

Continuation of the above entry. On the traditions of ancient literature: the *Man'yōshū*, the ballads and songs in *Kojiki* and *Nihon shoki*, and ancient narrative literature.

B15　シリーズ　古代の文学　古代文学会　編
Shiriizu Kodai no bungaku, ed. by Kodai Bungakkai. Musashino Shoin, 1974-82. 7v.

Ancient literature.

V.1 Poets of the *Man'yōshū*.
V.2 Language in the *Man'yōshū*.
V.3 The birth of literature.
V.4 Imagination and form in waka.
V.5 Stories and oral transmission.
V.6 The development of ancient literature.
V.7 Subject matter and style in poetry.

B16　土居光知　古代伝説と文学
Doi Kōchi. *Kodai densetsu to bungaku*. Iwanami Shoten, 1977. 467p. (Doi Kōchi chosakushū, v.2)

Explores the similarities between ancient Japanese literature and legends, and those of other lands.

B17　永藤　靖　古代日本文学と時間意識
Nagafuji Yasushi. *Kodai Nihon bungaku to jikan ishiki*. Miraisha, 1979. 247p.

Discusses the attitude of the ancient Japanese toward time, as it was expressed in literary works, such as *Kojiki*, *Nihon shoki*, *Man'yōshū*, *Makura no sōshi*, *Genji monogatari*, etc.

B18　上代日本文学史　中西　進　編
Jōdai Nihon bungakushi, ed. by Nakanishi Susumu. Yūhikaku, 1979. 220p. (Yūhikaku sōsho. Nyūmon, kiso chishiki hen)

A topical history of ancient Japanese literature. Contains a chronological table. Index.

By Period

B19　徳光久也　白鳳文学論
Tokumitsu Kyūya. *Hakuhō bungakuron*. Hōsei Daigaku Shuppanbu, 1959. 333p.

An introduction to Hakuhō literature and its historical and social background, with studies of Tenmu Tennō, *Kojiki* and early Man'yō poets.

B20　徳光久也　白鳳文学新論
Tokumitsu Kyūya. *Hakuhō bungaku shinron*: Kiki, Man'yō, Fudoki no hihyōteki kenkyū. Chikuma Shobō, 1978. 613p. (Chikuma sōsho)

A companion volume of the above entry, *Hakuhō bungakuron*. A critical study of the *Kojiki*, *Nihongi*, *Man'yōshū* , etc., which serves as an introduction to early Nara period art and culture.

B21　講座　飛鳥の歴史と文学　横田健一　等編
Kōza Asuka no rekishi to bungaku, ed. by Yokota Ken'ichi and Aboshi Yoshinori. Shinshindō Shuppan, 1980-. In progress.

Lectures on the history of Asuka literature.

Collected Works

B22 折口信夫 全集
Origuchi Shinobu zenshū, ed. by Origuchi Shinobu Hakushi Kinen Kodai Kenkyūjo. Chūō Kōronsha, 1965-68. 32v.

A complete collection of Professor Origuchi's works.

V.1 Studies in ancient literature.
V.2-3 Ancient folk literature.
V.4-5 Modern translation of the *Man'yōshū*.
V.6 *Man'yōshū* dictionary.
V.7-14 Studies of the classics.
V.15-16 Folk literature and traditions.
V.17-18 History of the performing arts.
V.19 The Japanese language.
V.20 The Shinto religion.
V.21-22 Professor Origuchi's tanka poetry.
V.23 'Shi' poetry.
V.24 Fiction.
V.25-26 Essays and lectures on poetry.
V.27-28 Critical essays.
V.29-30 Miscellaneous essays.
V.31 Diaries and letters.
V.32 Index.

B23 折口信夫 全集　ノート編
Origuchi Shinobu zenshū Nōtohen, ed. by Origuchi Shinobu Hakushi Kinen Kodai Kenkyūjo. Chūō Kōronsha, 1970-71. 19v.

A collection of lecture notes written by Professor Origuchi. On the history of Japanese literature and the performing arts.

B24 高崎正秀 著作集
Takasaki Masahide chosakushū. Ōfūsha, 1971. 8v.

A collection of Professor Takasaki's works, ed. by his students at Kokugakuin University.

V.1 The divine sword.
V.2 The pre-literary period.
V.3 *Man'yōshū*.
V.4 The time of the 'rokkasen' (the six poetic geniuses).
V.5 Monogatari (narrative) literature.
V.6 The Tale of Genji.
V.7 The birth of Kintarō.
V.8 Commentary on the classics.

B25 武田裕吉 著作集
Takeda Yūkichi chosakushū. Kadokawa Shoten, 1973. 8v.

Collected works of Takeda Yūkichi.

V.1 The literature of the gods.
V.2-4 *Kojiki*, (V.4 includes Fudoki).
V.5-7 *Man'yōshū*.
V.8 History of Japanese literature: poetry and prose.

B26 池田弥三郎 著作集
Ikeda Yasaburō chosakushū. Kadokawa Shoten, 1979-80. 10v.

A collection of selected essays by Professor Ikeda on ancient literature, folk literature, and performing arts. Each volume contains a dialogue between Professor Ikeda and the volume editor, and a bibliographical commentary on the subject.

V.1 Antiquity, ed. by Nishimura Tōru.
V.2 Folk literature and the performing arts, ed. by Iguchi Tatsuo.
V.3 Essays on folk traditions, ed. by Nakai Kōjirō.
V.4 Essays on literary traditions, ed. by Nishimura Tōru.
V.5 Folklore and literature, ed. by Iguchi Tatsuo.
V.6 Characters from folklore, ed. by Hinotani Akihiko.
V.7 Origuchi Shinobu's work, ed. by Iwamatsu Kenkichirō.
V.8 The language of folklore, ed. by Sekiba Takeshi.
V.9 Folkways, ed. by Nakao Tatsuo.
V.10 Miscellaneous essays, bibliographies, ed. by Ōshima Aki.

Festschrifts (a select list)

B27 上 代 文 学 論 叢　五味智英 先生
Jōdai bungaku ronsō: Gomi Tomohide Sensei Kanreki kinen, ed. by Kinen Ronbunshū Kankōkai. Ōfūsha, 1968. 601p.

Festschrift of 21 essays on ancient literature and linguistics. Contains a bio-bibliography.

B28 上代文学と言語　境田四郎 教授
Jōdai bungaku to gengo, ed. by Sakaida Kyōju Kiju Kinen Ronbunshū Kankōkai. Maeda Shoten, 1974. 650p.

Ancient Japanese language and literature. A study of the terms and names that appear in *Kojiki*, *Man'yōshū*, etc.

B29 古代文学論集　倉野憲司 先生
Kodai bungaku ronshū, ed. by Kurano Sensei Koki Kinen Ronbunshū Kankōkai. Ōfūsha, 1974. 691p.

Essays on ancient language and literature. A brief bio-biliography.

B30 上代文学論叢　五味智英 先生
Jōdai bungaku ronsō: Gomi Tomohide Sensei koki kinen, ed. by Kinen Ronbunshū Kankōkai and Man'yōshū Shichiyōkai. Chikuma shobō, 1977. 659p. (Ronshū jōdai bungaku, v.8)

Festschrift of 30 essays on ancient language and literature. A bio-biliography.

B31 上代文学考究　石井庄司 博士
Jōdai bungaku kōkyū: Ishii Shōji Hakushi Kiju Kinenkai ronbunshū, ed. by Itō Haku and Watase Masatada. Hanawa Shobō, 1978. 398p.

Festschrift of 23 essays on ancient literature. A short bio-bibliography.

B32 古代の文学と民俗　池田弥三郎 教授
Kodai no bungaku to minzoku, ed. by Keio Gijuku Daigaku Kokubungaku Kenkyūkai. Ōfūsha, 1980. 193p. (Kokubungaku ronsō, shinshū 2)

Festschrift in honor of Professor Ikeda, consisting of 7 essays on the relationship between literature and folk customs.

MYTHOLOGY

B33 松村健夫　日本神話の研究
Matsumura Takeo. *Nihon shinwa no kenkyū*. Baifūkan, 1954-58. 4v.

A general study of Japanese mythology. Author and subject indexes in each volume.

B34 上田正昭　日本神話の世界
Ueda Masaaki. *Nihon shinwa no sekai*. Sōgensha, 1967. 186p. (Sōgen shinsho)

Formation of the mythical world and the political exigencies of the *Nihon shoki* and *Kojiki*. Includes a list of reference materials.

B35 山上伊豆母　神話 の 原 像
Yamagami Izumo. *Shinwa no genzo*. Iwasaki Bijutsusha, 1969. 289p.

A study of the mythical prototypes indigenous to Japanese folklore and geography, before the formation of the *Kojiki* and *Nihon shoki* myths.

B36 青木紀元　日本神話の基礎的研究
Aoki Kigen. *Nihon shinwa no kisoteki kenkyū*. Kazama Shobō, 1970. 568p.

Basic studies in Japanese mythology.

Pt.1 Discusses the regional basis of the myths recorded in the fudoki.
Pt.2 Traces two mythical lines: Yamato and Izumo.
Pt.3 Treats the songs used in rites and ceremonies.
Pt.4 Contains studies on the ritual prayers (norito) found in *Kojiki* and *Engishiki*.

B37 松前　健　日本神話の形成
Matsumae Takeshi. *Nihon shinwa no keisei*. Hanawa Shobō, 1970. 509p.

The formation of Japanese myths and the people responsible for their transmission. Concentrates on the Izumo and Hyūga myths in an attempt to complete a historical reorganization of Japanese mythology.

B38 上田正昭　日 本 神 話
Ueda Masaaki. *Nihon shinwa*. Iwanami Shoten, 1970. 230p. (Iwanami shinsho)

An examination of the nature of Japanese myth as seen in the *Nihon shoki* and *Kojiki*.

B39 シンポジューム　日本の神話　伊藤清司 等編
Shinpojūmu Nihon no shinwa, ed. by Itō Kiyoshi and Ōbayashi Taryō. Gakuseisha, 1972-75. 5v.

Symposium on Japanese mythology, from antiquity to the development of the *Nihon shoki* and *Kojiki* myths, discussed by mythologists, folklorists, archeologists and historians. Index in each volume.

B40 守屋俊彦　記 紀 神 話 論 考
Moriya Toshihiko. *Kiki shinwa ronkō*. Yūzanku, 1973. 401p.

A textual and bibliographical search for the prototypes and stages of development of Japanese myths. Studies the mythology of the god of fire, the Takamagahara and Izumo myths, the descendants of the Sun Goddess, and Hyūga mythology.

B41 三谷栄一　日本神話の基盤
Mitani Eiichi. *Nihon shinwa no kiban*: Fudoki no kamigami to shinwa bungaku. Hanawa Shobō, 1974. 601p.

A collection of 16 studies, based on textual, literary, ethnological and historical methodologies. Discusses mythology in Fudoki.

B42 日本神話の比較研究　大林太良　編
Nihon shinwa no hikaku kenkyū, ed. by Ōbayashi Taryō. Hōsei Daigaku Shuppan Kyōkai, 1974. 433p.

A collection of essays on comparative mythological research. Divided into 3 parts: Pt.1 Comparison of Japanese and East Asian mythology. Pt.2 Comparison of Japanese and Southeast Asian/Oceanian mythology. Pt.3 Comparison of Japanese and northern Eurasian and Indian mythology.

B43 大林太良　日本神話の構造
Ōbayashi Taryō. *Nihon shinwa no kōzō*. Kōbundō, 1975. 285p.

The structure of Japanese mythology; a supplement to the author's previous works: *Nihon shinwa no kigen* (the origins of Japanese mythology) and *Inasaku no shinwa* (Mythology of rice culture). Divided into 3 sections:

Pt.1 The tripartite structure of the Japanese pantheon.

Pt.2 Correlations of heaven, earth and water.

Pt.3 The dialectic development of mythic plots.

Contains a list of reference materials. Index.

B44 講座　日本の神話
Kōza Nihon no shinwa: Essays on Japanese mythology, ed. by its Editorial committee. Yūseidō, 1976-78. 12v.

V.1 Research methods in Japanese mythology.

V.2 The formation and structure of Japanese myths.

V.3 The structure of creation myths and the founding of Japan.

V.4 The Takamagahara myths.

V.5 The myths of Izumo.

V.6 Heroic figures of ancient times.

V.7 Japanese myths and rituals.

V.8 Myth and Japan's ancient clans.

V.9 Japanese mythology and Korea.

V.10 Japanese mythology and the Ryukyus.

V.11 Comparative studies in Japanese mythology.

V.12 Japanese mythology and archeology.

CEREMONIES, FESTIVALS

B45 倉林正次　饗宴の研究　儀礼編
Kurabayashi Shōji. *Kyōen no kenkyū: gireihen*. Ōfūsha. 1965. 567p.

Study of ceremony, consisting of chapters on the organization of court ceremonies, the new year's ceremony, banquets for high ranking officials, dance and music performances for the Great Enthronement Thanksgiving ceremony, etc.

B46 倉林正次　饗宴の研究　文学編
Kurabayashi Shōji. *Kyōen no kenkyū: bungakuhen*. Ōfūsha, 1969. 861p.

Study of the court and religious ceremonies that gave rise to ballads and poetry. Covers the earliest ballads, from the *Nihon shoki*, *Kojiki*, and early poems from the Man'yōshū to the Shinto religious ballads of the medieval period.

B47 西角井正慶　古代祭祀と文学
Nishitsunoi Masayoshi. *Kodai saishi to bungaku*. Chūō Kōronsha, 1966. 505p.

Collection of the author's previously published essays on ancient Shinto rites. Contents: the ancient view of the gods; ancient Shinto rites; antiquity as it appears in literature; the ancient view of the spirits.

B48 岡田精司　古代王権の祭祀と神話
Okada Seishi. *Kodai ōken no saishi to shinwa*. Hanawa Shobō, 1970. 438p.

Rites and ceremonies conducted by royalty in antiquity and their relation to mythology.

B49 山上伊豆母　古代祭祀伝承の研究
Yamagami Izumo. *Kodai saishi denshō no kenkyū*. Yūzankaku, 1973. 475p.

Collection of the author's previously published essays. Divided into 5 sections: Shinto ceremony and the transmission of myths; the transmission and consolidation of the *Nihon shoki* and *Kojiki*; the performing arts and state ceremonies; ancient beliefs and festivals; the geneology of Shinto thought. Index.

B50 松前　健　古代伝承と宮廷祭祀
Matsumae Takeshi. *Kodai denshō to kyūtei saishi*: Nihon shinwa no shūhen. Hanawa Shobō, 1974. 410p.

Interdisciplinary studies on the origins of oral records and customs in ancient legends and court ceremonies.

RECORDS

Kojiki (Records of ancient matters)

B51 古事記大成
Kojiki Taisei. Heibonsha, 1956-58. 8v.

A complete study of the *Kojiki*:

V.1 The history of *Kojiki* research, ed. by
   Hisamatsu Sen'ichi.
V.2 *Kojiki* as literature, ed. by Takagi Ichinosuke.
V.3 Linguistics and literature, ed. by Takeda
   Yūkichi.
V.4 History and archeology, ed. by Sakamoto Tarō.
V.5 Mythology and folklore, ed. by Kazamaki
   Keijirō.
V.6 Text, ed. by Kurano Kenji.
V.7-8 Index, ed. by Takagi Ichinosuke and
   Tomiyama Tamizō.

B52 竹野長次　古事記の民俗学的研究
Takeno Chōji. *Kojiki no minzokugakuteki kenkyū.*
Bungadō Shoten, 1960. 520p.

The folkloristic studies of the *Kojiki*. Pt. 1 covers
the age of the gods; Pt.2, the period from Jinmu
Tennō to Kenso Tennō (660 B.C.-A.D. 487).

B53 校 本 古 事 記　倉野憲司 編
Kōhon Kojiki, ed. by Kurano Kenji. Zoku Gunsho
Ruijū Kanseikai, 1965. 732p.

The first fully collated text of the *Kojiki*, prepared
by the Kojiki Gakkai. Commentary section
appended.

B54 古 事 記 総 索 引　高木市之助 等編
Kojiki sōsakuin, ed. by Takagi Ichinosuke and
Tomiyama Tamizō. Heibonsha, 1974-77. 3v.

General index to the *Kojiki*, designed for the use of
specialists as well as for the interested layman. V.1
text; V.2 indexes; V.3 supplement.

B55 菅野雅雄　古事記説話の研究
Sugano Masao. *Kojiki setsuwa no kenkyū.* Ōfūsha,
1973. 340p.

A collection of essays on setsuwa found in the
Kojiki. Index.

B56 西郷信綱　古 事 記 研 究
Saigō Nobutsuna. *Kojiki kenkyū.* Miraisha, 1973.
319p.

Studies on the *Kojiki*. A collection of the author's
previously published essays on ''Hieda no Are'',
''Incest and myths'', ''The kuniyuzuri myth'' (Surrender of the land by Ōkuninushi to the Sun
Goddess), ''Daijōsai festival'', ''Jinmu Tenno'',
''The story of Yamato Takeru'', and ''Reflections on
the history of research on *Kojiki*'', etc.

B57 古 事 記　上田正昭 編
Kojiki, ed. by Ueda Masaaki. Shakai Shisōsha,
1977. 3l9p. (Nihon kodai bunka no tankyū)

Nine essays on the *Kojiki* from different points of
view: literary, historical, archeological, and
folkloristic. Also compares the *Kojiki* with the legends and writings of Okinawa, Korea, Burma, Java,
and the Ainu.

B58 徳光久也　古 事 記 研 究 史
Tokumitsu Kyūya. *Kojiki kenkyūshi.* Kasama Shoin,
1977. 443p. (Kasama sōsho)

Introduction to the history of research in the *Kojiki*.
Also indicates possible directions for the future of
this research. Divided into 2 periods: from the
medieval period to l945, in which the work of more
than 30 scholars is summarized; and l945-75, which
discusses in detail the work of contemporary scholars. Index.

Nihon Shoki (Chronicles of Japan)

B59 丸山二郎　日本書紀の研究
Maruyama Jirō. *Nihon shoki no kenkyū.* Yoshikawa
Kōbunkan, 1955. 359p.

A collection of essays on the *Nihon shoki*. Includes
the author's assessment of earlier scholarship.

B60 日 本 書 紀 研 究　三品彰英 等編
Nihon shoki kenkyū, ed. by Mishina Akihide and
Yokota Ken'ichi. Hanawa Shobō, 1969-(82) (12v.)

Mishina Akihide organized a research group of
historians, archeologists, folklorists and cultural an-
thropologists to study the *Nihon shoki*. The essays
are the product of that group, edited by Yokota
Ken'ichi after Mishina's death. An annual
publication.

B61 友田吉之助　日本書紀成立の研究
Tomoda Kichinosuke. *Nihon shoki seiritsu no kenkyū.* Kazama Shobō, 1969. 739p.

Research on the consolidation of the *Nihon shoki*.
Examines corrections between the Wadō period *Nihongi* and the extant *Nihon shoki*, and attempts to
delineate the character of the extant *Nihon shoki*
through textual criticism.

B62 校 本 日 本 書 紀　国学院大学日本文化研究所 編
Kōhon Nihon shoki, ed. by Kokugakuin Daigaku,
Nihon Bunka Kenkyūjo. Kadokawa Shoten,
1973-75. 2v.

The 4 volumes of the collated *Nihon shoki* were published in these 2 volumes to commemorate the 90th anniversary of the founding of Kokugakuin University.

B63　校本日本書紀総索引　中村啓信 編
Kōhon Nihon shoki sōsakuin, ed. by Nakamura Hirotoshi. Kadokawa Shoten, 1964-68. 4v.

General index to the collated *Nihon shoki*, indexes every kanji (character) and every word from the *Nihon shoki*, arranged so that any word from any part of the work, or in any writing system, can be easily found. Completed by Nakamura Hirotoshi after the death of Takeda Yūkichi, who conceived and began the project.

Fudoki

A collection of 8th century reports on the natural resources, geographical conditions, and oral traditions of each of approximately 60 Japanese provinces. Only five 'Fudoki' of substantial length are extant today.

B64　秋本吉郎　風土記 の 研究
Akimoto Kichirō. *Fudoki no kenkyū*. Osaka Keizei Daigaku Kōenkai, 1963. 1085p. (Osaka Keizai Daigaku kenkyū sōsho, no.4)

Collection of works on Fudoki. Contents: geographical distribution of Fudoki; their establishment, transmission, contents, and literary value; history of the study of the Fudoki.

B65　植垣節也　風土記の研究並びに漢字索引
Uegaki Setsuya. *Fudoki no kenkyū narabini kanji sakuin*. Kazama Shobō, 1972. 987p.

A study of Fudoki. An outline section lists works on Fudoki. An index section includes a kanji stroke index, a kana reading index, and a character pronunciation index.

POETRY

Kayō (songs and ballads)

B66　土橋　寛　古 代 歌 謡 論
Tsuchihashi Yutaka. *Kodai kayōron*. San'ichi Shobō, 1960. 456p.

Collection of 10 essays on ancient ballads.

B67　土橋　寛　古代歌謡と儀礼の研究
Tsuchihashi Yutaka. *Kodai kayō to girei no kenkyū*. Iwanami Shoten, 1965. 506p.

Study of the ballads sung during ancient ceremonies such as kunimi (land viewing) and utagaki (group singing and dancing).

B68　土橋　寛　古代歌謡の世界
Tsuchihashi Yutaka. *Kodai kayō no sekai*. Hanawa Shobō, 1968. 467p. (Hanawa sensho)

An introductory study on the world of the ancient ballads. Contains a general index, an index of songs and ballads, and waka.

B69　藤田徳太郎　古代歌謡の研究
Fujita Tokutarō. *Kodai kayō no kenkyū*. Yūseisha, 1969. 509p.

A study of songs and ballads in *Kojiki*, *Nihon shoki*, *Man'yōshū*, etc. Also discusses Muromachi period music and song. Illustrations include color plates. Index.

B70　益田勝実　記 紀 歌 謡
Masuda Katsumi. *Kiki kayō*. Chikuma Shobō, 1972. 337p. (Nihon shijin sen)

Nine essays on songs and ballads in the *Kojiki* and *Nihon shoki*, treating them as an early manifestation of lyricism.

B71　吉本隆明　初 期 歌 謡 論
Yoshimoto Takaaki. *Shoki kayōron*. Kawade Shobō Shinsha, 1977. 491p.

Critical commentary on early ballads: on the origins of poetry; on ballad prototypes; on 'uta makura' (fixed epithets in poetry); on poetic style; and the development of waka.

B72　渡辺昭五　歌 垣 の 研 究
Watanabe Shōgo. *Utagaki no kenkyū*. Miyai Shoten, 1981. 709p.

A study of utagaki (group singing and dancing) found in the *Kojiki* and *Nihon shoki*, etc.

B73　古橋信孝　古 代 歌 謡 論
Furuhashi Nobuyoshi. *Kodai kayōron*. Tōjusha, 1982. 434p.

Essays on ancient ballads. Contents: 1. the birthplace of literature; 2. the structure of the imperial system in antiquity; 3. Shinto ballads; 4. the development of 'shi' (Chinese style poetry); 5. the composition and development of song; 6. the early Man'yō period; 7. Kakinomoto no Hitomaro. Index to songs and ballads.

Man'yōshū

"Collection for ten thousand generations" or "Collection of myriad leaves". This is the earliest collection of waka poetry.

B74　万 葉 集 大 成
Man'yōshū taisei. Heibonsha, 1953-56. 22v.

The compendium of *Man'yōshū*: bibliographic, historical, linguistic, literary and folkloristic studies. Includes 5 volumes of indexes of words, and readings. V.22 contains a reference bibliography, chronology of studies. Index.

B75　平野仁啓　万葉批評史研究
Hirano Jinkei. *Man'yō hihyōshi kenkyū*: Kinseihen. Miraisha, 1965. 420p.

Man'yō studies in the Edo period. Chronology, 1640-1858, and index.

B76　万 葉 集 論 叢　沢瀉久孝 博士
Man'yōshū ronsō, Omodaka Hakushi kiju kinen. Suita, Ronbunshū Kankōkai, 1966. 751p.

Festschrift of essays on the *Man'yōshū* in honor of Professor Omodaka.

B77　渋谷虎雄　中世万葉集研究
Shibuya Torao. *Chūsei Man'yōshū kenkyū*. Kazama Shobō, 1967. 970p.

Medieval *Man'yōshū* research. Contains abstracts of the author's essays on ancient and medieval Man'yō research and a bibliography of his works on the history of research, and indexes.

B78　河野頼人　万 葉 学 研 究
Kawano Yorito. *Man'yōgaku kenkyū*: Kinsei. Ōfūsha, 1969. 293p.

Edo period studies on the *Man'yōshū*. Focuses on Kamo no Mabuchi, the first great figure in the study of Man'yō research. Divided into 3 sections: 1. An examination of Kamo no Mabuchi's Man'yō research; 2. An examination of the work for an enlarged and revised edition of Kamo no Mabuchi's work titled: *Man'yōkō* by Koma Moronari; 3. Introduction of new source materials. Contains an author/title index and an index to Man'yō poems.

B79　論集　上代文学　万葉七曜会 編
Ronshū jōdai bungaku, ed. by Man'yō Shichiyōkai. Kasama Shoin, 1970-(82) (V.12)

An annual publication on the *Man'yōshū*.

B80　万 葉 集 講 座　久松潜一 監修
Man'yōshū kōza. Hisamatsu Sen'ichi kanshū, ed. by Aso Mizue. Yūseidō, 1972-75. 7v.

Lecture series on *Man'yōshū*. Discusses the origins and influence of the *Man'yōshū*, the history of Man'yō studies, the Man'yō age, expression, style, poets and their poetry. The supplement volume contains a dictionary, with indexes, charts, and a chronology.

B81　万 葉 集 研 究　五味智英 等編
Man'yōshū kenkyū, ed. by Gomi Tomohide and Kojima Noriyuki. Hanawa Shobō, 1972-83. (11v.)

An annual publication of studies on the *Man'yōshū*.

B82　久松潜一　万葉集と上代文学
Hisamatsu Sen'ichi. *Man'yōshū to jōdai bungaku*. Kasama Shoin, 1973. 488p. (Kasama sōsho)

A collection of essays on the *Man'yōshū* and ancient literature. Discusses the literary, historical, and geographical aspects of the *Man'yōshū*, the *Kojiki* and Fudoki.

B83　万 葉 集 総 索 引
Man'yōshū sōsakuin. Heibonsha, 1974. 2v.

General index to the *Man'yōshū*. Reprint of the word index and the kanji index from *Man'yōshū taisei* (B74).

B84　伊藤　博　古代和歌史研究
Itō Haku. *Kodai wakashi kenkyū*. Hanawa Shobō, 1974-76. 7v.

Documented studies of ancient waka in 3 parts: organization of *Man'yōshū*; poets and their poetry; literary expression and the composition of waka. Supplement volume consists of a chronology and subject index.

B85　河野頼人　上代文学研究史の研究
Kawano Yorito. *Jōdai bungaku kenkyūshi no kenkyū*. Kazama Shobō, 1977. 446p.

Study of the history of research in ancient literature with emphasis on the studies of *Man'yōshū* by Kamo no Mabuchi.

B86　万 葉 の 発 想　森脇一夫 博士
Man'yō no hassō, ed. by Moriwaki Kazuo Hakushi Koki Kinen Ronbunshū Kankōkai, Ōfūsha, 1977. 649p.

Festschrift of 34 essays on the conception of the *Manyōshū*, by the students and colleagues of Professor Moriwaki. A bio-bibliography.

B87　万葉集を学ぶ
Man'yōshū o manabu. Yūhikaku, 1977-78. 8v.

This study of the *Man'yōshū* elucidates the current state of Man'yō research. Each volume contains a section titled 'Discovery of the ancient language' and a waka index.

B88　校 本 万 葉 集　佐竹昭広 等編
Kōhon Man'yōshū, ed. by Satake Akihiro, et al. New, revised and enlarged ed. Iwanami shoten, 1979-82. 17v.

A new revised text of the *Man'yōshū* which was first published in 1932, under the editorship of Sasaki Nobutsuna, et al.

B89　万 葉 集 年 表　土屋文明 編
Man'yōshū nenpyō, ed. by Tsuchiya Bunmei. 2nd ed. Iwanami Shoten, 1980. 567p.

Man'yōshū chronology: all the poems from the *Man'yōshū* are listed in order of composition. Poems and poets whose dates are uncertain are listed at the end. Each chapter includes an index to poems and poets.

B90　五味智英　万葉集の作家と作品
Gomi Tomohide. *Man'yōshū no sakka to sakuhin.* Iwanami Shoten, 1982. 477p.

Collection of essays on Man'yō poets, including Kakinomoto Hitomaro, Takechi no Kurohito, Yamabe no Akahito, Ōtomo no Tabito, Yamanoue no Okura, and others.

LANGUAGE

B91　馬淵和夫　上 代 の こ と ば
Mabuchi Kazuo. *Jōdai no kotoba.* Shibundō, 1968. 268p. (Nihon bunpō shinsho)

The language of antiquity. Attempts to unearth the language used by ancient Japanese. Contains a reference bibliography and an index.

B92　佐伯梅友　奈良時代の国語
Saeki Umetomo. *Nara jidai no kokugo.* Sanseidō, 1972. 213p. (Kokugo sōsho)

Reprint of the 1950 edition. A standard survey of Nara period Japanese. Gives grammatical analyses of the classics including *Man'yōshū*, etc.

B93　田辺正男　上代語中古語の研究
Tanabe Masao. *Jōdaigo Chūkogo no kenkyū.* Ōfūsha, 1976. 546p.

Study of the language of antiquity and the Heian period. A collection of previously published essays. In 4 sections: sentence and word use; vocabulary;

use of kana and kanji; history of the field; and comments on appreciation of the classics.

PERFORMING ARTS

B94　池田弥三郎　日本芸能伝承論
Ikeda Yasaburō. *Nihon geinō denshōron.* Chūō Kōronsha, 1962. 322p.

Folkloristic studies of the Japanese performing arts. A collection of essays on Japanese literature, song and dance.

B95　浜　一衛　日本芸能の源流
Hama Kazue. *Nihon geinō no genryū: sangakukō* (san yueh). Kadokawa Shoten, 1968. 442p.

Traces the relationship between early Japanese performing arts such as sarugaku and dengaku (music and dance) and Chinese 'san yueh' (popular music and dance). Index.

B96　山上伊豆母　日本芸能の起源
Yamagami Izumo. *Nihon geinō no kigen.* Yamato Shobō, 1977. 281p. (Nihon kodai bunka sōsho)

The rise of the ancient performing arts of Japan is studied in its origins in Chinese festivals and Japanese mythology, and its close relationship to the political, economic, religious and military customs of the time.

B97　荻　美津夫　日本古代音楽史論
Ogi Mitsuo. *Nihon kodai ongakushi ron.* Yoshikawa Kōbunkan, 1977. 305p.

Historical look at the changing role of music and its institutions in ancient Japanese society.

LIFE AND CULTURE

B98　関根真隆　奈良朝食生活の研究
Sekine Masataka. *Narachō shoku seikatsu no kenkyū.* Yoshikawa Kōbunkan, 1969. 586p. (Nihon shigaku kenkyū sōsho)

The eating habits of the Nara period, based on evidence found in Nara period documents on food, and references in the *Nihon shoki, Kojiki, Man'yōshū* and various local records. Also examines data on cooking utensils from the same sources. Contains a list of reference sources. Illustrations. Index.

B99　関根真隆　奈良朝服飾史の研究
Sekine Masataka. *Narachō fukushokushi no kenkyū.* Yoshikawa Kōbunkan, 1974. 2v.

Study of clothing of the Nara period, which was based on T'ang dynasty models, preserved in the Shōsōin. Both domestic and continental Asian influences on Japanese clothing are examined. V.2 consists of illustrations, charts, and diagrams. Index.

B100　町田甲一　上代彫刻史の研究
Machida Kōichi. *Jōdai chōkokushi no kenkyū*. Yoshikawa Kōbunkan, 1977. 353p.

Study of the 7th-8th century sculptures housed in the Hōryūji. Illustrations include plates.

B101　藤島亥治郎　上代詩歌の家と庭
Fujishima Gaijirō. *Jōdai shiika no ie to niwa*. Kokusho Kankōkai, 1977. 397p.

Discusses clothing, food, houses, and gardens based on the description of these given in the festival songs of the *Kojiki* and *Nihon shoki*, and in the poems of the *Man'yōshū*, *Kokinshū*, etc. Illustrations.

B102　武者小路　穣　天平芸術の工房
Mushakōji Minoru. *Tenpyō geijutsu no kōbō*. Kyōikusha, 1981. 221p. (Kyōikusha rekishi shinsho, Nihonshi)

Historical and cultural study of various studio arts and artisans of the Tenpyō era (729-65) with reference to their works and to biographical documents. Traces their gradual change of status from craftsmen dependent upon their patrons to independent artists.

C HEIAN OR CHŪKO PERIOD

In the early Heian period Japanese literature was over-shadowed by the influence of Chinese prose and poetry. But by 905, the year in which the *Kokinshū* was compiled, the native poetic tradition had reasserted itself. For several centuries Japanese poetry flourished, culminating in 1205 with the *Shinkokinshū*, greatest of the 21 Imperial Anthologies. Japanese prose literature also emerged in the Heian period, and reached its apogee in *Genji monogatari*.

Special terms:

> kanbungaku (classical Chinese literature)
> kanshi (poetry in Chinese)
> monogatari (tales, narrative literature)
> nikki (diaries)
> utaawase (poetry contest)
> utamonogatari (poem tales)
> zuihitsu (essays)

GENERAL

C1　佐藤謙三　平安時代文学の研究
Satō Kenzō. *Heian jidai bungaku no kenkyū*. Kadokawa Shoten, 1960. 352p.

Collection of previously published essays on Heian literature. Arranged by genre, including monogatari, nikki, waka, setsuwa, etc.

C2　阿部秋生　日本文学史
Abe Akio. *Nihon bungakushi: chūkohen*. Hanawa Shobō, 1966. 382p. (Hanawa sensho)

Study of Heian literature. Organized chronologically: 9th century: Chinese-style poetic literature; 10th century: The beginnings of prose; 11th century: The age of prose literature; 12th century: Prose and waka.

C3　平安朝文学史　秋山　虔　等編
Heianchō bungakushi, ed. by Akiyama Ken, et al. Meiji Shoin, 1965. 970p.

Collection of essays on various genres of Heian literature, including waka, monogatari, diaries, travel accounts, essays, and songs. Appended are a chronology and a bibliography of references written in Western languages. Index.

C4　鈴木知太郎　平安時代文学論叢
Suzuki Tomotarō. *Heian jidai bungaku ronsō*. Kasama Shoin, 1968. 558p.

Collection of 25 previously published essays on Heian literature, including tales, diaries, essays, and poetry.

C5　池田亀鑑選集
Ikeda Kikan senshū. Shibundō, 1968-69. 5v.

Selected works of Ikeda Kikan.

V.1 Diaries and poetry.
V.2 Tales, I.
V.3 Tales, II.
V.4 Essays.
V.5 *Makura no sōshi*.

C6　萩谷　朴　平安朝文学の史的考察
Hagitani Boku. *Heianchō bungaku no shiteki kōsatsu*. Hakuteisha, 1969. 364p.

Study of literature during the 60 years from the death of Fujiwara no Michinaga to the age of the cloistered emperor system. Discusses the literature written by women at court, Buddhist literature, humorous literature, etc.

C7　佐藤謙三　王朝文学前後
Satō Kenzō. *Ōchō bungaku zengo*. Kadokawa Shoten, 1969. 299p.

Collection of 19 essays on various literary works, including *Genji monogatari*, *Makura no sōshi*, *Ōkagami*, *Konjaku monogatari*, *Tsurezuregusa*, etc.

C8　今井源衛　王朝文学の研究
Imai Gen'e. *Ōchō bungaku no kenkyū*. Kadokawa Shoten, 1970. 462p.

Bibliographical and historical studies of literature with emphasis on *Ise monogatari*, *Makura no sōshi*, and *Genji monogatari*. Bibliography and index.

C9 角田文衛　王　朝　の　映　像
Tsunoda Bun'ei. *Ōchō no eizō*. Tokyodō, 1970. 612p.

Collection of essays on prominent historical and literary figures of the Heian period, including Ono no Komachi, Ariwara no Narihira, Sei Shonagon, etc. Arranged chronologically. Bibliographical references at the end of each chapter. Index.

C10 平安朝文学研究　岡　一男　博士
Heianchō bungaku kenkyū: sakka to sakuhin - Oka Kazuo Hakushi shōju kinen ronshū, ed. by Waseda Daigaku Heianchō Bungaku Kenkyūkai. Yūseidō, 1971. 743p.

Festschrift of essays on Heian period authors and their works.

C11 中古文学論考　山岸徳平　先生
Chūko bungaku ronkō, Yamagishi Tokuhci Sensei shōju, ed. by Yamagishi Tokuhei Sensei o Tataerukai. Yūseidō, 1972. 542p.

C12 西木忠一　平安文学論考
Nishiki Tadakazu. *Heian bungaku ronkō*. Kyoto, Daigakudō Shoten, 1973. 301p.

Collection of essays on Heian literature treating the study of diaries, waka, and monogatari.

C13 迫　徹郎　王朝文学の考証的研究
Hazama Tetsurō. *Ōchō bungaku no kōshōteki kenkyū*. Kazama Shobō, 1973. 680p.

Collection of essays on literature of the Nara and Heian periods, with emphasis on *Yamato monogatari*, *Ōkagami*, *Makura no sōshi*, *Man'yōshū*, and *Shinsen wakashū*. General index and index to waka.

C14 年表資料　中古文学史　犬養　廉　等編
Nenpyō shiryō: chūko bungakushi, ed. by Inukai Kiyoshi, et al. Chikuma Shobō, 1973. 339p.

A history of Heian period literature. Pt.1: Chronological table for the years 794-1200; Pt.2: Short excerpts from Heian literature, including Chinese poetry, waka, monogatari, diaries, etc. Genealogical charts are appended.

C15 高橋和夫　平　安　京　文　学
Takahashi Kazuo. *Heiankyō bungaku*: sono rekishi to fūdo. Kyoto, Akao Shōbundō, 1974. 476p.

A literature of the city of Heiankyō. Contains essays on the *Kokinshū*, diaries, the life of Hikaru Genji, etc. Includes an appendix on Heian period social life and customs. Illustrations and maps.

C16 山中　裕　平安朝文学の史的研究
Yamanaka Yutaka. *Heianchō bungaku no shiteki kenkyū*. Yoshikawa Kōbunkan, 1974. 454p.

Collection of essays on Heian period literature, including *Makura no sōshi*, *Genji monogatari*, *Eiga monogatari*, and *Ōkagami*. Bibliography. Index.

C17 平安朝文学の諸問題　岡　一男　先生
Heianchō bungaku no shomondai: Oka Kazuo Sensei kiju kinen ronshū, ed. by Heianchō Bungaku Kenkyūkai. Kasama Shoin, 1977. 419p.

Festschrift of essays by specialists. Discusses various issues of Heian literature.

C18 日本文学全史　巻2　中古　秋山　虔　編
Nihon bungaku zenshi v.2 Chūko, ed. by Akiyama Ken. Gakutōsha, 1978. 598p.

Collection of essays on the historical development of Heian literature. Discusses the following topics: Chinese-style poetry, *Kokin wakashū*, the appearance of monogatari and diaries, the period of *Gosen wakashū*, *Shūi wakashū*, the period of the Emperor Ichijō, *Genji monogatari*, later Heian monogatari and diaries, the birth of historical tales, Chinese literature and setsuwa literature.

C19 論叢王朝文学　上村悦子　編
Ronsō ōchō bungaku, ed. by Uemura Etsuko. Kasama Shoin, 1978. 711p.

Festschrift in honor of Professor Uemura Etsuko. Contains essays on various aspects of Heian literature, including *Kagerō nikki*, *Izumi shikibu nikki*, *Yamato monogatari*, *Genji monogatari*, etc.

C20 原田芳起　探　求　日　本　文　学
Harada Yoshioki. *Tankyū Nihon bungaku*: chūko chūseihen. Kazama Shobo, 1979. 457p.

Collection of essays on Heian literature, including *Kagerō nikki*, *Genji monogatari*, and other works of fiction, and on the literature of the medieval period, including waka, renga, haikai, and military tales. Bibliography of works by the author.

C21 中古　日本文学史　木村正中　編
Chūko Nihon bunkgakushi, ed. by Kimura Masanori. Yūhikaku, 1979. 272p.

Collection of introductory essays on various genres of Heian literature, including Japanese and Chinese poetry, monogatari, diaries, historical tales, setsu-wa, and songs. Bibliography. Chronology. Index.

C22　論集　中古文学　中古文学研究会　編
Ronshū chūko bungaku, ed. by Chūko Bungaku Kenkyūkai. Kasama Shoin, 1979- (4v.)

A serial publication of the Society for the Study of Heian Literature.

No.1　The structure and presentation of *Genji monogatari*.
No.2　Early monogatari.
No.3　Diaries, literary criticism.
No.4　Monogatari from the late Heian period, including historical fiction.

C23　平安時代の歴史と文学　山中　裕編
Heian jidai no rekishi to bungaku, ed. by Yamanaka Yutaka. Yoshikawa Kōbunkan, 1981. 2v.

Festschrift in honor of Professor Yamanaka Yutaka.

V.1　On the literature of the mid-Heian period, especially *Genji monogatari*.
V.2　On the historical background of Heian period literature.

WOMEN WRITERS

C24　山中　裕　平安時代の女流作家
Yamanaka Yutaka. *Heian jidai no joryū sakka*. Shibundō, 1962. 231p. (Nihon rekishi shinsho)

Women writers of the Heian period. Discusses the rise of the Fujiwara regency as a major factor in the development of literature written by women. Bibliographical references.

C25　岡崎知子　平安朝女流作家の研究
Okazaki Tomoko. *Heianchō joryū sakka no kenkyū*. Kyoto, Hōzōkan, 1967. 306p.

Collection of previously published essays on women writers of the Heian period, including Akazome Emon, Izumi Shikibu, Ise no Tayū, etc.

C26　木之下正雄　平安女流文学のことば
Kinoshita Masao. *Heian joryū bungaku no kotoba*. Shibundō, 1968. 246p.

An introduction to word usage in Heian women's literature. Pt.1 An outline of terminology; Pt.2 Grammar and idioms. Bibliography. Index.

C27　根來　司　平安女流文学の文章の研究
Negoro Tsukasa. *Heian joryū bungaku no bunshō no kenkyū*. Kasama Shoin, 1969-73. 2v. (Kasama sōsho)

A study of syntax in Heian women's literature, with emphasis on *Makura no sōshi*, *Genji monogatari*, and *Murasaki Shikibu nikki*. Also discusses the use of auxiliary verbs, honorifics, etc. Index in each volume.

C28　秋山　虔　王朝女流文学の形成
Akiyama Ken. *Ōchō joryū bungaku no keisei*. Hanawa Shobō, 1967. 260p.

Consists of three essays on the formative years of Heian period women's literature, including *Ise monogatari*, *Kagerō nikki*, etc.

C29　秋山　虔　王朝女流文学の世界
Akiyama Ken. *Ōchō joryū bungaku no sekai*, Tokyo Daigaku Shuppankai, 1972. 236p. (UP sensho)

The world of Heian period women's literature, with emphasis on *Genji monogatari*, *Makura no sōshi*, and diaries. Also describes the literary circles formed by ladies at court during the period of the Fujiwara Regency.

C30　森野宗明　王朝貴族社会の女性と言語
Morino Muneaki. *Ōchō kizoku shakai no josei to gengo*. Yūseidō, 1975. 232p. (Yūseidō sensho)

A study of the speech and behavior of Heian period aristocratic women as revealed in monogatari and diaries.

C31　上村悦子　王朝女流作家の研究
Uemura Etsuko. *Ōchō joryū sakka no kenkyū*. Kasama Shoin, 1975. 424p. (Kasama sōsho)

Collection of essays on Heian period women writers and their life style, including Izumi Shikibu, Murasaki Shikibu, Sei Shōnagon, etc. Reference bibliography. Illustrations. Indexes.

C32　山路麻芸　王朝の女人像
Yamaji Maki. *Ōchō no nyoninzō*. Shunjūsha, 1980. 333p.

Biographical studies of Heian period women writers:

Ono no Komachi

Ise

Michitsuna no haha

Sei Shōnagon

Murasaki Shikibu

Izumi Shikibu

Akazome Emon

Ise no Tayū

Sugawara Takasue no musume

Jōjin Ajari no haha

Sanuki no suke

LANGUAGE

C33 渡辺　実　平安朝文章史
Watanabe Minoru. *Heianchō bunshōshi*. Tokyo Daigaku Shuppankai, 1981. 239p.

A study of sentence structure and word usage in the major literary works of the Heian period.

C34 神尾暢子　王朝国語の表現映像
Kamio Nobuko. *Ōchō kokugo no hyōgen eizō*. Shintensha, 1982. 562p. (Shintensha kenkyū sōsho)

A collection of essays on imagery in Heian literature, with examples drawn from monogatari, poetry, etc.

C35 榊原邦彦　平安語彙論考
Sakakibara Kunihiko. *Heian goi ronkō*. Kyōiku Shuppan Sentā, 1982. 248p. (Kenkyū sensho)

A study of the honorifics used in Heian period Japanese.

C36 沼本克明　平安鎌倉時代における日本漢字音
Numoto Katsuaki. *Heian Kamakura jidai ni okeru Nihon kanjion ni tsuite no kenkyū*. Musashino Shoin, 1982. 1197p.

A study of the Japanese pronunciation of Chinese characters in the Heian and Kamakura periods.

CLASSICAL LITERATURE IN CHINESE

Kanbungaku (Chinese prose literature)

C37 川口久雄　平安朝日本漢文学史の研究
Kawaguchi Hisao. *Heianchō Nihon kanbungakushi no kenkyū*. Revised and enlarged ed. Meiji Shoin, 1975-(82) (3v.)

1st ed. published in 1959-61 in 2v.

Historical survey of classical Chinese literature from 800 to 1200. Discusses the revival of Chinese classical studies in the Heian period, the influence of Chinese literature on *Kokinshū*, *Tosa nikki*, *Genji*

monogatari, etc. Contains bibliographical references and genealogical charts. Indexes.

C38 後藤昭雄　平安朝漢文学論考
Gotō Akio. *Heianchō kanbungaku ronkō*. Ōfūsha, 1981. 480p.

Collection of previously published essays on Chinese style literature and literary circles in the Heian period. Indexes.

C39 川口久雄　平安朝の漢文学
Kawaguchi Hisao. *Heianchō no kanbungaku*. Yoshikawa Kōbunkan, 1981. 314p. (Nihon rekishi shinsho)

Traces the history of Heian literature in Chinese and its relationship to vernacular literature. Appended are a chronology, a chart, and reference sources. Index.

Kanshi (poetry in Chinese)

C40 小島憲之　国風暗国時代の文学
Kojima Noriyuki. *Kokufu ankoku jidai no bungaku*. Hanawa Shobō, 1967- (3v.) In progress.

An extensive study of Chinese style poetry from the early Heian period. Indexes in each volume.

V.1 Introduction to literature in antiquity.
V.2, pt.1 Literature of the late Nara, early Heian period.
      pt.2 The first imperial anthology of the Kōnin era (810-24), the *Ryōunshū*.
      pt.3 Forthcoming.
V.3 Forthcoming.

C41 小島憲之　古今集以前
Kojima Noriyuki. *Kokinshū izen*. Hanawa Shobō, 1976. 362p.

English title: Chinese influences on Japanese poetry - especially on the literature of the early Heian era (9thc. A.D.). A survey of the period between the *Man'yōshū* and the *Kokinshū*, when Chinese poetry was much admired. English abstract. Chronology. Index.

C42 金原　理　平安朝漢詩文の研究
Kinbara Tadashi. *Heianchō kanshibun no kenkyū*. Kyushu Daigaku Shuppankai, 1981. 464p.

Collection of 18 essays on men of letters, poetry, poetics, etc., in Chinese from the Heian period to the beginning of the medieval period. Indexes to personal names, titles, and poems.

POETRY

Waka

C43　峯岸義秋　平安時代和歌文学の研究
Minegishi Yoshiaki. *Heian jidai waka bungaku no kenkyū*. Ōfūsha, 1965. 357p.

Collection of previously published essays on the waka of Ōshikōchi Mitsune, Ki no Tsurayuki, Tsutsumi chūnagon Kanesuke, and on various utaawase. Waka index.

C44　藤岡忠美　平安和歌史論
Fujioka Tadaharu. *Heian wakashiron* - Sandaishū jidai no kichō. Ōfūsha, 1966. 372p.

A study of the three imperial anthologies *Kokin wakashū*, *Gosen wakashū*, and *Shūi wakashū*. Includes essays on the anthologies themselves, on Sone no Yoshitada and other prominent poets, and on Izumi Shikibu. A post-war essay of Heian period waka, appended.

C45　松田武夫　王朝和歌集の研究
Matsuda Takeo. *Ōchō wakashū no kenkyū*. Hakuteisha, 1968. 287p.

Bibliographical studies of 8 imperial anthologies and private collections of poetry from the Heian period. Also discusses the nature and historical development of utaawase.

C46　松田武夫　平安朝の和歌
Matsuda Takeo. *Heianchō no waka*. Yūseidō, 1968. 438p.

Collection of previously published essays concerning Heian period poetry. In 4 parts: an outline of Heian period waka; shikashū (private collections of waka); Kokinshū; and bibliographical studies.

C47　目崎徳衛　平安文化史論
Mezaki Tokue. *Heian bunkashiron*. Ōfūsha, 1968. 370p.

A study of Heian period waka from the standpoint of cultural history. Examines the lifestyle of the Imperial family, aristocrats, and courtiers as a source for poetry. Index.

C48　窪田敏夫　王朝和歌史論
Kubota Toshio. *Ōchō wakashiron*. Kadokawa Shoten, 1969. 317p.

Collection, issued posthumously, of Professor Kubota Toshio's essays, and lecture notes on the *Kokinshū* and other works of classical poetry.

C49　橋本不美男　王朝和歌集の研究
Hashimoto Fumio. *Ōchō wakashū no kenkyū*. Kasama Shoin, 1972. 566p.

Collection of previously published essays on the development of waka in the Heian period. Also discusses the life of Heian aristocrats, aesthetics, private anthologies, etc. Indexes.

C50　和歌文学新論　森本元子 編
Waka bungaku shinron, ed. by Morimoto Motoko. Meiji Shoin, 1982. 567p.

Festschrift of essays on Heian and medieval period waka by members of the Waka study group in honor of Professor Morimoto.

poetics

C51　小沢正夫　平安の和歌と歌学
Ozawa Masao. *Heian no waka to kagaku*. Kasama Shoin, 1979. 296p. (Kasama sōsho)

Heian period poetry and poetics. Contains a summary in English of waka scholarship in the Heian period.

C52　小沢正男　古代歌学の形成
Ozawa Masao. *Kodai kagaku no keisei*. Hanawa Shobō, 1963. 590p.

English title: the development and tradition of ancient poetics in Japan. A history of waka based on a comparison of Chinese and Japanese classical literature. Emphasizes the study of poetics as expressed in the preface to the *Kokinshū*, etc. Bibliographical references. English summary. Index.

poetry circle

C53　橋本不美男　院政期の歌壇史研究
Hashimoto Fumio. *Inseiki no kadanshi kenkyū*. Musashino Shoin, 1966. 338p.

History of poetry circles, especially that of the retired Emperor Horikawa, during the period of the cloistered government.

C54　山口　博　王朝歌壇の研究
Yamaguchi Hiroshi. *Ōchō kadan no kenkyū*. Ōfūsha, 1967, 1973, 1979. 3v.

A study of poetry circles in the Imperial court.

V.1 Covers the forty years of poetry reading from Murakami Tenno to En'yū Tennō in the latter part of the 10th century.

V.2 Covers the period from Uda Tenno to Sujaku Tennō.

V.3 (Suppl.) Lists officials of the Imperial House-hold Office (Kurōdo dokoro). Discusses literary circles of court nobles and civil servants who elevated waka composition to official literature.

(See also C56)

C55 杉崎重遠　平安中期歌壇の研究
Sugisaki Shigetō. *Heian chūki kadan no kenkyū*. Ōfūsha, 1977. 428p.

An evaluation of the major poets of the mid-Heian period, with emphasis on Fujiwara no Michinaga's poetry circle. Index to poems.

C56 山口　博　王朝歌壇の研究
Yamaguchi Hiroshi. *Ōchō kadan no kenkyū*. Ōfūsha, 1982. 804p.

Poetry circles active during the reign of eight Heian period emperors, from Emperor Kanmu to Emperor Kōkō. (See also C54)

poets

C57 臼田甚五郎　平安歌人研究
Usuda Jingorō. *Heian kajin kenkyū*. Miyai Shoten, 1976. 406p.

Collection of essays on life and thought at the Heian period court, men and women poets, etc.

C58 井上宗雄　平安後期歌人伝の研究
Inoue Muneo. *Heian kōki kajinden no kenkyū*. Kasama Shoin, 1978. 581p. (Kasama sōsho)

Biographical studies on poets active in the mid-11th century. Indexes to author's names, references, source books, and waka.

utaawase (poetry contests)

C59 萩谷　朴　平安朝歌合概説
Hagitani Boku. *Heianchō utaawase gaisetsu*. Hagitani, 1969. 399p. (Private publication)

A complete catalogue of Heian period utaawase. Reprinted in Heianchō utaawase taisei, v.10. (see the following entry)

C60 萩谷　朴　平安朝歌合大成
Hagitani Boku. *Heianchō utaawase taisei*. Kyoto, Dōhōsha, 1979. 10v.

A complete collection of Heian period utaawase.

V.1-8 Textual studies.
V.9 Index.
V.10 Historiography, survey histories, bibliography.

Imperial Anthologies

Kokin wakashū

C61 三代集の研究　小沢正男 編
Sandaishū no kenkyū, ed. by Ozawa Masao. Meiji Shoin, 1981. 487p.

Festschrift on the Sandaishū (*Kokinshū, Gosenshū, Shūishū*) in honor of Professor Ozawa Masao. Bio-bibliography.

Kokin wakashū

C62 久曽神　昇　古今和歌集成立論
Kyūsojin Hitaku. *Kokin wakashū seiritsuron*. Kazama Shobō, 1960-61. 4v.

On the probable date of publication of the *Kokinshū*.

V.1-3 Examines variant editions of the text.
V.4 Bibliographical studies of the poems in each text, which leads to the determination of the date.

C63 村瀬敏夫　古今集の基盤と周辺
Murase Toshio. *Kokinshū no kiban to shūhen*. Ōfūsha, 1971. 243p.

Discusses the compilation of the *Kokinshū*, the social status of the compilers: Ki no Tsurayuki and others.

C64 小沢正男　古今集の世界
Ozawa Masao. *Kokinshū no sekai*. Enlarged, revised ed. Hanawa Shobō, 1976. 332p. (Hanawa sensho)

History of the composition of the *Kokinshū*. Charts. Index.

C65 古今集校本　西下経一等 編
Kokinshū kōhon, ed. by Nishishita Keiichi and Takizawa Sadao. Kasama Shoin, 1977. 462p. (Kasama sōsho)

Definitive edition of the *Kokinshū* based on the text dating from the 2nd year of the Jōō era (1223).

C66 菊地靖彦　古今的世界の研究
Kikuchi Yasuhiko. *Kokinteki sekai no kenkyū*. Kasama Shoin, 1080. 479p. (Kasama sōsho)

The literary world of the *Kokinshū*, *Gosenshū*, and *Shūishū*. Traces the formulation and development of Kokin-style poetry.

C67　岡村恒哉　古今集の研究
Okamura Tsuneya. *Kokinshū no kenkyū*. Rinsen Shoten, 1980. 277p.

A study of the *Kokinshū*, with emphasis on the prefaces, the influence of the *man'yōshū*, problems of interpretation, etc.

C68　和田嘉寿男　万葉から古今へ
Wada Kazuo. *Man'yō kara kokin e*. Meiji Shoin, 1981. 205p.

Surveys the history of Japanese poetry from the *Man'yōshū* to the *Kokinshū*. Index to poems. Illustrations.

C69　中田武司　古今和歌集の形成
Nakada Takeshi. *Kokin wakashū no keisei*. Ōfūsha, 1982. 266p.

A study of the composition of the *Kokinshū*, its compiler, Ki no Tsurayuki, and others.

Kin'yōshū

C70　松田武夫　金葉集の研究
Matsuda Takeo. *Kin'yōshū no kenkyū*. Yamada Shoin, 1956. 431p.

A collection of previously published essays on the *Kin'yōshū*, discussing its compilation, poets, variant texts, etc.

Gosen wakashū

C71　小松茂美　後撰和歌集
Komatsu Shigemi. *Gosenwakashū*. Seishin Shobō, 1961. 2v.

Bibliographical studies of the *Gosenshū*.

V.1 Variant texts with annotations. Index of poems.
V.2 Textual studies and manuscript reproductions. Index.

C72　田島毓堂　後撰和歌集研究史
Tajima Ikudō. *Gosen wakashū kenkyūshi*. Nagoya, Tōkai Gakuen Joshi Tanki Daigaku Kokugo Kokubun Gakkai, 1970. 403p. (Tōkai Gakuen kokubun sōsho)

History of research on the *Gosenshū*. Sources, reference works, chronology of research appended. Index.

C73　片桐洋一　拾遺和歌集の研究
Katagiri Yōichi. *Shūi wakashū no kenkyū*. Kyoto, Daigakudō Shoten, 1970. 2v.

A textual study of the *Shūishū*. Charts.

C74　奥村恒哉　古今集・後撰集の諸問題
Okamura Tsuneya. *Kokinshū, Gosenshū no shomondai*. Kazama Shobō, 1971. 587p.

Collection of previously published essays on the *Kokinshū* and the *Gosenshū*. Index.

C75　上野　理　後撰集前後
Ueno Osamu. *Gosenshū zengo*. Kasama Shoin, 1976. 890p.

Traces the history of poetry from the end of the 10th century to the early 12th century. Also contains a history of the study of the *Gosenshū*. Indexes poetry by line, subject, and number in the *Gosenshū*.

Shikashū (private collections)

C76　森本元子　私家集と新古今集
Morimoto Motoko. *Shikashū to Shinkokinshū*. Meiji Shoin, 1974. 494p.

Study of Heian private poetry anthologies and their representation in the *Shinkokinshū*. Also includes an analysis of the private anthology *Saigū no nyōgoshū*. Appended are a table listing the poems from Heian period private anthologies that can be found in the *Shinkokinshū* and a chart of variant editions of the *Saigū no nyōgoshū*. Poetry index.

C77　安藤太郎　平安時代私家集歌人の研究
Andō Tarō. *Heian jidai shikashū kajin no kenkyū*. Ōfūsha, 1982. 320p.

Poets whose work appeared in the private anthologies of the Heian period, including Fujiwara no Michinobu, Tadamine, Minamoto no Nobuaki, and others.

PROSE LITERATURE

Monogatari (tales)

C78　石川　徹　古代小説史考
Ishikawa Tōru. *Kodai shōsetsushi kō*. Tōkō Shoin, 1958. 559p.

Collection of essays on Heian period fiction, especially *Genji monogatari*. Also discusses diaries, the relationship between waka and monogatari, the influence of Chinese literature, etc.

C79 目加田さくを　物語作家圏の研究
Mekada Sakuo. *Monogatari sakkaken no kenkyū.* Musashino Shoin, 1964. 968p.

Discusses the development of the novel in the Heian period by examining writers and their audiences, the education of men of letters in the Chinese classics and poetry, etc. Also describes the women's literary circles referred to in the *Genji monogatari.*

C80 三谷栄一　物語史の研究
Mitani Eiichi. *Monogatarishi no kenkyū.* Yūseidō, 1969. 559p.

Study of the monogatari genre examining its origins, its relationship to katarimono, its development, and its fruition in *Taketori monogatari, Utsubo monogatari, Genji monogatari,* etc. Indexes to names, titles, subjects, and poems.

C81 仲田庸幸　平安朝文学の文芸的研究
Nakata Tsuneyuki. *Heianchō bungaku no bungeiteki kenkyū.* Kazama Shobō, 1967. 538p.

Collection of essays on Heian period literature, including *Genji monogatari, Kagero nikki, Makura no sōshi,* etc. Index.

C82 松尾　聡　平安時代物語論考
Matsuo Satoshi. *Heian jidai monogatari ronkō.* Kasama Shoin, 1968. 625p.

Collection of essays on Heian period monogatari, from *Ise monogatari* to *Hamamatsu chūnagon monogatari.* Contains an appendix on the study of monogatari no longer extant.

C83 阿部俊子　歌物語とその周辺
Abe Toshiko. *Utamonogatari to sono shūhen.* Kazama Shobō, 1969. 1193p.

Study of Heian period utamonogatari, including *Henjōshū, Tōnomine Shōshō monogatari,* etc.

C84 中田武司　王朝歌物語の研究と新資料
Nakada Takeshi. *Ōchō uta monogatari no kenkyū to shin shiryō.* Ōfūsha, 1971. 477p.

An introduction to uta monogatari, with emphasis on *Ise monogatari, Heichū monogatari* and *Yamato monogatari.* Discusses the structure and subject matter of uta monogatari. contains newly found editions of *Ise monogatari.* Index.

C85 中野幸一　物語文学論攷
Nakano Kōichi. *Monogatari bungaku ronkō.* Kyōiku Shuppan Sentā, 1971. 537p.

Traces the development of monogatari from antiquity to the late Heian period.

C86 南波　浩　物語文学
Nanba Hiroshi. *Monogatari bungaku.* New ed. San'ichi Shobō, 1971. 240p. (Koten to sono jidai v. 3)

General discussion of the development of monogatari, from the *Kojiki* to *Ise monogatari* and *Genji monogatari.*

C87 鈴木弘道　平安末期物語についての研究
Suzuki Hiromichi. *Heian makki monogatari ni tsuite no kenkyū.* Kyoto, Akao Shōbundō, 1971. 580p.

Study of three important monogatari from the late Heian period: *Yowa no nezame, Hamamatsu chūnagon monogatari, and Torikaebaya monogatari.* Reference bibliography. Index.

C88 今井卓爾　物語文学史の研究
Imai Takuji. *Monogatari bungakushi no kenkyū.* Waseda Daigaku Shuppanbu, 1976-77. 3v.

History of Heian period monogatari.

V.1 Early Heian monogatari.

V.2 *Genji monogatari.*

V.3 Late Heian monogatari. List of sources. Bibliography.

C89 藤村　潔　古代物語研究序説
Fujimura Kiyoshi. *Kodai monogatari kenkyū josetsu.* Kasama Shoin, 1977. 445p. (Kasama sōsho)

Introduction to monogatari in antiquity. Analyzes *Genji monogatari, Sumiyoshi monogatari, Sagoromo monogatari,* etc.

C90 石川　徹　平安時代物語文学論
Ishikawa Tōru. *Heian jidai monogatari bungakuron.* Kasama Shoin, 1979. 588p.

Collection of previously published essays on Heian period monogatari, including *Utsuho monogatari, Genji monogatari, Ochikubo monogatari.* Also discusses diaries. Index.

C91 鈴木弘道　平安末期物語研究
Suzuki Hiromichi. *Heian makki monogatari kenkyū.* Kyoto, Daigakudō Shoten, 1979. 391p.

Summary of the author's studies in late Heian period monogatari. Analyzes the development of the genre, its subject matter, etc. Title/name index. (see also C88)

C92 盛岡常夫　平安朝物語の研究
Morioka Tsuneo. *Heianchō monogatari no kenkyū*. Enlarged ed. Kazama Shobō, 1981. 671p.

Study of *Genji monogatari* and of other monogatari from the late Heian period, including *Sagoromo*, *Hamamatsu chūnagon*, *Torikaebaya*, etc.

C93 樋口芳麻呂　平安鎌倉時代散逸物語の研究
Higuchi Yoshimaro. *Heian Kamakura jidai san'itsu monogatari no kenkyū*. Hitaku Shobō, 1981. 585p.

Study of 12 monogatari, dating from the Heian and Kamakura periods, that are no longer extant.

C94 小木　喬　散逸物語の研究
Ogi Takashi. *San'itsu monogatari no kenkyū*: Heian-Kamakura jidaihen. Kasama Shoin, 1973. 930p.

Study of monogatari no longer extant. Gives bibliographical explanations of source materials, followed by titles arranged in a-i-u-e-o order with citations of sources. Index.

C95 王朝物語とその周辺　南波　浩　編
Ōchō monogatari to sono shūhen, ed. by Nanba Hiroshi. Kasama Shoin, 1982. 512p. (Kasama sōsho)

Festschrift in honor of Professor Nanba Hiroshi. Traces the history of Heian period monogatari. Biobiliography appended.

C96 増渕勝一　平安朝文学成立の研究
Masubuchi Katsuichi. *Heianchō bungaku seiritsu no kenkyū: sanbunhen*. Kasama Shoin, 1982. 346p. (Kasama sōsho)

Collection of previously published essays on Heian period prose literature, including *Taketori monogatari*, *Genji monogatari*, *Ōkagami*, etc. Index.

C97 体系物語文学史　三谷栄一　編
Taikei monogatari bungakushi, ed. by Mitani Eiichi. Yūseidō, 1982- V.1-

A festschrift in honor of Professor Mitani Eiichi. To be completed in 5 volumes. V.1 A general introduction to monogatari.

Genji monogatari

C98 池田亀鑑　源氏物語大成
Ikeda Kikan. *Genji monogatari taisei*. Chūō Kōronsha, 1953-56. 8v.

A comprehensive collection of materials on *Genji monogatari*.

V.1-3 Standard text with variations, based on the copy by Fujiwara no Teika. Annotated.

V.4-6 Indexes to words, auxiliary verbs, suffixes.

V.7　Reference materials.

V.8 Reproductions of scrolls, screen paintings, fans, etc.

C99 阿部秋生　源氏物語研究序説
Abe Akio. *Genji monogatari kenkyū josetsu*. Tokyo Daigaku Shuppankyoku, 1959. 2v.

Introduction to the study of *Genji monogatari*.

C100 今井源衛　源氏物語の研究
Imai Gen'e. *Genji monogatari no kenkyū*. Miraisha, 1962. 345p.

Collection of essays on Genji monogatari.

C101 秋山　虔　源氏物語の世界
Akiyama Ken. *Genji monogatari no sekai*. Tokyo Daigaku Shuppankai, 1964. 434p.

Companion volume to the author's ''Ōchō joryū bungaku no sekai''. Discusses the development of literature written by women, thought and syntax in the *Murasaki Shikibu nikki*, etc. Book reviews of recent studies on *Genji monogatari*, appended.

C102 伊藤慎吾　風俗よりみたる源氏物語
Ito Shingo. *Fūzoku yori mitaru Genji monogatari byōsha jidai no kenkyū*. Kazama Shobō, 1968. 951p.

Examines life at court during the Heian period as described in the *Genji monogatari*.

C103 古代文学論叢　紫式部学会　編
Kodai bungaku ronsō, ed. by Murasaki Shikibu Gakkai. Musashino Shoin, 1969- (82)-. 8v.

Essays by members of the Murasaki Shikibu Society.

No.1 *Genji monogatari*: studies and sources.

No.2 The world of *Genji monogatari*.

No.3 *Genji monogatari* and *Makura no sōshi*: studies and sources.

No.4 Studies and sources of the poetry in *Genji monogatari* (1).

No.5 Women's diaries and *Genji monogatari*: studies and sources.

No.6 The influence of *Genji monogatari*: studies and sources.

No.7 Monogatari after *Genji monogatari*: studies and sources.

No.8 Studies and sources of the poetry in *Genji monogatari* (2).

C104　寺本直彦　源氏物語受容史論考
Teramoto Naohiko. *Genji monogatari juyōshi ronkō*. Kazama Shoin, 1970, 1984. 2v.

V.1 Traces the influence of *Genji monogatari* on medieval poetry and Edo period haikai. Reference bibliography. Indexes.

V.2 Zokuhen, 1984. Criticism of *Genji monogatari* found in the *Imakagami*, Genji-inspired folklore, etc. Includes various editions of the text. Reference bibliography. Indexes.

C105　重松信弘　源氏物語の思想
Shigematsu Nobuhiro. *Genji monogatari no shisō*. Kazama Shobō, 1971. 540p.

A collection of essays on philosophical aspects of *Genji monogatari*, including religion, Chinese classical thought, ethics, etc.

C106　源氏物語講座　山岸徳平　等編
Genji monogatari kōza, ed. by Yamagishi Tokuhei and Oka Kazuo. Yūseidō, 1971-73. 9v.

Lectures on *Genji monogatari*.

V.1 Theme and method in *Genji monogatari*.
V.2 Plot conception.
V.3 Characters.
V.4 Characters.
V.5 Philosophical background.
V.6 Life of Murasaki Shikibu.
V.7 Narrative style, syntax, word usage.
V.8 Variant editions, sources, influence on other stories, the performing arts, etc.
V.9 (Supplement) *Genji monogatari* dictionary.

C107　岩瀬法雲　源氏物語と仏教思想
Iwase Hōun. *Genji monogatari to Bukkyō shisō*. Kasama Shoin, 1972. 246p. (Kasama sōsho)

Collection of essays on Buddhist thought in *Genji monogatari*. Also contains an analysis of *Murasaki Shikibu nikki* and *Kagerō nikki*.

C108　源氏物語の探求　源氏物語探求会　編
Genji monogatari no tankyū, ed. by Genji Monogatari Tankyūkai. Kazama Shobō, 1974-(84) (9v.)

A serial publication. No.1 was edited by Shigematsu Nobuhiko Hakushi Shōjukai. Each number treats a specific topic in the study of *Genji monogatari*. No.8 contains 14 essays by women specialists on anaylsis of women in the monogatari.

C109　藤井貞和　源氏物語の始原と現在
Fujii Sadakazu. *Genji monogatari no shigen to genzai*. Tōjusha, 1980. 307p.

Collection of previously published essays on *Genji monogatari*. Discusses the origins of the monogatari genre, the composition of the story, etc.

C110　重松信弘　源氏物語研究叢書
Shigematsu Nobuhiro. *Genji monogatari kenkyū sōsho*. Kazama Shobō, 1980- (82). (4v.)

Genji monogatari research series.

No.1 Characters in the story.
No.2 A history of research on *Genji monogatari*.
No.3 Theme, structure, and development of the story.
No.4 An analysis of the plot of *Genji monogatari* and of Genji's character.

C111　講座　源氏物語の世界　秋山　虔　等編
Kōza Genji monogatari no sekai, ed. by Akiyama Ken, et al. Yūhikaku, 1980- (82). (7v.)

The world of *Genji monogatari*, with a chapter-by-chapter analysis of the book. To be completed in 9v.

C112　伊井春樹　源氏物語論考
Ii Haruki. *Genji monogatari ronkō*. Kazama Shobō, 1981. 415p.

Collection of previously published essays on *Genji monogatari*. Discusses the structure, character and composition of the story.

C113　文芸読本　源氏物語
Bungei tokuhon. Genji monogatari. Kawade Shobō Shinsha, 1981. 335p.

Collection of essays, intended for the general reader, on various aspects of *Genji monogatari*. Includes a section in modern Japanese transliteration. Reference bibliography. Illustrations.

C114　源氏物語　日本文学研究資料刊行会　編
Genji monogatari, ed. by Nihon Bungaku Kenkyū Shiryō Kankōkai. Yūseidō, 1969- (82) (4v.) (Nihon bungaku kenkyū shiryō sōsho)

Collection of essays on *Genji monogatari*.

C114a　源氏物語引歌索引　伊井春樹　編
Genji monogatari hikiuta sakuin, ed. by Ii Haruki. Kasama Shoin, 1977, 457p. (Kasama Shoin sōkan)

Collection of waka and song references in 30 major commentaries of the *Genji monogatari*, grouped by the order of chapters of the monogatari. Index.

C115　源 氏 物 語　鈴木一雄 編
Genji monogatari, ed. by Suzuki Kazuo. Shibundō, 1982. 3v. (Kokubungaku kaishaku to kanshō, special issue)

No.1 Origin and plot, March 1982.
No.2 Plot and theme, April 1982.
No.3 Style and presentation, May 1982.

other monogatari

C116　中田剛直　竹取物語の研究
Nakata Takenao. *Taketori monogatari no kenkyū*. Hanawa Shobō, 1965. 378p.

An annotated edition of *Taketori monogatari* collated from texts of the Keichō era. Indexes of words and subjects.

C117　鈴木弘道　寝覚物語の基礎的研究
Suzuki Hiromichi. *Nezame monogatari no kisoteki kenkyū*. Hanawa Shobō, 1965. 452p.

Collection of essays on the *Nezame monogatari*. An appendix includes annotations for the *Nezame monogatari emaki* and a bibliography of *Nezame monogatari* studies. Index.

C118　土岐武治　堤中納言物語の研究
Toki Takeji. *Tsutsumi chūnagon monogatari no kenkyū*. Kazama Shobō, 1967. 1005p.

Study of *Tsutsumi chūnagon monogatari*. Considers various aspects of the tale, its text, date of composition, etc. A separate essay on the standard text is included at the end. Bibliographical references. Index.

C119　鈴木弘道　とりかへばや物語の研究
Suzuki Hiromichi. *Torikaebaya monogatari no kenkyū*. Kasama Shoin, 1973. 471p. (Kasama sōsho)

A standardized, annotated text of the *Torikaebaya monogatari*. Contains essays on the author, texts, and origins. Bibliographical references.

C120　山田清市　伊勢物語の成立と伝本の研究
Yamada Seiichi. *Ise monogatari no seiritsu to denpon no kenkyū*. Ōfūsha, 1972. 701p.

Study of the *Ise monogatari*. Examines various texts to determine which are the closest to the original manuscript.

C121　山田清市　伊勢物語校本と研究
Yamada Seiichi. *Ise monogatari kōhon to kenkyū*. Ōfūsha, 1977. 747p.

Continuation of the above entry. Contains variant texts discovered since. Index to poems.

C122　野口元大　うつほ物語の研究
Noguchi Motohiro. *Utsuho monogatari no kenkyū*. Kasama Shoin, 1976. 494p.

Study of the *Utsuho monogatari*, examining the tale's structure, themes, texts, etc.

C123　中野幸一　うつほ物語の研究
Nakano Kōichi. *Utsuho monogatari no kenkyū*. Musashino Shoin, 1981. 757p.

Study of the *Utsuho monogatari* and its influence on later monogatari. Bibliography.

C124　高橋　元　竹取・伊勢物語の世界
Takahashi Gen. *Taketori, Ise monogatari no sekai*. Yoshikawa Kōbunkan, 1981. 340p.

History of thought, depicted in the *Taketori* and *Ise monogatari* in the early Heian period.

Historical Fiction (rekishi monogatari)

C125　山中　裕　歴史物語成立序説
Yamanaka Yutaka. *Rekishi monogatari seiritsu josetsu*. Tokyo Daigaku Shuppankai, 1962. 325p. (Tōdai Jinbun kagaku kenkyū sōsho)

Collection of essays on the development of historical fiction, with emphasis on *Genji monogatari* and *Eiga monogatari*. Index.

C126　松村博司　歴 史 物 語
Matsumura Hiroshi. *Rekishi monogatari*. Revised ed. Hanawa Shobō, 1979. 346p. (Hanawa sensho)

Traces the development of historical fiction; discusses *Eiga monogatari*, *Ōkagami*, *Imakagami*, *Mizukagami*, *Masukagami*, etc.

C127　松村博司　歴史物語研究序説
Matsumura Hiroji. *Rekishi monogatari kenkyū josetsu*. Izumi Shoin, 1981. 188p. (Izumi sensho)

Essays on various aspects of historical fiction. Also comments on the English translations of *Eiga monogatari* and *Ōkagami*.

C128　河北　騰　歴史物語の新研究
Kawakita Noboru. *Rekishi monogatari no shin-kenkyū*. Meiji Shoin, 1981. 402p.

Collection of essays on historical fiction and ancient chronicles. Includes bibliographical references to *Eiga monogatari*. Name index.

C129　保坂弘司　大鏡研究序説
Hosaka Hiroshi. *Ōkagami kenkyū josetsu*. Kōdansha, 1979. 697p.

Introduction to the *Ōkagami*, touching on the literary qualities of the work, its organization, etc. Appendices include a chronology, a genealogical chart, and maps. Index.

C130　目加田さくを　大鏡論
Mekada Sakuo. *Ōkagamiron*. Kasama Shoin, 1979. 947p.

Study of the *Ōkagami* as the first example of historical fiction that offers implicit political criticism in the Chinese tradition.

C131　論集　平將門研究　林　陸郎　編
Ronshū Taira Masakado kenkyū, ed. by Hayashi Rokuro. Gendai Shichōsha, 1975. 320p.

Collection of essays on the *Shōmonki*, which tells of the rebellion led by Taira no Masakado.

Setsuwa

C132　高橋　貢　中古説話文学研究序説
Takahashi Mitsugu. *Chūko setsuwa bungaku kenkyū josetsu*. Ōfūsha, 1974. 402p.

Introduction to Heian period setsuwa, with emphasis on *Konjaku monogatari* and *Nihon ryōiki*. A genealogical chart of the Tendai sect Buddhism derived from *Konjaku monogatari*, appended. p.375-392.

C133　黒沢幸三　日本古代の伝承文学の研究
Kurosawa Kōzō. *Nihon kodai no denshō bungaku no kenkyū*. Hanawa Shobō, 1976. 444p.

Collection of previously published essays on orally transmitted literature of the ancient period in Buddhist and Shinto related setsuwa. Also discusses the author of *Nihon ryōiki*. Index.

C134　守屋俊彦　日本霊異記の研究
Moriya Toshihiko. *Nihon ryōiki no kenkyū*. Miyai Shoten 1974-78. 2v.

Collection of essays on *Nihon ryōiki*. Both volumes contain detailed structural analysis of individual setsuwa. V.2, entitled "Zoku Nihon ryōiki no kenkyū."

C135　八木　毅　日本霊異記の研究
Yagi Tsuyoshi. *Nihon ryōiki no kenkyū*. Kazama Shobō, 1976. 564p.

Collection of previously published essays on the *Nihon ryōiki*. Examines the use of Ryōiki setsuwa in the *Konjaku monogatari*.

C136　日本霊異記の世界　日本霊異記研究会編
Nihon ryōiki no sekai, ed. by Nihon Ryōiki Kenkyūkai. Miyai Shoten, 1982. 362p. (Miyai sensho)

Collection of essays on tales, songs, grammar, etc. of the *Nihon ryōiki*. Reference bibliography.

C137　国東文麿　今昔物語集成立考
Kunisaki Fumimaro. *Konjaku monogatarishū seiritsukō*. Enlarged ed. Waseda Daigaku Shuppanbu, 1978. 529p.

Collection of essays on the *Konjaku monogatari*, its structure and development, its relationship to *Ōkagami*, etc.

C138　黒部通善　説話の生成と変容についての研究
Kurobe Michiyoshi. *Setsuwa no scisci to hen'yō ni tsuite no kenkyū*. Chūbu Nihon Kyōiku Bunkakai, 1982. 220p.

Collection of previously published essays on the origin and transformation of tales in *Uchigikishū*, *Konjaku monogatari*, etc. Index.

Nikki (diaries) See also *Hyakudai no kakaku*, A76

C139　今井卓爾　平安時代日記文学の研究
Imai Takuji. *Heian jidai nikki bungaku no kenkyū*. Meiji Shoin, 1957. 578p.

Discusses the historical and literary value of Heian period diaries.

C140　玉井幸助　日記文学の研究
Tamai Kōsuke. *Nikki bungaku no kenkyū*. Hanawa Shobō, 1965. 758p.

Companion volume to the author's "Nikki bungaku gaisetsu". Discusses 23 diaries from the Heian and medieval periods. Includes a chronology and a list of major commentaries. Index.

C141　玉井幸助　日記文学概説
Tamai Kōsuke. *Nikki bungaku gaisetsu*. Enlarged ed. Kokusho Kankōkai, 1982. 861p.

Reproduction of the 1945 edition. A survey of literary diaries. Indexes to personal names and titles.

C142 宮崎荘平　平安女流日記文学の研究
Miyazaki Sōhei. *Heian joryū nikki bungaku no kenkyū*. Kasama Shoin, 1972-80. 2v. (Kasama sōsho)·

Study of diaries written by women of the Heian period, with emphasis on *Kagerō nikki, Izumi Shikibu nikki, Murasaki Shikibu nikki*, etc.

C143 伊藤　博　蜻蛉日記研究序説
Itō Hiroshi. *Kagerō nikki kenkyū josetsu*. Kasama Shoin, 1976. 403p. (Kasama sōsho)

Study of various aspects of the *Kagerō nikki*, including its structure, characters, relationship to other diaries, etc.

C144 森田兼吉　和泉式部日記論攷
Morita Kaneyoshi. *Izumi Shikibu nikki ronkō*. Kasama Shoin, 1977. 375p. (Kasama sōsho)

Collection of essays on the *Izumi Shikibu nikki*, its authors, variant texts, relations to the authors' poetry, etc.

C145 木下　美　紫式部日記の研究と鑑賞
Kinoshita Miyoshi. *Murasaki Shikibu nikki no kenkyū to kanshō*. Fukuoka, Kyushu Daigaku Shuppankai, 1982. 662p.

Study of the life of Murasaki Shikibu, with an appreciation of her diary.

C146 西田禎元　更科日記研究序説
Nishida Sadamoto. *Sarashina nikki kenkyū josetsu*. Kyōiku Shuppan Sentā, 1982. 244p. (Kenkyū sensho)

Introductory study of the *Sarashina nikki*.

C147 津元信博　更科日記の研究
Tsumoto Nobuhiro. *Sarashina nikki no kenkyū*. Waseda Daigaku Shuppanbu, 1982. 711p.

Study of the *Sarashina nikki*, its author Sugawara no Takasue no musume, and the places she visited. Appended are a map and photographs of the locations mentioned in the diary.

Essays (zuihitsu)

C148 目加田さくを　枕草子論
Mekada Sakuo. *Makura no sōshi ron*. Kasama Shoin, 1975. 523p. (Kasama sōsho)

Discusses the cultural and literary background of *Makura no sōshi*, its literary style, its influence on the *Tsurezuregusa*, etc.

C149 枕草子講座　枕草子講座編集部 編
Makura no sōshi kōza. ed. by Makura no Sōshi Kōza Henshūbu. Yūseidō, 1975-76. 5v.

A lecture series on *Makura no sōshi*.

V.1 Sei Shonagon.
V.2-3 Interpretation and appreciation of *Makura no sōshi*.
V.4 The language and influence of *Makura no sōshi*.
V.5 Suppl. vol. Dictionary.

LIFE AND CULTURE

C150 赤木志津子　平安貴族の生活と文化
Akagi Shizuko. *Heian kizoku no seikatsu to bunka*. Kōdansha, 1964. 425p.

The lifestyle of the aristocracy in the Heian period. Pt.1 on the rank and financial status of the aristocracy; Pt.2 a description of various aspects of life at court. Index.

C151 池田亀鑑　平安時代の文学と生活
Ikeda Kikan. *Heian jidai no bungaku to seikatsu*. Shibundō, 1966. 646p.

Collection of essays on the Heian literary environment, including manners and customs, clothing, food, etc.

C152 池田源太　奈良平安時代の文化と宗教
Ikeda Genta. *Nara Heian jidai no bunka to shūkyō*. Kyoto, Nagata Bunshōdō, 1977. 520p.

Collection of previously published essays on culture and religion in the Nara and Heian periods. Examines the contrast between material and spiritual culture from the 8th century to the late Heian period.

C153 伊原　昭　平安朝の文学と色彩
Ihara Aki. *Heianchō no bungaku to shikisai*. Chūō Kōronsha, 1982. 212p. (Chūkō sensho)

Discusses the importance of the description of colors in ancient and Heian period literature. Contains a dictionary of color names, p. 157-205. Bibliographical references. Index.

Pictorial Sources

C154 鈴木敬三　初期絵巻物の風俗史的研究
Suzuki Keizō. *Shoki emakimono no fūzokushiteki kenkyū*. Yoshikawa Kōbunkan, 1960. 656p.

An analysis of picture scrolls, with emphasis on *Genji monogatari, Shigisan engi, Ban Dainagon*, and *Heiji monogatari*. Describes the special features of each scroll, the manners and customs pictured in them, etc. Index.

C155　秋山光和　平安時代世俗画の研究
Akiyama Terukazu. *Heian jidai sezokuga no kenkyū*. Yoshikawa Kōbunkan, 1964. 468p.

English title: Secular painting in early medieval Japan. Explains the development of painting that depicted the life of common folk in the Heian period. Illustrations.

C156　絵巻物による日本常民生活絵引　渋沢敬三 編
Emakimono ni yoru Nihon Jōmin seikatsu ebiki, ed. by Shibusawa Keizō. Kadokawa Shoten, 1964-68. 5v.

A pictorial dictionary of the life of the common folk as shown in illustrated handscrolls from the Heian, Kamakura, and Muromachi periods. Arranged by topics:

-1 dwellings

-2 clothing

-3 food

-4 furnishings

-5 occupation

-6 transportation

-7 trade

-8 social life, labor

-9 status, illnesses

-10 death, burial

-11 children

-12 entertainment

-13 annual events

-14 religion, festivals

-15 animals, plants, nature

Subject index in each volume.

C157　桜井清春　大和絵と戦記物語
Sakurai Seika. *Yamatoe to senki monogatari*. Moku-jisha, 1969. 337p.

A study of picture scrolls depicting scenes of battle. Also discusses scenes from *Genji monogatari, Shigisan engi*, etc.

C158　片野達郎　日本文芸と絵画の相関性の研究
Katano Tatsuro. *Nihon bungei to kaiga no sōkansei no kenkyū*. Kasama Shoin, 1975. 395p.

A study of the relationship between literature and art, with emphasis on waka. Pt.1 deals with the Heian and Kamakura periods; pt.2 treats the modern era.

C159　源　豊宗　大和絵の研究
Minamoto Toyomune. *Yamatoe no kenkyū*. Kadokawa Shoten, 1976. 501p.

A collection of essays on the development of Yamatoe (Japanese-style painting) in the 9th century and portrait painting of the Kamakura period. Illustrations. Index.

C160　亀田　孜　仏教説話絵の研究
Kameda Tsutomu. *Bukkyō setsuwae no kenkyū*. 1979. 237p.

A study of paintings done on Buddhist-related subjects including Heike nōkyō (sutras). Also included is a study of Buddhist-related song and dance.

C161　宮本常一　絵巻物に見る日本庶民生活史
Miyamoto Tsuneichi. *Emakimono ni miru Nihon shomin seikatsushi*. Chūō Kōronsha, 1981. 232p. (Chūkō shinsho)

A history of the life of common folk as seen in illustrated scrolls.

Education

C162　桃　裕行　上代学制の研究
Momo Hiroyuki. *Jōdai gakusei no kenkyū*. Meguro Shoten, 1947. 476p.

A study of the origins of the ancient educational system, the organization of national and private school systems, etc.

C163　久木幸雄　大学寮と古代儒教
Kuki Yukio. *Daigakuryō to kodai jukyō*. Saimaru Shuppan, 1968. 335p.

A history of education in ancient Japan, with emphasis on the Daigakuryō (office of education) and on the influence of Confucian thought.

D MEDIEVAL PERIOD

The medieval period which lasts from 1200 to 1600 was a turbulent age of political upheaval and war. The representative genre of literature from these years was gunki monogatari - tales that tell of the struggles between rival military clans. Other types of literature that were cultivated during this age include renga, setsuwa, sermons, essays, and Gozan poetry and prose.

Special terms:

 dengaku (an antecedent of the Nō)

 gagaku (court music)

 gunki monogatari (military tales)

 kagura (Shinto music)

 katarimono (dramatic recitation)

 kyōgen (farce)

 Nō drama

 renga (linked verse)

 sōka, enkyoku (banquet songs)

GENERAL

D1 唐木須三　中 世 の 文 学
Karaki Junzō. *Chūsei no bungaku.* New ed. Chikuma Shobō, 1955. 315p. (Chikuma sōsho; Karaki Junzō zenshū v.5, 1967)

Traces the philosophical development of medieval literature from Kamo no Chōmei and Yoshida Kenkō to Zeami and Dōgen.

D2 永積安明　中世文学の展望
Nagazumi Yasuaki. *Chūsei bungaku no tenbō.* Tokyo Daigaku Shuppankai, 1956. 309p.

A survey of medieval literature. Companion volume to the 1953 collection of essays "Chūsei bungakuron", which dealt with Kamakura literature. Mainly a history of monogatari, with emphasis on *Heike monogatari, Taiheiki,* and other writings in prose, including essays, diaries, etc. Index.

D3 荒木良雄　中世文学の形成と発展
Araki Yoshio. *Chūsei bungaku no keisei to hatten.* Kyoto Mineruba Shobō, 1957. 470p.

Surveys the development of medieval literature under the following topics: the development of linked verse; the role of poetry during the medieval period; sarugaku nō (an antecedent of Nō drama); kyōgen (comic farce); setsuwa, historical tales, short stories, fiction, etc. Subjects, titles, and personal names are indexed.

D4 中世文学の世界　西尾　実　先生
Chūsei bungaku no sekai: Nishio Minoru Sensei koki kinen ronbunshū, ed. by Nishio Minoru Sensei Koki Shukugakai. Iwanami Shoten, 1960. 386p.

A festschrift of 16 essays by prominent scholars in medieval literature. Includes essays on monogatari, poetry, Nō drama, etc.

D5 西尾　実　日本文芸史における中世的なもの
Nishio Minoru. *Nihon bungeishi ni okeru chūseiteki na mono to sono tenkai.* Enl. ed. Iwanami Shoten, 1961. 476p.

Discusses the development of a distinctively medieval literature. Covers some 600 years and three historical periods: Kamakura, Muromachi, and Edo.

D6 石津純道　中世の文学と芸道
Ishizu Jundō. *Chūsei no bungaku to geidō.* Shibundō, 1961. 267p.

The major part of this collection of essays examines certain principles of poetry and Nō, with examples drawn from the work of Fujiwara no Shunzei, the Priest Saigyō, Fujiwara no Teika, Zeami, etc. Also discusses *Heike monogatari,* travel accounts, and diaries. Index.

D7 谷　　宏　中世文学の達成
Tani Hiroshi. *Chūsei bungaku no tassei.* San'ichi Shobō, 1962. 274p.

Collection of essays on medieval literature. Includes essays on the following: how the people of Kyoto accepted the interpretation of historical events offered in the Heike monogatari; the accomplishment of Zeami, who depicted in Nō the inner desires of men living in a world of distress; the dramatic style of kyōgen in showing the relationship between the peasants and their superiors; the perfection of 'ushin renga' by Sōgi and others; on haikai renga.

D8 　永積安明　中世文学の成立
Nagazumi Yasuaki. *Chūsei bungaku no seiritsu.* Iwanami Shoten, 1963. 295p.

Collection of essays on the formation of medieval literature. Traces the changes in literary expression in the *Hōgen, Heiji,* and *Heike monogatari,* and in the *Hōjōki, Tsurezuregusa,* etc.

D9 　中世文学の研究　東京大学中世文学研究会 編
Chūsei bungaku no kenkyū, ed. by Tokyo Daigaku Chūsei Bungaku Kenkyūkai. Meiji Shoin, 1968. 285p.

Contemporary interpretations of medieval literature. Contains a bibliography of studies in medieval literature, arranged by genre, and covering the years 1964-67.

D10　田中　裕　中世文学論研究
Tanaka Yutaka. *Chūsei bungakuron kenkyū.* Hanawa Shobō. 1969. 500p.

Examines certain methods of expression discussed in the poetics of Fujiwara no Toshinari and Fujiwara no Teika, and the renga poetics of Nijō Yoshimoto and Shinkei. With chapters on renga poems and Zeami's theories of Nō drama.

D11　桑田忠親　大名と御伽衆
Kuwata Tadachika. *Daimyō to otogishū.* Enlarged new ed. Yūseidō, 1969. 276p.

An analysis of the occupation and organization of the Otogishū (story-tellers) from the Sengoku to the early modern period. Traces changes in the kinds of stories told to Daimyō, and the later development of otogizōshi from these stories.

D12　安良岡康作　中世的文学の探求
Yasuraoka Kōsaku. *Chūseiteki bungaku no tankyū.* Yūseidō, 1970. 327p.

A collection of essays on medieval literature including: the development of medieval literature from its roots in antiquity to the period of the Northern and Southern Courts; the works of Dōgen and Yoshida Kenkō; prose-style literature.

D13　安良岡康作　中世的文芸の理念
Yasuraoka Kōsaku. *Chūseiteki bungei no rinen.* Kasama Shoin, 1971. 397p. (Kasama sōsho)

A collection of essays on medieval literature. Discusses literary history, authors and their works, etc.

D14　久保田　淳　中世文学の世界
Kubota Jun. *Chūsei bungaku no sekai.* Tokyo Daigaku Shuppankai, 1972. 252p. (UP sensho)

Collection of essays on the world of medieval literature. Consists of a general survey of this literature, studies of prose works (such as the *Tsurezuregusa,* etc.), and studies of the poetry of, among others, Fujiwara no Teika and Shikishi Naishinnō.

D15　中世文学の研究　秋山　虔 編
Chūsei bungaku no kenkyū, ed. by Akiyama Ken. Tokyo Daigaku Shuppankai, 1972. 568p.

Festschrift of 22 essays written in honor of Professor Ichiko Teiji, and organized as 'prose works', 'poetry', and 'source materials'. Contains an article by Kubota Jun on postwar trends in the study of medieval literature. A bio-bibliography of Ichiko Teiji is appended.

D16　唐木須三　中世から近世へ
Karaki Junzō. *Chūsei kara kinsei e.* Chikuma Shobō, 1973. 318p. (Karaki Junzō Bunko 7)

Collection of essays on the changes in thought, religion, literature, and art from the medieval to the Edo period. The author holds that a Zen-inspired sense of humility was the basis for attaining the beautiful in the middle ages, but was replaced in the Edo period by a worldly culture.

D17　前田妙子　中世文芸の理念
Maeda Taeko. *Chūsei bungei no rinen.* Ōfūsha, 1974. 267p.

Study of certain features of literature in the medieval period, including the elegant simplicity of the Nō and renga. Reference bibliography.

D18　福田秀一　中世文学論考
Fukuda Hideichi. *Chūsei bungaku ronkō.* Meiji Shoin, 1975. 554p.

Collection of essays on medieval literature, especially writings in prose, such as monogatari, diaries and travel accounts, literary essays, etc. Index.

D19　米原正義　戦国武士と文芸の研究
Yonehara Masayoshi. *Sengoku bushi to bungei no kenkyū*. Ōfūsha, 1976. 1012p.

Study of the literature produced by six warrior clans during the period of the Northern and Southern Courts. The six clans are: the Hatakeyama clan of Noto province; the Asakura clan of Echizen province; the Takeda clan of Wakasa province; the Amako clan of Izumo province; the Ōuchi clan of Suō province; and the Imagawa clan of Suruga province.

D20　永積安明　中世文学の可能性
Nagazumi Yasuaki. *Chūsei bungaku no kanōsei*. Iwanami Shoten, 1977. 425p.

Continuation of the author's *Chūsei bungaku no seiritsu* (D8). Treats the study of medieval literature, with emphasis on sermons, setsuwa, war chronicles, etc. With bibliographical notes at the end of each chapter.

D21　中世文学　資料と論考　伊地知鉄男 編
Chūsei bungaku: shiryō to ronkō, ed. by Ijichi Tetsuo. Kasama Shoin, 1978. 669p.

Festschrift on medieval literature and source materials. A bio-bibliography on Professor Ijichi is appended.

D22　中世日本文学史　有吉　保 編
Chūsei Nihon bungakushi, ed. by Ariyoshi Tamotsu. Yūhikaku, 1978. 262p. (Yūhikaku sōsho: Nyūmon kiso chishiki hen)

Introductory text on the history of medieval literature, grouped by genre and illustrated with excerpts from pertinent sources. With a reference bibliography, chronology, indexes.

D23　長野甞一　著作集
Nagano Jōichi chosakushū, ed. by Nagano Jōichi Chōsakushū Henshū Iinkai. Kasama Shoin, 1979-80. 3v.

A collection of essays:

V.1 *Konjaku monogatari*.

V.2 Studies in setsuwa literature.

V.3 Medieval literature. Includes a bio-bibliography.

D24　佐々木八郎　中世文学の構想
Sasaki Hachirō. *Chūsei bungaku no kōsō*. Meiji Shoin, 1981. 368p.

Posthumous collection of essays treating the development of commentaries on literature from the medieval period, such as *Heike monogatari*, *Hōjōki*, and Muromachi period fiction.

By Period

D25　斉藤清衛　南北朝時代文学通史
Saitō Kiyoe. *Nanbokuchō jidai bungaku tsūshi*. Furukawa Shobō, 1972. 229p.

A general history of literature in the Nanboku Era, chronologically and topically arranged and giving sources, important authors, and works.

D26　室町ごころ，中世文学資料集　岡見正雄 博士
Muromachi gokoro: chūsei bungaku shiryōshū, ed. by Okami Masao Hakushi Kanreki Kinen Kankōkai. Kadokawa Shoten, 1978. 597p. (Chūsei bungaku shiryōshū)

Festschrift in honor of Professor Okami Masao. Consists of an introductory essay on 'the spirit of Muromachi literature' by Okami Masao, and reproductions of source materials, edited by specialists. A bio-bibliography is appended.

D27　荒木良雄　安土桃山時代文学史
Araki Yoshio. *Azuchi Momoyama jidai bungakushi*. Kadokawa Shoten, 1969. 558p.

History of literature in the Azuchi-Momoyama periods (1543-1610). In 2 parts:

Pt.1 Survey of waka-renga, classical literature, works on Oda Nobunaga, the development of Nō, etc.

Pt.2 Studies of individual authors and their works including Hosokawa Yūsai, etc. A chronological table of Azuchi-Momoyama literature. Index.

Thought

D28　唐木須三　無　常
Karaki Junzō. *Mujō*. Chikuma Shobō, 1964. 354p.

History of literature and thought from the Heian to the medieval period, centered on the concept of nihilism (mujō).

D29　小林智昭　中世文学の思想
Kobayashi Tomoaki. *Chūsei bungaku no shisō*. 1964. 295p.

Study of literary thought, with emphasis on *Heike monogatari* and the *Tsurezuregusa*.

D30 小林智昭　続中世文学の思想
Kobayashi Tomoaki. *Zoku chūsei bungaku no shisō*. 1974. 390p.

Continuation of the above entry. Also contains essays on Buddhist literature, sermons, and the relationship between Buddhism and literature.

D31 桜井好朗　隠 者 の 風 貌
Sakurai Yoshirō. *Inja no fūbō*. Hanawa Shobō, 1967. 272p. (Hanawa shinsho)

Describes medieval hermits, who led lives devoted to simplicity and spiritual discipline. Discusses the Priest Saigyō, Kamo no Chōmei, etc.

D32 石田吉貞　隠 者 の 文 学
Ishida Yoshisada. *Inja no bungaku*. Hanawa Shobō, 1968. 251p. (Hanawa shinsho)

The literature of Japanese 'inja', or anchorite poets. Subtitled 'beauty in suffering', the book discusses Saigyō, Yoshida Kenkō, Kamo no Chōmei with reference to the *Hōjōki*, renga and the tea ceremony

D33 桜井好朗　日 本 の 隠 者
Sakurai Yoshirō. *Nihon no inja*. Hanawa Shobō, 1969. 228p.

On the life of hermits in ancient and medieval Japan.

D34 石田吉貞　中世草庵の文学
Ishida Yoshisada. *Chūsei sōan no bungaku*. Revised ed. Kitazawa Tosho Shuppan, 1970. 270p.

Literature written by hermits in the medieval period. Describes the life of these men, their spiritual background and the literature they wrote. Also discusses the tea ceremony as a symbol of simplicity.

D35 桜井好朗　中世日本人の思惟と表現
Sakurai Yoshirō. *Chūsei Nihonjin no shii to hyōgen*. Miraisha, 1970. 367p.

Collection of essays on the *Hōjōki*, *Gukanshō*, *Heike monogatari*, *Taiheiki*, and other works, seeking to define the spiritual life of medieval period Japanese.

D36 桜井好朗　中世日本の精神的景観
Sakurai Yoshirō. *Chūsei Nihon no seishinteki keikan*. Hanawa Shobō, 1974. 380p.

Continuation of the above entry. Discusses the culture and thought of those who led a life of seclusion. Also discusses the development of the

Kitano Shrine picture scroll (Kitano Tenjin engi). Bibliographical note at the end of each chapter.

D37 伊藤博之　隠 遁 の 文 学
Itō Hiroyuki. *Inton no bungaku - mōnen to kakusei*. Kasama Shoin, 1975. 272p. (Kasama sensho)

Collection of previously published essays on the literature of disillusionment and reality written by hermits. Emphasizes the works of Saigyō, Kamo no Chōmei, Yoshida Kenkō, etc.

D38 小林智昭　法語文学の世界
Kobayashi Tomoaki. *Hōgo bungaku no sekai*. Kasama Shoin, 1975. 309p. (Kasama sensho)

The world of Buddhist literature, especially sermons. Explains representative sermons by the priests Hōnen, Dōgen, Nichiren, and Ippen.

D39 久保田　淳　日本人の美意識
Kubota Jun. *Nihonjin no biishiki*. Kōdansha, 1978. 322p.

Collection of previously published essays discussing the Japanese sense of beauty as expressed in classical poetry, the *Shinkokinshū*, war chronicles, etc.

D40 藤原正義　中世作家の思想と方法
Fujiwara Masayoshi. *Chūsei sakka no shisō to hōhō*. Kazama Shobō, 1981. 230p.

Collection of essays on the systems of thought which influenced men of letters in the medieval period, the religious beliefs of Yoshida Kenkō, etc.

LANGUAGE

D41 湯沢幸吉郎　室町時代言語の研究
Yuzawa Kōkichirō. *Muromachi jidai gengo no kenkyū*. Kazama Shobō, 1955. 387p.

Study of Muromachi period Japanese, focusing on commentaries (shōmono). Gives grammatical explanation of the Japanese notes and comments added to the Chinese classics, Buddhist scriptures, etc. Index.

D42 土井忠生　吉利支丹語学の研究
Doi Tadao. *Kirishitan gogaku no kenkyū*. New ed. Sanseidō, 1971. 355p.

On the Jesuits' study of the Japanese language. Organized as follows:

1. Introduction.

2. Organization and characteristics of the Jesuits' language study.

3. The editorship of the Japanese/Portuguese dictionary.
4. *Rakuyoshū* (collection of fallen leaves) a dictionary of Chinese characters. An English resume is appended.
5. Biography of Father Rodriguez.
6. Rodriguez's theory of adjectives.
7. Rodriguez's interpretation of Japanese grammar, including the uses of 'te-ni-o-ha'.
8. Honorifics used by the Jesuits.

D43　根來　司　中世文語の研究
Negoro Tsukasa. *Chūsei bungo no kenkyū*. Kasama Shoin, 1976. 221p. (Kasama sōsho)

Examines certain grammatical usages in the literature of the Kamakura and Muromachi periods. Compares the honorific verbs (tamō, obosu, etc.), the auxiliary verbs used in the *Tsurezuregusa*, and various editions of the 'te-ni-o-ha' secret manuals (hidensho). Index.

D44　山口明穂　中世国語における文語の研究
Yamaguchi Akiho. *Chūsei kokugo ni okeru bungo no kenkyū*. Meiji Shoin, 1976. 249p.

A study of the style, composition, and grammar of medieval Japanese, with references taken from books of poetics and commentaries on the classics.

D45　鎌倉時代語研究　鎌倉時代語研究会 編
Kamakura jidaigo kenkyū, ed. by Kamakura Jidaigo Kenkyūkai. Musashino Shoin, 1978-(1983). (7v.)

This study of Kamakura period Japanese covers some 350 years, centering on the years of the Kamakura Bakufu, the period of the Insei government, and the period of the Northern and Southern Courts. Consists of comparative studies of grammar and of the Chinese characters used in documents. Volumes 1 and 2 contain a preliminary draft of a bibliography for the study.

D46　山田　巖　院政期言語の研究
Yamada Iwao. *Inseiki gengo no kenkyū*. Ōfūsha, 1982. 216p.

Collection of essays on grammatical changes from ancient to modern Japanese, with emphasis on the medieval period language used in *Konjaku* and *Heike* monogatari.

POETRY

Waka

D47　太田水穂　日本和歌史論
Ōta Mizuho. *Nihon wakashiron: chūseihen*. Kondō Shoten, 1957. (Ōta Mizuho Zenshū v.9)

History of waka in the medieval period. Begins with the 'Six Poetic Geniuses' (Rokkasen), then moves through the *Kokinshū, Senzaishū, Shinkokinshū*, Fujiwara no Teika, and ends with the Muromachi period.

D48　前田妙子　和歌十体論研究
Maeda Taeko. *Waka jutteiron kenkyū*. Kōbundō, 1957. 271p. (Kansai Daigaku Bungakubu kenkyū sōsho v.2)

Analyzes the poetics of the medieval period with emphasis on the 'ten styles' articulated by Fujiwara no Teika in the *Teika juttei*.

D49　井上宗雄　中世歌壇史の研究
Inoue Muneo. *Chūsei kadanshi no kenkyū*. Meiji Shoin, 1961-72. 3v.

Examines the activities of poetic circles between the late Kamakura and early Edo period, with reference to books of poems and other source materials. V.1 covers the period of the Northern and Southern Courts; V.2 the early Muromachi period; V.3 the late Muromachi period. Each volume contains indexes to personal names, subjects, titles, and the first lines of waka.

D50　藤平春男　新古今歌風の形成
Fujihira Haruo. *Shinkokin kafū no keisei*. Meiji Shoin, 1969. 388p.

Collection of essays on the Shinkokin style, with emphasis on the poetics of Fujiwara no Shunzei and Fujiwara no Teika.

D51　福田秀一　中世和歌史の研究
Fukuda Hideichi. *Chūsei wakashi no kenkyū*. Kadokawa Shoten, 1972. 884p.

History of medieval waka in 5 parts:
1. Survey.
2. Poets and their circles.
3. Poetics and books of poetics.
4. Waka of the late medieval period.
5. Explanations of source materials and a chronology of mid-Kamakura period waka. Index.

D52　石田吉貞　新古今世界と中世文学
Ishida Yoshisada. *Shinkokin sekai to chūsei bungaku*. Kitazawa Shoten, 1972. 2v.

Collection of essays summarizing the author's work on the *Shinkokinshū* and medieval literature. In 4 parts:

V.1,

    pt.1 The formation of Shinkokin poetic style, including poems by Saigyō, Fujiwara no Shunzei, Fujiwara no Teika, Princess Shikishi, etc.

    pt.2 Poets and their works: the Horikawa Tennō's collection of 100 poems, *Gyokuyō wakashū*, etc.

V.2,

    pt.1 Critical biographies of poets, including Fujiwara no Tameie, Ton'a, etc.

    pt.2 Essays on renga, literature written by hermits, diaries and travel accounts etc.

D53 久保田　淳　新古今歌人の研究
Kubota Jun. *Shinkokin kajin no kenkyū*. Tokyo Daigaku Shuppankai, 1973. 1021p.

Biographical and literary studies of the Shinkokin poets: Fujiwara no Teika, Fujiwara no Shunzei, Fujiwara no Ietaka, Fujiwara no Yoshitsune, and the Priests Jien and Saigyō.

D54 石村雍子　和歌連歌の研究
Ishimura Yasuko. *Waka renga no kenkyū*. Musashino Shoin, 1975. 306p.

Study of waka and renga leading up to the Muromachi period. Discusses the social and economic aspects of renga poets and their gatherings. Well documented with source materials.

D55 和歌と中世文学　峯村文人　先生
Waka to chūsei bungaku, Minemura Fumito Sensei taikan kinen ronbunshū, ed. by Tokyo Kyōiku Daigaku Chūsei Bungaku Danwakai. 1977. 468p.

Festschrift of 28 essays written in honor of Professor Minemura Fumito by members of the medieval literature society of Tokyo Kyōiku Daigaku.

D56 梁瀬一雄　中世和歌研究
Yanase Kazuo. *Chūsei waka kenkyū*. Katō Chūdōkan, 1982. 511p. (Yanase Kazuo chosakushū, v.4)

Essays on medieval period waka, with emphasis on the anthologies lost to history.

D57 糸賀きみ江　中世の抒情
Itoga Kimie. *Chūsei no jojō*. Kasama Shoin, 1979. 429p. (Kasama sōsho)

Study of lyricism in the *Shinkokinshū*, *Gyokuyoshū*, and *Fūgawakashū*. Also contains a study of women poets and their work in the Shinkokin period.

Poetics

D58 久松潜一　日本歌論史の研究
Hisamatsu Sen'ichi. *Nihon karonshi no kenkyū*. Kazama Shobō, 1963. 430p.

Introduction to the history of poetics with emphasis on medieval poets.

D59 釘本久春　中世歌論の性格
Kugimoto Hisaharu. *Chūsei karon no seikaku*. Enlarged ed. Kokugo o Aisurukai, 1969. 257p.

Study of medieval period poetics, with emphasis on the methods of poetic analysis and expression introduced by Fujiwara no Shunzei.

D60 細谷直樹　中世歌論の研究
Hosoya Naoki. *Chūsei karon no kenkyū*. Kasama Shoin, 1976. 432p.

Collection of essays on medieval period poetics, with emphasis on Fujiwara no Teika's ideas concerning the change of style from the *Shinkokinshū* to the *Shinchokusenshū*.

D61 水上甲子三　中世歌論と連歌
Mizukami Kashizō. *Chūsei karon to renga*. 1977. 254p. Privately published.

Collection of essays including book reviews, studies of poetics, and studies of renga. With a bio-bibliography.

D62 武田元治　中世歌論をめぐる研究
Takeda Motoharu. *Chūsei karon o meguru kenkyū*. Ōfūsha, 1978. 257p.

Study of medieval period poetics from the standpoint of literary criticism.

D63 奥田久輝　新古今的発想論
Okuda Hisateru. *Shinkokinteki hassōron*. Ōfūsha, 1981. 358p.

Studies in the characteristic style of Shinkokin poetry, including the works of Teika, Sōgi, etc.

Renga

D64 伊地知鉄男　連　歌　の　世　界
Ijichi Tetsuo. *Renga no sekai*. Yoshikawa Kōbunkan, 1967. 463p.

Explains many of the features of renga practice: format, poetry meetings, formalities observed, etc. Also traces the history of renga from the 11th to the 15th century. Contains a chronology, a reference bibliography. Index.

D65 連歌とその周辺　金子金治郎 博士
Renga to sono shūhen: Kaneko Kinjirō Hakushi kanreki kinen ronbunshū, ed. by Hiroshima Chūsei Bungei Kenkyūkai. 1967. 455p.

Festschrift of 22 essays on renga.

D66 福井久蔵　連歌の史的研究
Fukui Kyuzō. *Renga no shiteki kenkyū*. Yūseido, 1969. 715p.

History of renga in 2 parts.

Pt.1 Deals with the origins and developments of renga, based on the activities of important poets and the traditional customs governing renga meetings.

Pt.2 Lists about 2,400 works on renga and collections of selected poems with explanations, arranged chronologically by date of publication.

D67 島津忠夫　連歌史の研究
Shimazu Tadao. *Rengashi no kenkyū*. Kadokawa Shoten, 1969. 331p.

History of renga from its beginnings to the age of the poet Shōyū and his circle. Contains a chapter on the *Sarumino*. Reprints of source material appended. Index.

D68 木藤才蔵　連歌史論考
Kidō Saizō. *Rengashi ronkō*. Meiji Shoin, 1971-73. 2v.

Survey history covering some 900 years, from the beginnings of renga to the publication of the *Shinsen Tsukubashū*. Contains a chronology of the years 720-1500, with reference notes. Indexes to sources, personal names, subjects, renga, waka, Chinese poems.

D69 島津忠夫　連歌の研究
Shimazu Tadao. *Renga no kenkyū*. Kadokawa Shoten, 1973. 489p.

Study of various aspects of renga: its style and form, poets, relationship to haikai, etc. Contains reproductions of source materials. Index.

D70 連歌と中世文芸　金子金治郎 博士
Renga to chūsei bungei, ed. by Kaneko Kinjirō Hakushi Koki Kinen Ronbunshū Hensan Iinkai. Kadokawa Shoten, 1977. 453p.

Festschrift of 22 essays. Covers topics on biographical studies of poets, rules of composition, renga meetings, scholarship of renga poets, etc.

Kayō (songs and ballads)

D71 淺野健二　日本歌謡の研究
Asano Kenji. *Nihon kayō no kenkyū*. Tokyodō, 1961. 421p.

Study of Japanese songs and ballads, especially of the medieval and early modern period. Traces the history of kouta (little songs) and lists collections of kouta from the medieval period. Also discusses dance songs and folk songs of the early modern period. Contains a bibliography of Kayō, p.367-392. Indexes to subjects and songs. (See also A79)

D72 外村久江　早歌の研究
Tonomura Hisae. *Sōka no kenkyū*. Shibundō, 1965. 343p.

Study of sōka, songs of praise sung by warriors in the Kamakura period. Also touches on the relationship between sōka and sarugaku. Contains a bibliographical study of collections of sōka. Index.

D73 武石彰夫　仏教歌謡の研究
Takeishi Akio. *Bukkyō kayō no kenkyū*. Ōfūsha, 1969. 440p.

History of Buddhist song. Explains Buddhist songs of praise, including Jishū-sect songs, popular songs in the collection titled *Ryōjin hishō* and enkyoku (banquet music). Reference bibliography. Index.

D74 吾郷寅之進　中世歌謡の研究
Ago Toranoshin. *Chūsei kayō no kenkyū*. Kazama Shobō, 1971. 710p.

Collection of essays on the development of medieval songs, including popular songs and ceremonial songs, their relation to Zen literature, and to Nō and kyōgen. Contains indexes of poems, songs, and special phrases.

D75 乾　克己　宴曲の研究
Inui Katsumi. *Enkyoku no kenkyū*. Ōfūsha, 1972. 574p.

Studies the sources of enkyoku with reference to waka, renga, *Genji monogatari*, *Wakan rōeishū*, etc. Also traces enkyoku to the performing arts. Indexes to songs and titles.

D76 田植草紙の研究　田唄研究会 編
Tauezōshi no kenkyū, ed. by Tauta Kenkyūkai. Miyai Shoten, 1872. 707p.

Collection of essays on the *Tauezōshi* (a book of rice-planting songs), discussing the musical, cultural, and ethnological aspects of these songs.

Explanations of terms, p.616-675, and a bibliography, p.676-702.

D77　武石彰夫　仏 教 歌 謡
Takeishi Akio. *Bukkyō kayō*. Hanawa Shobō, 1973. 270p. (Hanawa sensho)

Traces the development of Buddhist hymns by sect. Also discusses enkyoku and rice-planting songs.

D78　武石彰夫　仏 教 歌 謡 集 成
Takeishi Akio. *Bukkyō kayō shūsei*. Daitō Bunka Daigaku. Tōyō Kenkyūjo, 1976-77. 2v.

Collection of Buddhist hymns, prayer books, and devotionals arranged by sect. Contains explanations of each entry and an analytical list of hymns given in collected works. V.2 consists of commentaries and source material on Buddhist chants (shōmyō).

D79　渡辺昭五　田植歌謡と儀礼の研究
Watanabe Shōgo. *Taue kayō to girei no kenkyū*. Miyai Shoten, 1979. 1052p.

Examines the cultural background of rice-planting songs, the ceremonies surrounding them, their literary character, etc. A history of the study of these songs and a bibliography are appended. Index.

D80　真鍋昌弘　中世近世歌謡の研究
Manabe Masahiro. *Chūsei kinsei Kayō no kenkyū*. Ōfūsha, 1982. 614p.

Study of song in the medieval and early modern periods. Traces the development of rice-planting songs, children's and folk songs, etc. Index to songs.

PROSE LITERATURE

Military Tales (Gunki monogatari)

D81　軍記物とその周辺　佐々木八郎 博士
Gunkimono to sono shūhen: Sasaki Hachirō Hakushi koki kinen ronbunshū. Waseda Daigaku Shuppankyoku, 1969. 944p.

Festschrift of 48 essays on military tales. Written in honor of Professor Sasaki Hachirō, an authority on the *Heike monogatari*.

D82　山下宏明　軍記物語と語り物文芸
Yamashita Hiroaki. *Gunki monogatari to katarimono bungei*. Hanawa Shobō, 1972. 357p.

Collection of previously published essays on the literary art of military tales and katarimono (recited stories), with emphasis on *Heike, Heiji*, and *Hōgen monogatari*. Includes various war chronicles from the period of the Northern and Southern Courts, including the *Gikeiki, Soga monogatari*, etc.

D83　安部元雄　軍記物の原像とその展開
Anbe Motoo. *Gunkimono no genzō to sono tenkai*. Ōfūsha, 1976. 311p.

Traces the history of military tales from their origins in the *Shōmonki* and *Mutsuwaki*, to their development in *Hōgen* and *Heiji monogatari*, and their consummation in *Heike monogatari*.

D84　渥美かをる　軍 記 物 と 説 話
Atsumi Kaoru. *Gunki mono to setsuwa*. Kasama Shoin, 1979. 529p. (Kasama sōsho)

Collection of essays, issued posthumously, on military tales, including *Heike, Heiji*, and *Hōgen monogatari*. Also contains essays on the music for *Heike monogatari* and on setsuwa. With a bio-bibliography.

Heike monogatari

D85　石母田　正　平 家 物 語
Ishimoda Shō. *Heike monogatari*. Iwanami Shoten, 1957. 227p. (Iwanami shinsho)

Examines the characters, the theme of fatalism, and literary style in the Heike monogatari. Contains a chronological table of the story. Illustrations.

D86　むしやこうじみのる　平家物語と琵琶法師
Mushakōji Minoru. *Heike monogatari to biwa hōshi*. Awaji Shobō Shinsha, 1957. 254p.

Describes the forces of historical change between the ancient and medieval periods as evidenced in the performing arts, with emphasis on the *Heike mongatari* and biwa hōshi (monks who performed katarimono to lute accompaniment). With an annotated bibliography.

D87　佐々木八郎　平家物語の研究
Sasaki Hachirō. *Heike monotari no kenkyū*. Enlarged ed. Waseda Daigaku Shuppanbu, 1967. 1264p.

A general study of the *Heike monogatari*. In two parts: 1. the organization and meaning of the story; 2. the influence of the story on drama and the performing arts. Contains a history of commentaries on the *Heiki monogatari*.

D88　上横手雅敬　平家物語の虚構と真実
Uwayokote Masataka. *Heike monogatari no kyokō to shinjitsu*. Kōdansha, 1973. 397p.

Fact and fancy in *Heike monogatari*. Looks at how 12 heroes from the Heike story (including Taira Kiyomori, Taira Shigemori, Minamoto Yorimasa, etc.) responded to the political and social crises of their times. With bibliographical references.

D89　館山漸之進　平家音楽史
Tateyama Zennoshin. *Heike ongakushi*. Kamakura, Geirinsha, 1974. 359p.

Reprint of the 1910 edition. History of Heike music. Also discusses Shōmyō (Buddhist chants) and the biwa lute. Provides source material for the study of this music. Illustrated.

D90　渥美かをる　平家物語の基礎的研究
Atsumi Kaoru. *Heike monogatari no kisoteki kenkyū*. Kasama Shoin, 1978. 445p.

Study of *Heike monogatari*, its author and the time he lived, etc. Lists various editions with comments.

Taiheiki, Hōgen, Heiji monogatari

D91　増田　欣　太平記の比較文学的研究
Masuda Motomu. *Taiheiki no hikaku bungakuteki kenkyū*. Kadokawa Shoten, 1976. 654p.

A comparative study of the *Taiheiki* and various works in Chinese. Verifies author and date of publication. With bibliographical references and an index.

D92　水原　一　保元平治物語の世界
Mizuhara Hajime. *Hōgen Heiji monogatari no sekai*. Nihon Hōsō Shuppan Kyōkai, 1979. 311p. (Hōsō raiburari)

An introduction, first broadcast over NHK radio, to *Hōgen* and *Heiji monogatari*. Kana readings are given for difficult words.

Setsuwa (tales, legends)

D93　西尾光一　中世説話文学論
Nishio Kōichi. *Chūsei setsuwa bungakuron*. Hanawa Shobō, 1963. 301p. (Hanawa sensho)

A historical survey of the development of setsuwa from the ancient to the modern period, with emphasis on the medieval period.

D94　菊地良一　中世の唱導文芸
Kikuchi Ryōichi. *Chūsei no shōdō bungei*. Hanawa Shobō, 1968. 304p. (Hanawa sensho)

Examines the literary art of sermons and sutra recitation. Includes a discussion of the Priest

Dōgen's sermons and their relationship to the *Tsurezuregusa*.

D95　菊地良一　中世説話の研究
Kikuchi Ryōichi. *Chūsei setsuwa no kenkyū*. Ōfūsha, 1972. 270p.

Studies the literary aspects of medieval Buddhist sermons and the setsuwa-influenced style of prose used in the writing of Priests' biographies. Reference bibliography.

D96　築瀬一雄　説話文学研究
Yanase Kazuo. *Setsuwa bungaku kenkyū*. Miyai Shoten, 1974. 317p.

A collection of previously published essays on various aspects of setsuwa literature.

D97　春田　宣　中世説話文学論序説
Haruta Akira. *Chūsei setsuwa bungakuron josetsu*. Ōfūsha, 1975. 425p.

An introduction to medieval period setsuwa literature. Discusses setsuwa style passages in *Heike monogatari*, *Konjaku monogatari*, etc. Index.

D98　藤本徳明　中世仏教説話論
Fujimoto Akira. *Chūsei Bukkyō setsuwaron*. Kasama Shoin, 1977. 249p. (Kasama sōsho)

Examines medieval period Buddhist setsuwa in the context of the history of thought. In 3 parts:
1. *Shasekishū* (a collection of setsuwa in 10v., 1283)
2. *Kankyo no tomo* (a collection of setsuwa in 2v., 1222) and *Hosshinshū* (a collection of setsuwa ed. by Kamo no Chōmei
3. Methodology in the study of setsuwa.

D99　中世説話の世界　北海道説話文学研究会　編
Chūsei setsuwa no sekai, ed. by Hokkaidō Setsuwa Bungaku Kenkyūkai. Kasama Shoin, 1979. 565p. (Kasama sōsho)

Festschrift published in honor of Professor Koizumi Hiroshi. Consists of essays on the world of medieval period setsuwa and setsuwa source material.

D100　安藤直太郎　説話と俳諧の研究
Andō Naotarō. *Setsuwa to haikai no kenkyū*. Kasama Shoin, 1979. 433p.

A continuation of the author's "Setsuwa to haikai" (1962). A collection of essays on setsuwa and haikai as a witty literature of the people, with emphasis on the *Sangoku denki*, *Shasekishō*, etc.

D101　説 話 文 学 論 集　馬渕和夫 博士
Setsuwa bungaku ronshū, Mabuchi Kazuo Hakushi
taikan kinen, ed. by the Publishing Committee.
Taishūkan Shoten, 1981. 314p.

Festschrift of essays on setsuwa in honor of Professor Mabuchi by the members of the Setsuwa
Study Group.

D102　志村有弘　説話文学の構想と伝承
Shimura Kunihiro. *Setsuwa bungaku no kōsō to
denshō*. Meiji Shoin, 1982. 341p.

Study of medieval period setsuwa, its transmission,
etc. List of references.

D103　原田行造　中世説話文学の研究
Harada Kōzō. *Chūsei setsuwa bungaku no kenkyū*.
Ōfūsha, 1982. 2v.

Study of medieval period setsuwa.

V.1 Concentrates on 2 setsuwa collections:
Hosshinshū and *Kankyo no tomo*.

V.2 Contains a study of characters often found in
setsuwa, a printed reproduction of *Nezame ki*,
etc.

Both volumes have bibliographical notes. Indexes.

Fiction

D104　市古貞次　中世小説の研究
Ichiko Teiji. *Chūsei shōsetsu no kenkyū*. Tokyo
Daigaku Shuppankai, 1955. 498p.

Surveys the scope, meaning, and historical background of medieval fiction. Classified by subject:
aristocracy, religion, warrior class, commoners, foreign country, and miscellaneous. Contains a
chronological table of the years 1334-1624 and a
catalog of medieval period fiction reprinted since
1868. Index.

D105　小木　喬　鎌倉時代物語の研究
Ogi Takashi. *Kamakura jidai monogatari no kenkyū*. Tōhō Shobō, 1961. 412p.

A survey of Kamakura period monogatari, including
individual authors and their works.

D106　大島建彦　お伽草子と民間文芸
Ōshima Tatehiko. *Otogizōshi to minkan bungei*.
Iwasaki Bijutsusha, 1967. 207p. (Minzoku mingei
sōsho)

Collection of essays on folk literature and
otogizōshi. Compares the differences and sim-

ilarities between otogizōshi and stories transmitted
orally. Illustrated. Index.

D107　佐竹昭広　下 剋 上 の 文 学
Satake Akihiro. *Gekokujō no bungaku*. Chikuma
Shoin, 1967. 264p.

Collection of essays on the otogizōshi, kyōgen, and
folk tales that depicted this period of revolt against
established authority. The essays are based on linguistic and historical sources.

D108　桑原博史　中世物語の基礎的研究
Kuwabara Hiroshi. *Chūsei monogatari no kisoteki
kenkyū*. Kazama Shobō, 1969. 559p.

The historical basis of medieval stories. Contains
essays on Fujiwara no Takafusa and his works,
Torikaebaya, etc. Also includes texts of *Iwashimizu
monogatari*, *Sayogoromo*, etc.

D109　大島建彦　咄　の　伝　承
Ōshima Tatehiko. *Hanashi no denshō*. Iwasaki Bijutsusha, 1970. 239p. (Minzoku mingei sōsho)

Collection of essays on the oral transmission of
setsuwa, waka, Nō, kyōgen, proverbs, etc. Illustrated. Index.

D110　佐竹昭広　民 話 の 思 想
Satake Akihiro. *Minwa no shisō*. Heibonsha, 1973.
260p. (Heibonsha sensho)

Analyzes heroes and villains in folk tales. Also
searches out whatever foreign influence there may
be in these tales.

D111　室町時代物語大成　横山　重 等編
Muromachi jidai monogatari taisei, ed. by
Yokoyama Shigeru and Matsumoto Takanobu. Kadokawa Shoten, (1973-83) to be completed in 13
volumes.

Complete collection of Muromachi period fiction.

D112　市古貞次　中世小説とその周辺
Ichiko Teiji. *Chūsei shōsetsu to sono shūhen*. Tokyo
Daigaku Shuppankai, 1981. 321p.

A continuation of the author's ''Chūsei shōsetsu no
kenkyū'' (see D104). Contains a chronology of
medieval fiction and a chronology of Kōwaka
dance.

D113　西沢正二　中世小説の世界
Nishizawa Masaji. *Chūsei shōsetsu no sekai*. Miyai
Shoten, 1982. 240p. (Miyai sensho)

Study of four otogizōshi from the medieval period:
Aki no yonaga monogatari, Akimichi, Sannin hōshi,

and *Oyō no ama*. A photo reproduction of *Akimichi* appended. Bibliographical notes included.

Essays (Zuihitsu)

Tsurezuregusa

D114　徒 然 草 講 座　三谷栄一 編
Tsurezuregusa kōza, ed. by Mitani Eiichi. Yūseidō, 1974-77. 5v.

Lectures, by over 80 specialists, on the *Tsurezuregusa*.

V.1　Yoshida Kenkō and the age in which he lived.

V.2-3　Appreciations of the *Tsurezuregusa*.

V.4　Linguistic studies, sources, and influence.

V.5　(Suppl.) dictionary consisting of important words, indexes, a chronology, a genealogical table, and a reference bibliography.

D115　上田三四二　俗　と　無　常
Ueda Miyoji. *Zoku to mujō*. Kōdansha, 1976. 214p.

'Worldliness and transiency' in the *Tsurezuregusa*. A collection of essays on Kenkō's consciousness of time, and his views on life, death, etc.

D116　桑原博史　徒然草の鑑賞と批評
Kuwabara Hiroshi. *Tsurezuregusa no kanshō to hihyō*. Meiji Shoin, 1977. 411p.

Appreciation and criticism of the *Tsurezuregusa*. Examines Kenkō's thoughts on such topics as philosophy, life, priests, aestheticism, etc. Contains a chronology and reference works. Indexes.

D117　永積安明　徒然草を読む
Nagazumi Yasuaki. *Tsurezuregusa o yomu*. Iwanami Shoten, 1982. 218p. (Iwanami shinsho)

An introduction to the spiritual world of Yoshida Kenkō as revealed in the *Tsurezuregusa*.

D118　細野哲雄　鴨長明の周辺, 方丈記
Hosono Tetsuo. *Kamo no Chōmei no shūhen: Hōjōki*. Kasama Shoin, 1978. 213p. (Kasama sōsho)

Consists of essays on people who knew Kamo no Chōmei, (e.g., his father Nagatsugu, his friend the Priest Zenjaku), and essays on the spiritual background of the *Hōjōki*.

Travel Accounts

D119　白井忠功　中世の紀行文学
Shirai Tadanori. *Chūsei no kikō bungaku*. Bungaku Shobō, 1976. 225p.

Medieval travel diaries. With excerpts and a chronology.

D119a　日本紀行文学便覧　福田秀一 等編
Nihon kikō bungaku benran, ed. by Fukuda Hideichi and Herbert E. Plutschow. Musashino Shoin, 1975. 271p.

English title: A handbook for the study of classical Japanese travel diaries. Lists 69 travel accounts of the Heian and medieval periods, giving for each entry the author, duration of the travel, places visited, date of publication and location of the book in collected works. Bibliography of references, illustrations, maps, included.

RELIGION AND LITERATURE

D120　西尾　実　道元と世阿弥
Nishio Minoru. *Dōgen to Zeami*. Iwanami Shoten, 1965. 310p.

Examines the influence of Zen on the *Shōbō genzō* (a collection of sermons written in kana by the Priest Dōgen) and on the artistry of Zeami in the Nō.

D121　武石彰夫　仏教文学論考
Takeishi Akio. *Bukkyō bungaku ronkō*. Hakuteisha, 1974. 172p.

An introduction to medieval period Buddhist literature, with emphasis on the *Tsurezuregusa*, Buddhist ballads and songs, setsuwa, etc.

D122　寺田　透　道元の言語宇宙
Terada Tōru. *Dōgen no gengo uchū*. Iwanami Shoten, 1974. 518p.

Collection of essays on the *Shōbō genzō* and the Priest Dōgen.

D123　石田瑞麿　中世文学と仏教の交渉
Ishida Mizumaro. *Chūsei bungaku to Bukkyō no kōshō*. Shunjūsha, 1975. 284p.

Explains the realtionship of Buddhism and medieval literature by examining the *Hōbutsushū* (a collection of setsuwa) and *Ōjōyōshū* (The essentials of salvation, a collection of sermons), and other literary works.

D124　筑土鈴寛　著作集
Tsukudo Reikan chosakushū. Serika Shobō, 1976-77. 5v.

Collected works of Tsukudo Reikan.

V.1　A general introduction to religious literature.

V.2 On the Priest Jien, including a reference bibliography and a bibliographical chronology, 1155-1225.

V.3-4 Medieval period religious literature.

V.5 Japanese Buddhist culture, especially Buddhist ceremonies and literature.

Jishū

D125　金井清光　時衆文芸研究
Kanai Kiyomitsu. *Jishū bungei kenkyū*. Kazama Shobō, 1967. 619p.

Explains the importance of the Jishū sect of Buddhism in the development of medieval period literature. Discusses the sermons and waka of the Priest Ippen, and the traveling Priests who followed warriors to their battle sites in order to record what happened at them.

D126　金井清光　一遍と時衆教團
Kanai Kiyomitsu. *Ippen to jishū kyōdan*. Kadokawa Shotcn, 1975. 557p.

History of the Jishū sect and its founder, the Priest Ippen. Describes the 12 factions of the sect, and also covers literature and the performing arts. Indexed by personal names, titles, and the names of temples and shrines.

D127　金井清光　時衆と中世文学
Kanai Kiyomitsu. *Jishū to chūsei bungaku*. Tokyo Bijutsu Shuppan, 1975. 568p.

A continuation of the author's "Jishū bungei kenkyū" (D125). A collection of essays on the Jishū sect and medieval literature, covering such topics as kyōgen, hymns, chant, etc. The major part of the book is an annotated bibliography of the Jishū sect, p.247-554.

Gozan Bungaku

D128　玉村竹二　五山文学
Tamamura Takeji. *Gozan bungaku*. Shibundō, 1955. 290p. (Nihon rekishi shinsho)

Historical survey of Gozan literature, tracing its origins, development, and decline. Contains a bibliography, p.279-290. Illustrated.

D129　芳賀幸四郎　中世禪林の学問および文学に関する研究
Haga Kōshirō. *Chūsei zenrin no gakumon oyobi bungaku ni kansuru kenkyū*. Nihon Gakujutsu Shinkōkai, 1956. 438p.

Study of the learning and literature practice by Zen priests in the medieval period.

D130　五山文学新修　玉村竹二　編
Gozan bungaku shinshū, ed. by Tamamura Takeji. Tokyo Daigaku Shuppankai, 1967-81. 8v.

New and revised collection of Gozan literature, covering the years between the Kamakura and the Edo period. A continuation of the "Gozan bungaku zenshū", a collection of Chinese-style poetry written by Gozan priests which was first published in 1906-1916 and reprinted in 1973 by Shibunkaku.

D131　蔭木英雄　五山詩史の研究
Kageki Hideo. *Gozan shishi no kenkyū*. Kasama Shoin, 1977. 519p.

History of Gozan poetry. Analyzes the works of 52 representative Gozan poets between the years 1279-1615. Contains bibliographical references and an index of personal names.

PERFORMING ARTS

D132　林屋辰三郎　中世芸能史の研究
Hayashiya Tatsusaburō. *Chūsei geinōshi no kenkyū*. Iwanami Shoten, 1960. 593p.

An introduction to the performing arts of the medieval period, including gagaku, sarugaku, dengaku, Nō, kyōgen, etc. Also sketches the development of theater in the same period.

D133　森末義彰　中世芸能史論考
Morisue Yoshiaki. *Chūsei geinōshi ronkō*. Tokyodō, 1971. 336p.

Essays on the medieval performing arts with emphasis on the Nō and its supporters: shōgun, court nobles, temples and shrines, etc. Contains essays on Zeami, professional performers, and female performers.

D134　盛田嘉徳　中世賤民と雑芸能の研究
Morita Yoshinori. *Chūsei senmin to zōgeinō no kenkyū*. Yūzankaku, 1974. 395p.

Collection of essays on the performing arts popular among the lower classes, including female kabuki, and management of their business.

D135　田井庄之助　中世芸能の研究
Tai Shōnosuke. *Chūsei geinō no kenkyū*. Ōfūsha, 1976. 267p.

Study that compares Nō and the tea ceremony with other performing arts of the same period for their use of zen and waka influenced ideas and terms.

D136　徳江元正　芸能・能芸
Tokue Gensei. *Geinō, nōgei*. Miyai Shoten, 1976. 288p. (Miyai sensho)

Collection of essays on the ethnological and literary background of Nō in the Muromachi period. Documented with records, diaries, etc. Provides kana readings for difficult words. Bibliographical references, illustrations. Index.

Nō, kyōgen

D137　戸井田道三　能芸論
Toida Michizō. *Nōgeiron*. Enlarged ed. Keisō Shobō, 1965. 392p.

On the art of Nō, surveying the history of Nō and kyōgen as a part of Japanese culture. Documented with examples drawn from classical literature. Illustrated.

D138　小西甚一　能楽論研究
Konishi Jin'ichi. *Nōgakuron kenkyū*. Hanawa Shobō, 1967. 324p. (Hanawa sensho)

Historical study of the principles of Nō from Zeami to Konparu Zenchiku. Analyzes these principles in relation to the poetic theories of Nijō Yoshimoto and the Priest Shinkei.

D139　後藤　淑　能の形成と世阿弥
Gotō Hajime. *Nō no keisei to Zeami*. Mokujisha, 1966. 299p.

On the history of Nō in the Muromachi period and the life of Zeami. Traces the development of sarugaku from its beginnings in Yamato province to its perfection under the guiding hand of Zeami. Illustrated.

D140　戸井田道三　観阿弥と世阿弥
Toida Michizō. *Kan'ami to Zeami*. Iwanami Shoten, 1969. 205p. (Iwanami shinsho)

Study of the life and times of Kan'ami and Zeami, who perfected the Nō in the turbulent years of the Muromachi period. Also describes the world of the *Taiheiki*, and village theaters.

D141　金井清光　能の研究
Kanai Kiyomitsu. *Nō no kenkyū*. Ōfūsha, 1969. 1167p.

Collection of essays on Nō as a performing art, and on Kan'ami and Zeami, etc.

D142　戸井田道三　能—神と乞食の芸術
Toida Michizō. *Nō - Kami to kojiki no geijutsu*. Enlarged ed. Serika Shobō, 1972. 317p.

An invitation to the Nō of today. Explains stage settings, masks, etc., and gives a retrospective history of the theater and a chronology of Zeami's life.

D143　小林靜雄　謡曲作者の研究
Kobayashi Shizuo. *Yōkyoku sakusha no kenkyū*. 2nd ed. Nōgaku Shobō, 1974. 294p.

Essays on the chanted texts of Nō (yōkyoku) and biographies of selected Nō composers, including Zeami, Kan'ami, Konparu Zenchiku, etc.

D144　後藤　淑　能楽の起源
Gotō Hajime. *Nōgaku no kigen*. Mokujisha, 1975. 586p.

The origins of Nō. A thorough study of sarugaku, the antecedent of Nō, from the Heian to the Muromachi period. Documented with literary evidence and other source material, including local histories, masks, etc. Bibliographical references. Index.

D145　後藤　淑　続能楽の起源
Gotō Hajime. *Zoku Nōgaku no kigen*. Mokujisha, 1982. 470p.

Continuation of the above entry. A study of Kagura (Shinto music), dengaku as the origin of Nō.

D146　金井清光　能と狂言
Kanai Kiyomitsu. *Nō to kyōgen*. Meiji Shoin, 1977. 668p.

Collection of essays on the original forms of Nō, the separation of kyōgen from Nō, waka in Nō and kyōgen, etc. Also contains studies of 20 Nō songs. Illustrations. Index.

D147　田口和夫　狂言論考
Taguchi Kazuo. *Kyōgen ronkō*. Miyai Shoten, 1977. 347p. (Miyai sensho)

Survey of the history of kyōgen, from its origins in the setsuwa of the Kamakura period to its development in the Muromachi period. Bibliographical references. Index.

D148　能楽全書　野上豊一郎　編
Nōgaku zensho, ed. by Nogami Toyoichirō. Complete, new edition. Sōgensha, 1979. 7v.

Complete collection of studies on Nō.

V.1 The thought and art of Nō.
V.2 History.
V.3 Literature.
V.4 Stage production of Nō.
V.5 Nō and kyōgen.
V.6 Appreciation of Nō and kyōgen.
V.7 Performance techniques.

D149　家永三郎　猿楽能の思想史的考察
Ienaga Saburō. *Sarugakunō no shisōshiteki kōsatsu*. Hōsei Daigaku Shuppankyoku, 1980. 256p.

An inquiry into the religious view of life underlying sarugakunō. Based on Nō songs about court nobles, warriors, women, etc. Kana readings are given for each excerpt from a Nō text.

Katarimono (dramatic recitation)

D150　福田　晃　中世語り物文芸
Fukuda Akira. *Chūsei katarimono bungei*. Miyai Shoten, 1981. 350p. (Miyai sensho)

Essays on late medieval katarimono (recited literature), its history and structure. Discusses *Ōkagami, Soga monogatari, Gikeiki*, etc.

D151　室木弥太郎　（増訂）語り物の研究
Muroki Yatarō. *Katarimono no kenkyū*. Enlarged ed. Kazama Shobō, 1981. 596p.

Describes the decline of katarimono after *Heike monogatari*, and the rise of jōruri (narrative shamisen music). (See also E137)

LIFE AND CULTURE

D152　横井　清　中世民衆の生活文化
Yokoi Kiyoshi. *Chūsei minshū no seikatsu bunka*. Tokyo Daigaku Shuppankai, 1975. 376p.

Cultural life of the masses in the medieval period. Describes the social aspects of recreation, ideology, occupations, etc. Bibliography of the author's works. Index.

D153　伊藤鄭爾　中世住居史
Itō Teiji. *Chūsei jūkyoshi*. Tokyo Daigaku Shuppankai, 1958. 295p. (Tōdai gakujutsu sōsho)

Historical and structural analysis of medieval period dwellings. Covers the years 1394-1704, with emphasis on rural family structures, farm houses, and merchant houses. Illustrations, plans, and charts are included.

D154　川上　貢　日本中世住宅の研究
Kawakami Mitsugu. *Nihon chūsei jūtaku no kenkyū*. Bokusui Shobō, 1968. 377p.

Essays on domestic architecture of the medieval period, focusing on the dwellings of court nobles, warriors and priests. Indexes for buildings, persons, and documents.

D155　野地脩左　日本中世住宅史研究
Noji Shūsa. *Nihon chūsei jūtakushi kenkyū*. Nihon Gakujutsu Shinkōkai, 1981. 661p.

Surveys the history of medieval period dwellings, with emphasis on residential buildings and ceremonial tea houses. Illustrated. Index.

D156　森　暢　鎌倉時代の肖像画
Mori Tōru. *Kamakura jidai no shōzōga*. Misuzu Shobō, 1971. 287p.

Collection of essays on portrait painting in the Kamakura period, including portraits of Minamoto no Yoritomo, the Priest Myōe, Fujiwara no Nobuzane, Kasen'e (paintings of the master poets), etc. Illustrated.

D157　渋江二郎　鎌倉彫刻史の研究
Shibue Jirō. *Kamakura chōkokushi no kenkyū*. Yūrindō, 1974. 280p.

History of Buddhist sculpture. Examines the work of various sculptors from the Kamakura area, and the distinctive traits of the Kamakura school. Illustrations. Index.

D158　三山　進　鎌倉彫刻史論考
Miyama Susumu. *Kamakura chōkokushi ronkō*. Yūrindō, 1981. 350p.

Essays on the artistic importance of sculpture in the Kamakura and Muromachi periods. Illustrations. Index

E EDO OR EARLY MODERN PERIOD

The Edo period gave rise to a vital plebian culture, product of the influential class of merchants and shop-keepers that filled the larger cities. The development and spread of literature was aided by a healthy mercantile economy, and by the growth of commercial publishing. Popular literature followed three courses: poetry, with Bashō, Buson, and others; fiction, with Saikaku, Bakin, and the gesaku writers; and drama, with Chikamatsu and the late Edo Kabuki playwrights.

Nor was this all. Scholarship engaged many of the finest minds of the period, including the Confucian Arai Hakuseki and Motoori Norinaga of the National Learning school.
Special terms:

> bunraku (puppet theater)
>
> gesaku (popular fiction)
>
> gidayū (music used in bunraku)
>
> jōruri (narrative shamisen music)
>
> kibyōshi (gesaku fiction in yellow covered book jackets)
>
> kokugaku (national learning)
>
> senryū (humorous haiku)
>
> yomihon (''reading books'')

GENERAL

E1　重友　毅　日本近世文学史
Shigetomo Ki. *Nihon Kinsei bungakushi*. Iwanami Shoten, 1950. 288p. (Iwanami zensho)

A handy, though dated, introduction to early modern Japanese literature. Divided into two periods - early and late Edo - with studies of fiction, haiku and drama for each period. Contains bibliographical references, chronology. Index.

E2　森山重雄　封建庶民文学の研究
Moriyama Shigeo. *Hōken shomin bungaku no kenkyū*. San'ichi Shobō, 1960. 381p.

On the development of a plebian literature in the feudal society of the Edo period. Discusses Saikaku, Chikamatsu, Akinari and others. Index.

E3　阿部次郎　徳川時代の芸術と社会
Abe Jiro. *Tokugawa jidai no geijustsu to shakai*. Kadokawa Shoten, 1961. 468p. (Abe Jiro zenshū, v.8)

An important study of the cultural and philosophical background of Edo period popular arts, especially the literature of Saikaku and Chikamatsu, and ukiyoe.

E4　重友　毅　近世文学史の諸問題
Shigetomo Ki. *Kinsei bungakushi no shomondai*. Meiji Shoin, 1963. 457p.

Examines various issues in the study of early modern literature, with emphasis on individual authors and their works: Saikaku, Bashō, Chikamatsu, Akinari, etc. Index.

E5　野田寿雄　近世文学の背景
Noda Hisao. *Kinsei bungaku no haikei*. Hanawa Shobō, 1964. 251p.

Examines the cultural background of early modern literature, including the characteristics of the people of Edo, Kyoto, and Osaka, the publishing industry, readership, etc. Also gives a decade-by-decade survey of changes in literary trends.

E6　森山重雄　中世と近世の原像
Moriyama Shigeo. *Chūsei to kinsei no genzō*. Shin-dokushosha, 1965. 334p.

Collection of essays on the thought which underlies literature of the early modern period. Discusses the sense of tragedy and impermanence in the *Gikeiki*, *Soga monogatari*, etc., and the significance of Edo period adventure stories.

E7　松田　修　日本近世文学の成立
Matsuda Osamu. *Nihon kinsei bungaku no seiritsu*. Hōsei Daigaku Shuppankyoku, 1972. 345p. (Sōsho Nihon bungakushi kenkyū)

Collection of essays on the establishment of early modern literature. Discusses the characteristics and limitations of Genroku literature, especially in the work of Saikaku and Chikamatsu.

E8   中村幸彦　近世文芸思潮攷
Nakamura Yukihiko. *Kinsei bungei shichōkō.* Iwanami Shoten, 1975. 402p.

Collection of essays on fiction, poetics, and literary criticism in the Edo period. Includes discussions of the poetics of Ishikawa Jōzan, the literary criticism written by Goi Ranshū, and the fiction of Ueda Akinari and Takizawa Bakin.

E9   森山重雄　近世文学の溯源
Moriyama Shigeo. *Kinsei bungaku no sōgen.* Ōfūsha, 1976. 226p.

Collection of essays on thought and tradition in early modern literature, with emphasis on the work of Saikaku, Chikamatsu, Ueda Akinari, etc.

E10   福井久蔵　諸大名の学術と文芸の研究
Fukui Kyūzō. *Shodaimyō no gakujutsu to bungei no kenkyū.* Reprint ed. Hara Shobō, 1976. 2v. (Meiji hyakunen shi sōsho)

Records the cultural accomplishments of over 300 Edo period clans. Arranged topically, with sections on literature, science, fine arts, and the performing arts. Contains a bibliography of the author's works.

E11   前田　愛　鎖国世界の映像
Maeda Ai. *Sakoku sekai no eizō.* Mainichi Shinbunsha, 1976. 238p. (Edo shiriizu)

Collection of essays on literature written during the Edo period, when Japan was closed to all foreign intercourse. Divided into 4 sections: the Genroku era; gesaku fiction; the end of the Edo period; the transition from Edo to Meiji.

E12   宗政五十緒　日本近世文苑の研究
Munemasa Isoo. *Nihon Kinsei bun'en no kenkyū.* Miraisha, 1977. 445p.

Collection of essays on Edo period men of letters, scholars of Chinese, including Arai Hakuseki, Tachibana Nankoku, etc. Also covers the subject of publishing in Kyoto during the Bunka-Bunsei period (1804-30).

E13   近世日本文学史　神保五弥　編
Kinsei Nihon bungakushi, ed. by Jinbo Kazuya. Yūhikaku, 1978. 248p. (Yūhikaku nyūmon, kiso chishiki sōsho)

Guide to Edo literature introducing various types of fiction, including kanazōshi, ukiyozōshi, yomihon, etc. Gives kana readings for difficult words and titles. Bibliography, chronology. Index.

By Period

E14   小高敏郎　近世初期文壇の研究
Odaka Toshio. *Kinsei shoki bundan no kenkyū.* Meiji Shoin, 1964. 672p.

Study of early Edo period literary circles. Organized by period: the Oda-Toyotomi regime; the Kan'ei era (1624-44); the Kanbun era (1661-73); and the Genroku era (1688-1704). Gives biographies of both little- and well-known members of these circles. Name/title index.

E15   広末　保　元禄文学研究
Hirosue Tamotsu. *Genroku bungaku kenkyū.* Enlarged ed. Tokyo Daigaku Shuppankai, 1979. 372p. (Fukkan gakujutsusho)

Collection of essays on the development of Genroku literature as seen in the work of Bashō, Saikaku, and Chikamatsu. Appended are essays on the Kabuki.

E16   広末　保　元禄期の文学と俗
Hirosue Tamotsu. *Genrokuki no bungaku to zoku.* Miraisha, 1979. 241p.

A study of 'zoku' (worldliness) in the literature of Bashō, Chikamatsu, and Saikaku in the Genroku era. Also includes essays on Kabuki and Jōruri.

E17   青山忠一　近世前期文学の研究
Aoyama Tadakazu. *Kinsei zenki bungaku no kenkyū.* Ōfūsha, 1981. 342p.

Collection of essays on the development of kanazōshi (stories written in kana) in the early Edo period. Explains the social background and educational aims of this form of literature.

E18   近世中期文学の研究　近世文学史研究の会　編
Kinsei chūki bungaku no kenkyū, ed. by Kinsei Bungakushi Kenkyū no Kai. 1961-

Studies of literature written during the mid-Edo period. A serial publication of the Society for the Study of the History of Early Modern Literature. The first two numbers of the series were published under the title: "Kinsei chūki bungaku no shomondai". Contains essays on poetry, fiction, drama, language, Chinese classical studies, etc. Index.

E19　中野三敏　近世新畸人伝
Nakano Mitsutoshi. *Kinsei shinkijinden*. Mainichi
Shinbunsha, 1977. 230p. (Edo shiriizu)

Biographical studies of five eccentric men of letters
who lived in Edo during the Hōreki era (1751-64).

E20　前田　愛　幕末維新期の文学
Maeda Ai. *Bakumatsu-Ishinki no bungaku*. Hōsei
Daigaku Shuppankyoku, 1972. 378p.

Collection of essays on literature written during the
transitional period from the end of the Bakufu to
Meiji. Includes a discussion of Kitamura Tōkoku,
etc. Contains a chronology for the years 1827-77.
Indexes of personal names and titles.

Collected Works (select list)

E21　森　銑三　著作集
Mori Senzō chosakushū. Chūō Kōronsha, 1970-72.
13v.

V.1-9　Biographical studies of Edo period men of
letters, artists, scholars of the classics, etc.

V.10-11　Bibliographical studies of works by
Saikaku, various forms of fiction, Chinese
poetry, etc.

V.12　Miscellaneous studies.

V.13　Indexes of personal names and titles and a list
of publications by the author.

E22　重友　毅　著作集
Shigetomo Ki chosakushū. Bunri Shoin, 1971-74.
5v.

V.1　Saikaku.

V.2　Bashō.

V.3　Chikamatsu.

V.4　Akinari.

V.5　Essays on Edo period literature.

Index in each volume.

E23　山口　剛　著作集
Yamaguchi Takeshi chosakushū. Chūō Kōronsha,
1972. 6v.

V.1-4　Saikaku, Chikamatsu, and various types of
fiction.

V.5　Japanese translations of Chinese drama.

V.6　Miscellaneous essays. A list of the author's
publications.

E24　水谷不倒　著作集
Mizutani Futō chosakushū. Chūō Kōronsha,
1973-78. 8v.

Grouped by topic: fiction, jōruri, illustrated books,
and the book trade in the Meiji, Taisho eras. V.8
contains the author's memoirs and a list of his
publications. Index.

E25　三田村鳶魚　全集
Mitamura Engyo zenshū. Chūō Kōronsha, 1975-77,
83. 28v.

Mitamura Engyo was a noted scholar of Edo literature and cultural history. The last three volumes of
this series consist of Mitamura's diaries. A supplementary volume, published in 1983, contains a list
of his works and indexes to personal names, titles,
and subjects for the entire set.

E26　近藤忠義　日 本 文 学 論
Kondō Tadayoshi. *Nihon bungakuron*. Shin Nihon
Shuppansha, 1974. 3v.

Studies in Japanese literature.

V.1　Introduction.

V.2　Kabuki and Jōruri.

V.3　Edo fiction and haikai. Includes a bio-
bibliography.

E27　穎原退蔵　著作集
Ebara Taizō chosakushū. Chūō Kōronsha, 1971-81.
20v.

V.1　Edo literature.

V.2　Renga.

V.3-5　History of haikai.

V.6-8　Commentaries on haikai.

V.9-12　Bashō.

V.13　Buson.

V.14-15　Senryū.

V.16　Language of the Edo period.

V.17-18　Fiction and jōruri.

V.19　Catalogue of haikai books held by the Waro
library in Tenri University.

V.20　Miscellaneous essays.

E28　中村幸彦　著述集
Nakamura Yukihiko chojutsushū. Chūō Kōronsha,
1982- (15v.) (In progress)

Each volume illustrated.

V.1　Early modern literary trends.

V.2　Early modern literary expression.

V.3　Studies in early modern literature.

V.4　not yet published.

V.5　Early modern fiction.

V.6　Early modern authors and their works.

V.7 not yet published.
V.8 Gesaku.
V.9 Haikai.
V.10 Recited literature.
V.11 Scholars of classical Chinese.
V.12 Scholars of national learning (kokugaku).
V.13 not yet published.
V.14 Bibliographical essays.
V.15 not yet published.

Festschrifts (select list)

E29 近世国文学　研究と資料　守随憲治 編
Kinsei Kokubungaku. Kenkyū to shiryō, ed. by
Shuzui Kenji. Sanseidō, 1960. 564p.

Festschrift in honor of Professor Shuzui. Consists of
essays on Edo literature, drama, the Hachimonjiya
publishing house, and relations between author and
publisher in the Edo period. Includes reproductions
of rare items on drama. Kana readings given for
difficult titles.

E30 近 世 文 学 論 叢　中村俊定 先生
Kinsei bungaku ronsō, Nakamura Shunjō Sensei
koki kinen, ed. by Sōdai Haikai Kenkyūkai.
Ōfūsha, 1970. 693p.

Festschrift in honor of Professor Nakamura. Consists of 35 essays by members of the Waseda
University Society for Haikai Studies. Bio-
bibliography.

E31 近世文学　作家と作品　中村幸彦 教授
Kinsei bungaku: Sakka to sakuhin, ed. by Kinen
Ronbunshū Kankōkai, Chūō Kōronsha, 1973. 626p.

Festschrift in honor of Professor Nakamura. Consists of 27 essays on Edo period writers and their
works. Bio-bibliography.

E32 近世大阪芸文叢談　大谷篤蔵 編
Kinsei Osaka geibun sōdan, ed. by Ōtani Tokuzō.
Osaka. Osaka Geibunkai, 1973. 709p.

Festschrift in honor of Professor Ōtani Tokuzō.
Consists of 19 essays by members of the Study
Group for Osaka literature.

E33 近 世 の 学 芸　三古会 編
Kinsei no gakugei, ed. by Sankokai. Yagi Shoten,
1976. 433p.

Festschrift published in honor of the 40th anniversary of the founding of the Sankokai study group
and the 80th birthday of the group's founder, Mori

Senzō. Consists of 31 essays on such figures as
Arai Hakuseki, Mamiya Rinzō, Rai San'yō, Santō
Kyōden, etc.

E34 芸 能 と 文 学　井浦芳信 博士
Geinō to bungaku, Inoura Yoshinobu Hakushi kako
kinen ronbunshū, ed. by the publishing committee.
Kasama Shoin, 1977. 529p.

Festschrift in honor of Professor Inoura. Consists of
essays on the performing arts and literature of the
Edo period.

E35 近 世 文 芸 論 叢　暉峻康隆 編
Kinsei bungei ronsō, ed. by Teruoka Yasutaka.
Chūō Kōronsha, 1978. 551p.

Festschrift in honor of Professor Teruoka. Consists
of essays on haikai, fiction, drama, etc.

E36 天明文学　資料と研究　浜田義一郎 編
Tenmei bungaku: shiryō to kenkyū, ed. by Hamada
Giichirō. Tokyodō, 1979. 547p.

Festschrift in honor of Professor Hamada. Consists
of essays on the literature of the Tenmei era
(1781-89). Contains reproductions of unpublished
source materials.

THOUGHT

Confucian Studies

E37 相良　享　近世日本における儒教運動の系譜

Sagara Tōru. *Kinsei Nihon ni okeru jukyō undō no
keifu*. Risōsha, 1965. 538p. (Tetsugaku zensho)

A study of the rise and fall of the Edo period
movement to inculcate Confucian ethics.

E38 田原嗣郎　徳川思想史研究
Tahara Tsuguo. *Tokugawa shisōshi kenkyū*. Miraisha, 1967. 528p.

A study of the thought of several Edo period
scholars on the classics: Yamaga Sokō, Ogyū Sorai,
and Itō Jinsai. Index.

E39 藤原　暹　日本近世思想の研究
Fujiwara Noboru. *Nihon kinsei shisō no kenkyū*.
Hōritsu Bunkasha, 1971. 237p.

Traces changes in thought in the feudal society of
the Edo period, from the Dutch studies of Ogyū
Sorai to the enlightenment movement anticipating
the Meiji period. At the beginning of the book is a
summary in English.

E40 岡田武彦　江戸期の儒学
Okada Takehiko. *Edoki no jugaku*. Mokujisha, 1982. 440p.

Traces the history of Confucian studies in the Edo period, with emphasis on the late Edo period scholars who followed the philosophy of Wang Yang-ming and Chu-tzu.

E41 日野龍夫　徂徠学派—儒学から文学へ
Hino Tatsuo. *Soraigakuha - jugaku kara bungaku e*. Chikuma Shobō, 1975. 230p.

Examines the thought of the Confucian scholar Ogyū Sorai and his conception of literary life.

E42 吉川幸次郎　仁斉・徂徠・宣長
Yoshikawa Kōjirō. *Jinsai, Sorai, Norinaga*. Iwanami Shoten, 1975. 388p.

Collection of essays on the Edo period scholars Itō Jinsai, Ogyū Sorai, and Moroori Norinaga. Contains an article in English: Itō Jinsai. 46p.

E43 日野龍夫　江戸人とユートピア
Hino Tatsuo. *Edojin to yūtopia*. Asahi Shinbunsha, 1977. 224p. (Asahi sensho)

Collection of essays on the decadent state of literature and culture at the end of the Edo period.

Kokugaku (National Learning)

E44 大久保　正　江戸時代の国学
Ōkubo Tadashi. *Edo jidai no kokugaku*. Shibundō, 1963. 278p. (Nihon rekishi shinsho)

Study of the development of national learning in the Edo period, with emphasis on the work of the Priest Keichū, Kada no Azumamaro, Kamo no Mabuchi, and Motoori Norinaga. Index.

E45 三枝康高　国学の運動
Saegusa Yasutaka. *Kokugaku no undō*. Kazama Shobō, 1966. 529p.

Study of kokugaku as a literary movement, with emphasis on the works of the Priest Keichū, Kada no Azumamaro, and Kamo no Mabuchi. Illustrations.

E46 塙　保己一　記念論文集
Hanawa Hokiichi Kinen ronbunshū, ed. by Hanawa Hokiichi Kengyō 150 nensai Ronbushū Henshū Iinkai. Onko Gakkai, 1971. 475p.

Collection of 24 essays issued in commemoration of the 150th year since the death of the scholar Hanawa Hokiichi, compiler of the *Gunsho ruijū*.

Covers history, literature, education, etc. Bibliographical references.

E47 重松信弘　近世国学の文学研究
Shigematsu Nobuhiro. *Kinsei kokugaku no bungaku kenkyū*. Kazama Shobō, 1974. 332p.

Study of the literary work produced by scholars of the national learning school, including that of the Priest Keichū, Kada no Azumamaro, Kamo no Mabuchi, and Motoori Norinaga.

E48 丸山季夫　国学史上の人々
Maruyama Sueo. *Kokugakushijō no hitobito*, ed. by Maruyama Sueo Ikōshū Kankōkai, Yoshikawa Kōbunkan, 1979. 885p.

Collection of essays, issued posthumously, on Edo period scholars of national learning and men of letters, including Ueda Akinari, Katō Umaki, etc. Contains a bio-bibliography.

E49 清原貞雄　国学発達史
Kiyohara Sado. *Kokugaku hattatsushi*. Kokusho Kankōkai, 1981. 434p.

Photo reproduction of the 1935 edition. A standard work on the the history of Kokugaku (national learning). Index.

LANGUAGE

E50 湯沢幸吉郎　江戸言葉の研究
Yuzawa Kōkichirō. *Edo kotoba no kenkyū*. Reprint ed. Meiji Shoin, 1954. 753p.

A study of the colloquial language used in the city of Edo at the end of the Tokugawa period. Based on an analysis of this langauge as found in works of fiction, Kabuki plays, rakugo, etc. Bibliographical references. Index.

E51 湯沢幸吉郎　徳川時代言語の研究
Yuzawa Kōkichirō. *Tokugawa jidai gengo no kenkyū*: Kamigatahen. Kazama Shobō, 1955. 650p.

Reprint of the 1936 edition. A study of the colloquial language used in the Kyoto/Osaka area in the early Edo period, as seen in Kabuki, Jōruri, etc. Bibliographical references. Index.

E52 杉本つとむ　江戸時代蘭語学の成立とその展開
Sugimoto Tsutomu. *Edo jidai rangogaku no seiritsu to sono tenkai*. Waseda Daigaku Shuppanbu, 1976-(1981) (4v)

English title: Dutch linguistics, its formation, growth, and development. Each volume is illustrated.

V.1 General survey.

V.2 Edo scholars of Western learning such as Arai Hakuseki, etc.

V.3 The compilation of the Dutch-Japanese dictionaries.

V.4 Personal histories and scientific works of the Dutch scholars. Contains extensive notes for vol.1-3.

E53 芳賀　登　江戸語の成立
Haga Noboru. *Edogo no seiritsu*. Kaitakusha, 1982. 221p. (Kaitakusha gengo bunka sōsho)

Linguistic and social development of speech in the city of Edo.

PROSE LITERATURE

Fiction

E54 中村幸彦　近世小説史の研究
Nakamura Yukihiko. *Kinsei shōsetsushi no kenkyū*. Ōfūsha, 1961. 368p.

Collection of essays on Edo period fiction, including sharebon, yomihon, etc. Also contains essays on the Hachimonjiya publishing house, and the Edo period reading public. Index.

E55 中村幸彦　近世作家研究
Nakamura Yukihiko. *Kinsei sakka kenkyū*. San'ichi Shobō, 1961. 365p.

Collection of essays on Edo period writers, including Ihara Saikaku, Tada Nanrei, Itō Jinsai and his disciples, Ueda Akinari, Jippensha Ikku, Tamenaga Shunsui, etc. Index.

E56 野田寿雄　近世小説史論考
Noda Hisao. *Kinsei shōsetsushi ronkō*. Hanawa Shobō, 1961. 409p.

Collection of 11 essays on some of the less-studied genres of late Edo period fiction, including kana-zōshi, ukiyozōshi, dangibon, etc. Index.

E57 中村幸彦　戯作論
Nakamura Yukihiko. *Gesakuron*. Kadokawa Shoten, 1966. 321p.

A comprehensive study of the history, style, and structure of fiction. Also discusses the publishing business. Illustrations, index.

E58 長谷川　強　浮世草子の研究
Hasegawa Tsuyoshi. *Ukiyozōshi no kenkyū*. Ōfūsha, 1969. 634p.

History of ukiyozōshi and the Hachimonjiya publishing firm, from its rise in the Genroku era (1688-1704) to its decline in the Genbun era (1736-41). Chronology. Index.

E59 武藤禎夫　江戸小咄の比較研究
Mutō Sadao. *Edo kobanashi no hikaku kenkyū*. Tokyodō Shuppan, 1970. 310p.

A study comparing Edo period kobanashi (short tales) with Chinese comic stories, senryū poems, kyōgen, folk tales, etc.

E60 森　銑三　黄表紙解題
Mori Senzō. *Kibyōshi kaidai*. Chūō Kōronsha, 1972-74. 2v.

Study of Edo period kibyōshi. V.1 discusses 130 titles published between 1772-85; V.2 discusses 121 titles published between 1786-93. Illustrated.

E61 尾崎久弥　近世庶民文学論考
Ozaki Kyūya. *Kinsei shomin bungaku ronkō*, ed. by Nakamura Yukihiko. Chūō kōronsha, 1973. 374p.

Collection of 22 essays on bibliographical aspects of late Edo period popular literature. Also contains the author's autobiography.

E62 横山邦治　読本の研究
Yokoyama Kuniharu. *Yomihon no kenkyū - Edo to Kamigata to*. Kazama Shobō, 1974. 876p.

History of yomihon from the late Tenmei era to the end of the Edo period (1780's-1869). Also relates the history of yomihon studies. Index.

E63 水野　稔　江戸小説論叢
Mizuno Minoru. *Edo shōsetsu ronsō*. Chūō Kōronsha, 1974. 416p.

Collection of 20 essays on late Edo fiction. Concentrates especially on the sharebon of Santō Kyōden and the gōkan (collected volumes) of Kyokutei Bakin.

E64 田中　伸　仮名草子の研究
Tanaka Shin. *Kanazōshi no kenkyū*. Ōfūsha, 1974. 393p.

History of kanazōshi and other prose writings. Contains reproductions of rare editions. Illustrations. Index.

E65 浅野三平　近世中期小説の研究
Asano Sanpei. *Kinsei chūki shōsetsu no kenkyū.* Ōfūsha, 1975. 331p.

Collection of 14 essays on the history of fiction and tales of famous sites in the 18th century.

E66 坂巻甲太　仮名草子新攷
Sakamaki Kōta. *Kanazōshi shinkō.* Kasama Shoin, 1978. 242p. (Kasama sōsho)

Study of kanazōshi, including Asai Ryōi's *Edo meishoki*, *Tokaidō meishoki*, etc.

E67 太刀川　清　近世怪異小説研究
Tachikawa Kiyoshi. *Kinsei kaii shōsetsu kenkyū.* Kasama Shoin, 1979. 346p. (Kasama sōsho)

On Edo period ghost stories. Selected from various genres of fiction.

E68 青山忠一　近世前期文学の研究
Aoyama Tadakazu. *Kinsei zenki bungaku no kenkyū.* Revised ed. Ōfūsha, 1981. 342p.

Study of the moral teachings found in early Edo period kanazōshi. (See also A17)

E69 中野三敏　戯　作　研　究
Nakano Mitsutoshi. *Gesaku kenkyū.* Chūō Kōronsha, 1981. 418p.

Collection of essays on gesaku, the eastward movement of the publishing trade from the Kyoto area to Edo, and dangibon and their writers. Indexes.

E70 広瀬朝光　戯　作　文　芸　論
Hirose Tomomitsu. *Gesaku bungeiron.* Kasama Shoin, 1982. 515p. (Kasama sōsho)

Study of kibyōshi and biographies of gesaku writers, with emphasis on Koikawa Harumachi. Contains reference sources on Koikawa and a catalog of kibyōshi, arranged by name of author, and with kana readings for unusual titles.

Individual Authors

Saikaku, 1642-93

E71 西　　鶴　天理図書館　編
Saikaku, ed. by Tenri Toshokan. 1965. 2v.

Festschrift commemorating the 60th birthday of Nakayama Shōzen, Archbishop of the Tenri sect. Consists of reproductions of biographcial materials, block copies, and first editions of Saikaku's works, with bibliographical explanations of important editions. Chronology. Index.

E72 宗政五十緒　西　鶴　の　研　究
Munemasa Isoo. *Saikaku no kenkyū.* Miraisha, 1969. 346p.

Collection of essays on Saikaku, including such topics as the intellectual and spiritual basis of Saikaku's fiction; concerning Saikaku's disciple Hōjō Dansui; the readership for Saikaku's works, etc.

E73 吉江久弥　西　鶴　文　学　研　究
Yoshie Hisaya. *Saikaku bungaku kenkyū.* Kasama Shoin, 1974. 623p.

Introduction to Saikaku's fiction, its relationship to Ukiyozōshi, the structure of the kōshokumono, etc. Index.

E74 西　鶴　論　叢　野間光辰　編
Saikaku ronsō, ed. by Noma Kōshin. Chūō Kōronsha, 1975. 562p.

Festschrift in honor of Noma Kōshin. Consists of essays by 28 scholars, including one by Donald Keene titled "The humor of Ihara Saikaku". Illustrated.

E75 檜谷昭彦　井原西鶴研究
Hinotani Teruhiko. *Ihara Saikaku kenkyū.* Miyai Shoten, 1979. 445p.

A collection of 16 essays on different facets of Saikaku's work. Organized into three parts: 1, the structure of Saikaku's works; 2, Saikaku's dealings with the publishing industry; 3, the elements of folklore in Saikaku's fiction.

E76 乾　裕幸　俳　諧　師　西　鶴
Inui Hiroyuki. *Haikaishi Saikaku.* Maeda Shoten, 1979. 302p. (Maeda kokubun sensho)

Essays on Saikaku's years as a haikai poet of the Danrin school.

E77 野間光辰　西　鶴　新　新　攷
Noma Kōshin. *Saikaku shinshinkō.* Iwanami Shoten, 1981. 640p.

New, revised edition of "Saikaku shinkō", published by Chikuma Shobō in 1953.

E78 谷脇理史　西　鶴　研　究　論　攷
Taniwaki Masachika. *Saikaku kenkyū ronkō.* Shintensha, 1981. 438p. (Shintensha kenkyū sōsho)

A collection of the author's previously published essays on various aspects of Saikaku's work.

E79 谷脇理史　元禄文化西鶴の世界
Taniwaki Masachika. *Genroku bunka Saikaku no sekai*. Kyōikusha, 1982. 227p. (Kyōikusha rekishi shinsho)

An introduction to Genroku culture through Saikaku's fiction. Reference bibliography. Chronology.

E80 広末　保　西　鶴　の　小　説
Hirosue Tamotsu. *Saikaku no shōsetsu*. Heibonsha, 1982. 265p. (Heibonsha sensho)

A study of Saikaku's novels. The author holds that Saikaku's stories have an unfinished quality about them unique to the age in which Saikaku wrote. Hence his fiction should not be regarded as a forerunner of the modern novel.

Ueda Akinari, 1734-1809

E81 高田　衛　上田秋成年譜考説
Takada Mamoru. *Ueda Akinari nenpu kōsetsu*. Meizendō, 1964. 427p.

A chronological study of Ueda Akinari. Contains essays on Akinari's parentage and on the probable date of publication of *Ugetsu Monogatari*. Illustrations. Index.

E82 高田　衛　上田秋成研究序説
Takada Mamoru. *Ueda Akinari kenkyū josetsu*. Nara Shobō, 1968. 488p.

An introduction to the study of Ueda Akinari and his works.

E83 鷲山樹心　秋成文学の思想
Washiyama Jushin. *Akinari bungaku no shisō*. Kyoto, Hōzōkan, 1979. 460p.

Traces the intellectual development of Akinari by examining the influence of National Learning (kokugaku), Buddhism, and Confucianism on Akinari's fiction. Foreword in English.

E84 大輪靖宏　上田秋成
Ōwa Yasuhiro. *Ueda Akinari*. Shunjūsha, 1982. 368p.

A literary biography of Ueda Akinari.

others

E85 小池藤五郎　山　東　京　伝
Koike Tōgorō. *Santō Kyōden*, ed. by Nihon Rekishi Gakkai. Yoshikawa Kōbunkan, 1961. 311p. (Jinbutsu sōsho)

Biography of Santō Kyōden - gesaku writer, ukiyoe artist, shopkeeper. Contains a chronology, bibliographical references, and illustrations.

E86 本多康雄　式亭三馬の文芸
Honda Yasuo. *Shikitei Sanba no bungei*. Kasama Shoin, 1973. 414p.

The life and work of the gesaku writer Shikitei Sanba. Each chapter includes bibliographical information. Contains a chronology, illustrations. Index.

Travel Accounts

E87 内田武志　菅江真澄の旅と日記
Uchida Takeshi. *Sugae Masumi no tabi to nikki*. Miraisha, 1970. 292p.

Study of the travel diaries written by the Kokugaku scholar Sugae Masumi between the years 1784-1814. Contains a chronology.

E88 鈴木棠三　近世紀行文芸ノート
Suzuki Tōzō. *Kinsei kiko bungei nōto*. Tokyodō, 1974. 303p.

Study of travel diaries of literary value written during the Edo period.

POETRY

Haiku, Senryū, Zappai

E89 俳句シリーズ　人　と　作　品
Haiku shiriizu: Hito to sakuhin. Ōfūsha, 1963-67. 18v.

Discusses Bashō, Buson, Kobayashi Issa, Masaoka Shiki, etc. Supplement volumes treat the history of modern haiku poetics and haiku forms.

E90 栗山理一　俳　諧　史.
Kuriyama Riichi. *Haikaishi*. Hanawa Shobō, 1963. 369p. (Hanawa sensho)

A general history of haikai from the times of Bashō to modern haiku.

E91 阿達義雄　江戸川柳の史的研究
Adachi Yoshio. *Edo senryū no shiteki kenkyū*. Kazama Shobō, 1967. 1035p.

A survey history of Edo senryū. Concentrates on the development of senryū in the 18th century. Chronology. Indexes.

E92　乾　裕幸　初期俳諧の展開
Inui Hiroyuki. *Shoki haikai no tenkai*. Ōfūsha,
1968. 341p.

Collection of 11 essays tracing the history of haikai
from the Danrin school to the Shōmon school.
Contains a name/title/subject index and a first word
index for haiku.

E93　能勢朝次　連句芸術の性格
Nose Asaji. *Renku geijustu no seikaku*. Kadokawa
Shoten, 1970. 232p. (Kadokawa sensho)

Collection of essays on the development of linked
verse in the Edo period.

E94　岡崎義恵　芸術としての俳諧
Okazaki Yoshie. *Geijutsu toshite no haikai*. New
ed. Hōbunkan, 1970. 379p. (Okazaki Yoshie
chosakusen)

Collection of essays on the view of nature expressed
in Bashō's haiku.

E95　荻野　清　著作集
Ogino Kiyoshi chosakushū. Akao Shōbundō,
1970-71. 2v.

V.1　Essays on haikai of the Genroku era
　　　(1688-1704) and the revival of haikai by
　　　Bashō.
V.2　Comments on 159 haiku in the *Sarumino*.

E96　山本唯一　元禄俳諧の位相
Yamamoto Yuiichi. *Genroku haikai no isō*. Kyoto,
Hōzōkan, 1971. 302p.

A survey of Genroku haikai, with studies of the
work of Onitsura, Bashō, Kikaku, etc.

E97　宮田正信　雑俳史の研究
Miyata Masanobu. *Zappaishi no kenkyū*. Kyoto,
Akao Shōbundō, 1972. 599p.

Traces the development of zappai (comic haikai).
Contains an annotated bibliography. Index.

E98　鈴木勝忠　俳諧史要
Suzuki Katsutada. *Haikaishiyō*. Meiji Shoin, 1973.
213p.

Outlines stylistic changes in linked verse from renga
to modern haiku.

E99　尾形　仂　俳諧史論考
Ogata Tsutomu. *Haikaishi ronkō*. Ōfūsha, 1977.
270p. (Kokugo Kokubungaku kenkyū sōsho, v.3)

Traces the development of haikai. Concentrates especially on the origins of various schools, such as
Danrin, Bashō, etc.

E100　江藤保定　近世初期俳諧論考
Etō Yasusada. *Kinsei shoki haikai ronkō*. Kasama
Shoin, 1977. 311p.

A study of the representative features of four different schools active in the early years of haikai:
Moritake, Sōin, Teimon, and Danrin. Bibliographical notes at the end of each chapter.

E101　山本唯一　俳文学の系譜
Yamamoto Yuiichi. *Haibungaku no keifu*. Kyoto,
Hōzōkan, 1978. 374p.

A collection of essays on the spiritual influence of
haikai on Japanese culture, as seen in the work of
Bashō, Issa, etc.

E102　小西甚一　俳句の世界
Konishi Jin'ichi. *Haiku no sekai*. Revised ed. Kenkyūsha Shuppan, 1981. 320p.

Traces the history of haiku in 2 parts: pt.1 pre-Meiji
haikai; pt.2 post-Meiji and contemporary haiku.
Index.

E103　俳文学論集　宮本三郎　先生
Haibungaku ronshū, ed. by Miyamoto Saburō
Sensei Tsuitō Ronbunshū Kankōkai. Kasama Shoin,
1981. 383p. (Kasama sōsho)

Collection of essays on haikai literature. Written by
Professor Miyamoto Saburō's colleagues in his
honor. Contains a bio-bibliography.

Matsuo Bashō (died 1695)

E104　大内初雄　芭蕉と蕉門の研究
Ōuchi Hatsuo. *Bashō to Shōmon no kenkyū*.
Ōfūsha, 1968. 325p.

Collection of essays on Bashō and the Shōmon
school. Contains a chapter on the publishing done
by this school, discussing publishing expenses,
number of copies printed, etc.

E105　芭蕉の本　中村幸彦　等編
Bashō no hon, ed. by Nakamura Yukihiko, et al.
Kadokawa Shoten, 1969-72. 8v.

Concerning Bashō. Each volume contains a reference bibliography.

V.1　Personality, thought and the world of the poet,
　　　ed. by Nakamura Yukio.
V.2　The poet's life, ed. by Katō Shūson.

V.3 The spread of Bashō-style haikai to various localities, ed. by Ogata Tsutomu.

V.4 Ideas and their expression, ed. by Kadokawa Motoyoshi.

V.5 The world of the master poets (kasen), ed. by Yamamoto Kenkichi.

V.6 Wandering sage, ed. by Imoto Nōichi.

V.7 Artistic refinement in Bashō's work, ed. by Konishi Jin'ichi.

V.8 (Suppl.) Illustrations, charts, etc., ed. by Okada Rihei.

E106　芭蕉　蕪村　一茶　栗山理一　編
Bashō, Buson, Issa, ed. by Kuriyama Riichi. Yūzankaku, 1978. 411p.

A festschrift in honor of Professor Kuriyama Riichi. Consists of 21 essays on the poets Bashō, Buson, and Issa. Bio-bibliography appended.

E107　芭 蕉 講 座
Bashō Kōza. Yūseidō, 1982- (5v.)

Lectures on Bashō.

V.1 Biography of Bashō and his disciples. Chronology.

V.2 Style of presentation in haikai, poetics.

V.3 forthcoming.

V.4 Appreciation of hokku and renga.

V.5 Prose works, travel accounts.

Waka

E108　山本嘉将　近 世 和 歌 史 論
Yamamoto Kashō. *Kinsei wakashiron*. Bunkyō Tosho Shuppan, 1958. 635p.

Traces the history of waka in the Edo period from the revival of the classical style by Kamo no Mabuchi and his disciples.

E109　山本嘉将　賀 茂 真 渕 論
Yamamoto Kashō. *Kamo no Mabuchi ron*. Kyoto, Hatsune Shobō, 1963. 325p.

Study of Kamo no Mabuchi as poet and reformer of waka.

E110　梁瀬一雄　近 世 和 歌 研 究
Yanase Kazuo. *Kinsei waka kenkyū*. Katō Chūdōkan, 1978. 843p. (Yanase Kazuo chosakushū, v.5)

A study of some of the lesser known poets of the early modern period, including the Priest Keichū, Yokoi Senshū, Takabatake Shikibu, etc.

E111　辻森秀英　近世後期歌壇の研究
Tsujimori Shūei. *Kinsei kōki kadan no kenkyū*. Ōfūsha, 1978. 462p.

Collection of essays on the circles of waka poets at the end of the Edo period in Edo and other places. Includes a study of the waka written during this period in the style of the *Shin Kokinshū*.

Kanshi (poetry in Chinese)

E112　富士川英郎　江戸後期の詩人たち
Fujikawa Hideo. *Edo kōki no shijintachi*. Chikuma Shobō, 1973. 397p. (Chikuma sōsho)

Traces the history of Chinese-style poetry written in the last 100 years of the Edo period. Index.

E113　野口武彦　江戸文学の詩と真実
Noguchi Takehiko. *Edo bungaku no shi to shinjitsu*. Chūō Kōronsha, 1971. 257p.

A modern interpretation of the poetry of Gion Nankai, Dōmyaku Sensei, Ōta Nanpo, and Dazai Shundai.

E114　頼　桃三郎　近 世 文 壇 史 話
Rai Momosaburo. *Kinsei bundan shiwa - Shijin no tegami*. Bunka Hyōronsha, 1974. 283p.

Describes life of poets and poetic circles in the Kyoto/Osaka area between the years, 1764-81, based on letters and notes left by those poets.

E115　中村真一郎　頼山陽とその時代
Nakamura Shin'ichirō. *Rai San'yō to sono jidai*. Chūō Kōronsha, 1971. 654p. (Chūkō bunko, 1976-77. 3v.)

The life and times of Rai San'yō, his family, friends, disciples, etc. A chronology, genealogy. Personal name index.

PERFORMING ARTS AND DRAMA

E116　関山和夫　中京芸能風土記
Sekiyama Kazuo. *Chūkyō geinō fudoki*. Seiabō, 1970. 295p.

Survey of the performing arts in Edo period Nagoya, including drama, story-telling, popular songs, etc. Index.

E117　田井庄之助　近世演劇の研究
Tai Shōnosuke. *Kinsei engeki no kenkyū*. Ōfūsha, 1972. 622p.

Study of the characteristic features of Kabuki, with reference to the works of Tsuruya Nanboku and Kawatake Mokuami. Includes chapters on the kabuki plays and jōruri written by Chikamatsu Monzaemon.

E118　松田　修　日本芸能史論考
Matsuda Osamu. *Nihon geinōshi ronkō.* Hōsei Daigaku Shuppankyoku, 1974. 289p. (Sōsho Nihon bungakushi kenkyū)

Thesis on the Japanese performing arts which holds that, because these arts originated in the satirical sketches performed by wandering minstrels, their mature forms are characterized by certain philosophical contrasts, such as sacred vs. vulgar, light vs. darkness, beauty vs. ugliness, etc.

E119　松崎　仁　元禄演劇研究
Matsuzaki Hitoshi. *Genroku engeki kenkyū.* Tokyo Daigaku Shuppankai. 1979. 292p.

Collection of essays on the performing arts of the Genroku era (1688-1704), especially Genroku kabuki and the jōruri of Chikamatsu. Index.

Kabuki

E120　守随憲治　著作集
Shuzui Kenji chosakushū. Kasama Shoin, 1976-79. 6v.

Collected works of Shuzui Kenji.

V.1 Structure of kabuki, bibliographical research on kabuki and jōruri, etc.

V.2 History of Edo period drama, collection of annotated scripts, etc.

V.3 Introduction to kabuki, on Tsuruya Nanboku and Kawatake Mokuami, etc.

V.4 Giri, Chikamatsu, Jōruri.

V.5 Essays on fiction, the performing arts, and actors.

V.6 (Suppl.) Charts and illustrations, explanatory notes.

E121　河竹繁俊　河竹黙阿弥
Kawatake Shigetoshi. *Kawatake Mokuami,* ed. by Nihon Rekishi Gakkai. Yoshikawa Kōbunkan, 1961. 271p. (Jinbutsu sōsho)

Contains a biography of the playwright Kawatake Mokuami and an annotated list of his plays. Chronology and reference bibliography included.

E122　和辻哲郎　歌舞伎と操り浄瑠璃
Watsuji Tetsurō. *Kabuki to ayatsuri jōruri.* Iwanami Shoten, 1963. 730p. (Watsuji Tetsurō zenshū V.16)

A study of the historical development of kabuki and the puppet theater.

E123　農村舞台の総合的研究　角田一郎 編
Nōson butai no sōgōteki kenkyū, ed. by Tsunoda Ichirō. Ōfūsha, 1971. 845p.

Report of a field survey that investigated the existence and condition of theaters in rural areas. Indicates the distribution of theaters by district. Contains a reference bibliography. Illustrations.

E124　諏訪春雄　元禄歌舞伎の研究
Suwa Haruo. *Genroku kabuki no kenkyū.* Kasama Shoin, 1967, 425p. (Kasama sōsho)

A survey of kabuki in the Genroku era (1688-1704), with emphasis on the actor Ichikawa Danjuro, kabuki's relationship to kyōgen, jōruri, etc.

E125　郡司正勝　歌舞伎：様式と伝統
Gunji Masakatsu. *Kabuki: yōshiki to dentō.* Gakugei Shoin, 1969. 330p.

First published in 1954 by Nara Shobō. Examines the folkloric origins of kabuki and its forms of performance. Illustrations. Index.

E126　今尾哲也　変身の思想
Imao Tetsuya. *Henshin no shisō.* Hōsei Daigaku Shuppankyoku, 1970. 324p. (Sōsho. Nihon bungakushi kenkyū)

Collection of essays on the principles of acting in double roles employed by kabuki actors, and on the establishment of kyōgen in Genroku kabuki, etc.

E127　小笠原恭子　かぶきの誕生
Ogasawara Kyōko. *Kabuki no tanjō.* Meiji Shoin, 1972. 447p.

Collection of essays on the development of kabuki, from its origins to the Genroku era.

E128　諏訪春雄　歌舞伎史の画証的研究
Suwa Haruo. *Kabukishi no gashōteki kenkyū.* Asuka Shobō, 1974. 482p.

Pictorial history of kabuki. Examines kabuki in its early years by referring to illustrated evidence, including screens, scrolls, etc. Also includes ukiyoe prints of actors.

E129　服部幸雄　変化論―歌舞伎の精神史
Hattori Yukio. *Hengeron - Kabuki no seishinshi.* Heibonsha, 1975. 269p.

Study of the influence of folklore and religion on kabuki, ghost stories, etc.

E130　服部幸雄　歌舞伎成立の研究
Hattori Yukio. *Kabuki seiritsu no kenkyū.* Revised ed. Kazama Shobō, 1980. 613p.

Collection of essays on the history of Kabuki and related performing arts such as kabuki dancing, kyōgen, etc. Contains a reference bibliography. Illustrations. Index.

E131　服部幸雄　江戸歌舞伎論
Hattori Yukio. *Edo kabukiron.* Hōsei Daigaku Shuppankai, 1980. 429p. (Sōsho Nihon bunkashi kenkyū)

Collection of 15 essays on Edo Kabuki from the point of view of cultural history. Includes essays on the organization of kabuki, make up, audiences, haikai-like elements in kabuki performances, etc. Illustrated. Index.

E132　中村哲郎　西洋人の歌舞伎発見
Nakamura Tetsurō. *Seiyōjin no kabuki hakken.* Geki Shobō, 1982. 280p.

The West's 'discovery' - from the Edo period to modern times - of kabuki and Japanese drama. Contains a chronology and a bibliography. Illustrations.

Jōruri

E133　内海繁太郎　人形浄瑠璃と文楽
Utsumi Shigetarō. *Ningyō jōruri to bungaku.* Hakusuisha, 1958. 769p.

Introduction to the puppet theater. Explains the basics of puppet theater music, the puppets, the stage, etc. Reference bibliography. Index.

E134　角田一郎　人形劇の成立に関する研究
Tsunoda Ichirō. *Ningyōgeki no seiritsu ni kansuru kenkyū.* Osaka, Asahiya Shoten, 1963. 978p.

Historical study of the puppet theater in Japan. Traces the origins to Chinese puppet theater and Japanese kugutsu of the ancient and medieval periods. Contains a list of reference books in Chinese and Japanese. Index.

E135　近石泰秋　操浄瑠璃の研究
Chikaishi Yasuaki. *Ayatsuri jōruri no kenkyū.* Kazama Shobō, 1961-65. 2v.

V.1 Study of the structure of the music used in Bunraku, its conventions, etc. V.2 discusses the image of feudal society offered in the texts of the puppet theater.

E136　横山　正　浄瑠璃操芝居の研究
Yokoyama Tadashi. *Jōruri ayatsurishibai no kenkyū.* Kazama Shobō, 1963. 781p.

Study of the development of literary style in the plays of the puppet theater, with examples drawn mainly from the work of Chikamatsu.

E137　室木弥太郎　語り物の研究
Muroki Yatarō. *Katarimono (mai, sekkyō, kojōruri) no kenkyū.* Kazama Shobō, 1970. 512p.

Historical study of several forms of narrated literature popular in the early Edo period.

E138　水谷不倒　新修絵入浄瑠璃史
Mizutani Futō. *Shinshū eiri jōrurishi.* Enlarged and revised ed. Chūō Kōronsha, 1974. 406p. (Mizutani Futō chōsakushū, v.4)

Collection, with commentary, of illustrated jōruri texts. Index.

E139　祐田善雄　浄瑠璃史論考
Yūda Yoshio. *Jōrurishi ronkō.* Chūō Kōronsha, 1975. 651p.

Collection of essays on various aspects of the puppet theater, its history, music, stagecraft, etc.

E140　横山　正　近世演劇論叢
Yokoyama Tadashi. *Kinsei engeki ronsō.* Seibundō Shuppan, 1976. 580p.

Companion volume to the author's ''Jōruri ayatsuri shibai no kenkyū''. A collection of essays on the plays of Ki no Kaion, a bibliographic study of maruhon, the dramatic character of local performing arts, etc.

E141　横山　正　近世演劇
Yokoyama Tadashi. *Kinsei engeki.* Ōfūsha, 1981. 296p.

Collection of essays on gidayū recitation and jōruri. Contains reprints of jōruri in modern typescript with kana readings.

Chikamatsu Monzaemon

E142　森　修　近松門左衛門
Mori Osamu. *Chikamatsu Monzaemon.* San'ichi Shobō, 1959. 234p.

Introduction to the life and work of the famous playwright. Contains a chronological list of his works.

E143　近松門左衛門研究入門　近松研究会 編
Chikamatsu Monzaemon kenkyū nyūmon, ed. by Chikamatsu Monzaemon Kenkyūkai. Tokyo Daigaku Shuppankai, 1963. 306p.

Collection of essays on the life, work, and philosophy of Chikamatsu. Contains a chronological list of works and a reference bibliography.

E144　広末　保　増補近松序説
Hirosue Tamotsu. (Zōho) *Chikamatsu josetsu*. Enlarged ed. Miraisha, 1963. 438p.

Collection of essays on Chikamatsu as a writer of tragedies for the stage.

E145　正本近松全集　近松書誌研究会 編
Shōhon Chikamatsu zenshū, ed. by Chikamatsu Shoshi Kenkyūkai. Benseisha, 1977-(84) (v.24)

Consists of photo reproductions of 148 of Chikamatsu's works. Will be complete in 36 vols., including 23 volumes of works that can be certainly identified as Chikamatsu's, and 11 volumes of works which are thought to be his. A supplementary volume will contain reproductions of colophons, indexes to titles, publishers, actors, gidayū chanters, etc.

E146　滝口　洋　近松戯曲の世界
Takiguchi Hiromi. *Chikamatsu gikyoku no sekai*. Kasama Shoin, 1981. 240p.

Collection of essays on various aspects of Chikamatsu's plays, including 'The religious character of sewamono', 'Some problems concerning the dramatic structure of sewamono', etc.

Katarimono (recited literature)

E147　関山和夫　説教と話芸
Sekiyama Kazuo. *Sekkyō to wagei*. Seiabō, 1964. 320p.

Study of the influence of sermons on story-telling. Illustrations.

E148　前田　勇　上方落語の歴史
Maeda Isamu. *Kamigata rakugo no rekishi*. Revised and enlarged ed. Osaka, Sugimoto Shoten, 1966. 292p.

History of rakugo in the Kyoto/Osaka area.

E149　関根黙庵　講談落語考
Sekine Mokuan. *Kōdan rakugokō*. Yūzankaku, 1967. 403p.

History of yose (variety halls) in the city of Edo. Traces the sources of stories told there, and discusses famous performers and their methods of impersonation.

E150　関山和夫　説教の歴史的研究
Sekiyama Kazuo. *Sekkyō no rekishiteki kenkyū*. Kyoto, Hōzōkan, 1973. 422p.

History of Jōdo-sect and Jōdo shin-sect sermons and their relationship to the origins of story-telling. (see also F147)

E151　前田　勇　上方まんざい 800 年史
Maeda Isamu. *Kamigata manzai 800 nenshi*. Osaka, Sugimoto Shoten, 1975. 264p.

800 years of comic dancers (manzai) in the Kyoto/Osaka area.

E152　暉峻康隆　落語の年輪
Teruoka Yasutaka. *Rakugo no nenrin*. Kōdansha, 1978. 518p.

History of rakugo, from the Edo period to the postwar period. Also treats various genres of story-telling performed to the accompaniment of the shamisen. A chronological reference list appended.

E153　噺本大系　武藤禎夫 等編
Hanashibon taikei, ed. by Mutō Sadao, et al. Tokyodō, 1976-79. 20v.

Collection of Edo period hanashibon (story books). V.20 consists of reproductions of Chinese style humorous stories written by Japanese and translations of Chinese humorous stories. Each volume contains explanatory notes.

LIFE AND CULTURE

E154　小野忠重　版画—日本の暮しの絵
Ono Tadashige. *Hanga - Nihon no kurashi no e*. Dabidosha, 1958. 192p.

Study of the depiction of everyday life in hanga (wood block prints). Also discusses illustrated books, nishikie of the Meiji era, and the life of the ukiyoe artist. Illustrations.

E155　高橋誠一郎　新修浮世絵 250 年
Takahashi Seiichirō. (Shinshū) *Ukiyoe 250 nen*. Chūō Kōron Bijustu Shuppan, 1961. 427p.

Study of the woodblock print and print makers in the Edo period. Contains both color and black and white plates. With a brief outline in English at the back of the book. Indexed by name of artist.

E156　生 活 史 叢 書
Seikatsushi sōsho. Yūzankaku, 1965- (31v.)

Collection of studies on certain Edo period groups i.e. warriors, policemen, townsmen, retainers, the Shogun's family, early Meiji entertainers, etc.

E157　岡田利兵衛　俳 画 の 世 界
Okada Rihei. *Haiga no sekai*. Tankō Shinsha, 1966. 131p.

Surveys the development of haiga (haiku pictures) with reference to Sōin, Saikaku, Bashō and his disciples, etc. Contains references and a brief chronology.

E158　平井　聖　日本の近世住宅
Hirai Kiyoshi. *Nihon no kinsei jūtaku*. Kashima Kenkyūjo, 1968. 234p.

Describes the residences of the shōgun, daimyō, etc. of the Momoyama and Edo periods. Illustrations and charts.

E159　守屋　毅　歌 舞 伎 の 時 代
Moriya Takeshi. *Kabuki no jidai*. Kadokawa Shoten, 1976. 234p. (Kikan ronsō: Nihon bunka 5)

Describes the social life and customs of people in what the author terms the 'Kabuki era' - late 17th-early 18th century.

E160　江 戸 シ リ ー ズ
Edo shiriizu. Mainichi Shinbunsha, 1976-78. 12v.

Edo series:

V.1 Life during the period of national seclusion, by Maeda Ai.

V.2 On social and political reform from the feudal to the modern period, by Haga Noboru.

V.3 The foundation of kabuki, by Kawatake Toshio.

V.4 The influence of Chinese literature on Edo period literature, ed. by Suwa Haruo and Hino Tatsuo.

V.5 Double suicide and the literature of Chikamatsu, by Suwa Haruo.

V.6 Belief in the gods (kami) during the feudal period, by Tamamura Fumio and Miyata Noboru.

V.7 Anti-establishment literati in the Hōreki era (1751-64), by Nakano Mitsutoshi.

V.8 Life of the master wood-block artists Sharaku, Utamaro, and Hokusai, by Tazaki Yonosuke.

V.9 History of religious movements, especially the 'ee ja nai ka' movement of the late Edo period, by Nishigaki Harutsugu.

V.10 Ukiyoburo - the public bath house in the Edo period, by Jinbo Kazuya.

V.11 The beginnings of publishing, by Suwa Haruo.

V.12 Life of the people during the 300 years of the Edo period, by Sugimoto Sonoko.

E161　小野忠重　浮 世 絵
Ono Tadashige. *Ukiyoe*. Tōkai Daigaku Shuppankai, 1980. 240p. (Tōkai Daigaku bunka sensho)

Study of ukiyoe print makers as artists who documented the art and culture of their times. Illustrations.

E162　近 世 風 俗 図 巻　菊地貞夫 等編
Kinsei fūzoku zukan, ed. by Kikuchi Sadao, et al. Mainichi Shinbunsha, 1973-74. 3v.

Reproductions of paintings and scrolls depicting the social life and customs of people during the Edo period.

V.1 Manners and customs, annual events in Edo.

V.2 Manners and customs, annual events outside Edo.

V.3 The performing arts and various occupations.

E163　近 世 風 俗 図 譜
Kinsei fūzoku zufu. Shōgakkan, 1982-(84). (13v.)

Series of illustrated books depicting the social life and customs of people during the Edo period.

V.1 Annual events.

V.2 Recreation.*

V.3 Kyoto and its vicinity 1.

V.4 Kyoto and its vicinity 2.*

V.5 Shijō Kawara entertainment district (Kyoto).

V.6 Gay quarters.

V.7 *

V.8 Festivals 1.

V.9 Festivals 2.

V.10 Kabuki.*

V.11 Manners and customs of nobles and warriors.

V.12 Occupations.*

V.13 Foreigners.*

* forthcoming.

Education

E164　和島芳男　昌平校と藩学
Wajima Yoshio. *Shōheikō to Hangaku*. Shibundō, 1962. 194p. (Nihon rekishi shinsho)

History of education under the Tokugawa regime. Traces the development of Confucian studies at the Shōheikō (Bakufu school) in Edo and at local schools established by the Han administrations. Reference bibliography. Illustrations.

E165　山下　武　江戸時代庶民教化政策の研究
Yamashita Takeshi. *Edo jidai shomin kyōka seisaku no kenkyū*. Azekura Shobō, 1969. 454p.

Studies in the educational policy of the Bakufu.

Pt.1　Bakufu and Han policy for the education of the masses.
Pt.2　Educational institutions and texts.
Pt.3　Publications for the education of the masses and banned books.
Pt.4　The influence of Bakufu policy on early Meiji period publishing.

Contains bibliographical references, illustrations, index.

E166　日本の藩校　奈良本辰也　編
Nihon no Hankō, ed. by Naramoto Tatsuya. Tankō-sha, 1970. 319p.

Shōheikō of the Bakufu and 11 prominent Han schools. Contains a list of Han schools. Illustrated.

E167　石川松太郎　藩校と寺小屋
Ishikawa Matsutarō. *Hankō to terakoya*. Kyōikusha, 1978. 246p. (Rekishi shinsho. Nihon rekishi)

Study of the education given warriors at the Han schools and that given commoners at the terakoya. References. Illustrated.

Publishing

E168　笠井助治　近世藩校における出版書の研究
Kasai Sukeharu. *Kinsei hankō ni okeru shuppansho no kenkyū*. Yoshikawa Kōbunkan, 1962. 787p.

Study of 800 works published by some 120 Edo period Han schools. Arranged by geographical region and Han, giving school name, year founded, status of clan, etc. Illustrated. Index.

E169　上里春生　江戸書籍商史
Uesato Shunsei. *Edo shoseki shōshi*. Meicho Kankōkai, 1965. 224p. Photo reproduction of 1930 edition.

A history of the book trade in the city of Edo. Describes publishing and the book-making process in the early Edo period.

E170　井上和雄　慶長以來書賈集覧
Inoue Kazuo. *Keichō irai shoka shūran*. Revised and enlarged edition by Sakamoto Muneko. Osaka, Takao Shoten, 1970. 111p.

Directory of bookstores in Kyoto, Osaka, and Edo from the Keichō to the Keiō era (1596-1868). Lists 3022 stores, giving location, name, dates of existence, and list of publications.

E171　矢島玄亮　徳川時代出版社出版物集覧
Yajima Genryō. *Tokugawa jidai shuppansha, shuppanbutsu shūran*. Man'yōdō Shoten, 1976. 2v.

Directory of approximately 3,200 publishers and 17,000 titles of trade books issued during the Edo period. Arranged by name of publisher. Author/title index.

E172　今田洋三　江戸の本屋さん
Konda Yōzō. *Edo no hon'yasan - kinsei bunkashi no sokumen*. Nihon Hōsō Shuppan Kyōkai, 1977. 206p. (NHK Books)

A cultural history of Edo period publishing. Covers the state of publishing in Kyoto, and the development of publishing from the Genroku era to the end of the Edo period. Reference bibliography.

E173　井上和雄　書物三見
Inoue Kazuo. *Shomotsu sanken*. Enlarged ed. Seishōdō Shoten, 1978. 348p. (Nihon shoshigaku taikei 4)

Collection of essays on publishing, publishers, and the rare book trade from the Edo to the Meiji period.

E174　諏訪春雄　出版事始—江戸の本
Suwa Haruo. *Shuppan koto hajime - Edo no hon*. Mainichi Shinbunsha, 1978. 222p. (Edo shiriizu, v.11)

Introduction to the publishing industry in Edo. Includes a short history of printing.

E175　鈴木敏夫　江戸の本屋
Suzuki Toshio. *Edo no hon'ya*. Chūō Kōronsha, 1980. 2v. (Chūkō shinsho)

History of the book trade in the Edo period. V.1 describes the publishing boom inspired by the introduction of moveable type, popular fiction by Saikaku, the jōruri of Chikamatsu, and the new genres of fiction associated with Edo. V.2 describes the rise and fall of Tsutaya Shigesaburō's publishing enterprise and government control of the book trade.

E176　本 屋 の 話　長沢規久也 編

Hon'ya no hanashi, ed. by Nagasawa Kikuya. Seishōdō Shoten, 1981. 532p. (Nihon shoshigaku taikei 16)

Collection of sources on book dealers from the Edo period to the early Meiji period.

E177　今田洋三　江 戸 の 禁 書

Konda Yōzō. *Edo no kinsho*. Yoshikawa Kōbunkan, 1981. 204p.

History of banned books in the Edo period, describing publishing regulations of the Tokugawa government, etc.

E178　蒔田稲城　京 阪 書 籍 商 史

Makita Tōjō. *Keihan shosekishōshi*. Revised and reprinted ed. Rinsen Shoten, 1982. 534p.

History of the book trade in the Kyoto/Osaka area during the Edo period. Examines publishing expenses, organizations, reprinting permits, laws for banning books, etc.

E179　宗政五十緒　近世京都出版文化の研究

Musemasa Isoo. *Kinsei Kyoto shuppan bunka no kenkyū*. Dōmeisha, 1982. 254p.

Traces the history of publishing in Kyoto in the Edo period, including the publishing industry, book dealers and their guilds, book collectors, etc. Bibliography. Index.

E180　長友千代治　近世貸本屋の研究

Nagatomo Chiyoji. *Kinsei kashihonya no kenkyū*. Tokyodō Shuppan, 1982. 258p.

Traces the development of the book-lending business in the Edo period. Illustrated.

F MODERN AND CONTEMPORARY PERIOD

At the beginning of the modern period, 1868- , new literary models were introduced to Japan from the West. Modern forms of literature took precedence over traditional literary style, and within a few decades Japanese writers began to produce work that took its place beside that of Western writers.

An outline history of modern Japanese literature can be found in "Japanese literature of the Showa era: a guide to Japanese reference and research materials", by Joseph K. Yamagiwa. (University of Michigan Center for Japanese Studies. *Bibliographical series*, no.8 1959)

GENERAL

F1　現代日本文学論争史　平野　謙 等編
Gendai Nihon bungaku ronsōshi, ed. by Hirano Ken, et al. Miraisha, 1956-1957. 3v.

History of literary disputes concerning modern Japanese literature:

V.1 Collection of essays on formalism, explanation by Hirano Ken.

V.2 Collection of 44 essays on the artistic value of proletarian literature and 'tenkō' (conversion), explanation by Odagiri Hideo.

V.3 Collection of 40 essays on novels, 'geijutsu-ha' (artistic school), and national literature, explanation by Hirano Ken.

F2　川副国基　近代日本文学論
Kawazoe Kunimoto. *Kindai Nihon bungaku ron.* Waseda Daigaku Shuppanbu, 1959. 484p.

Collection of essays on modern literature, arranged by topic: nationalism, new romanticism, etc. Contains a bibliography on Mori Ōgai and a reference guide to the work of Natsume Sōseki.

F3　飛鳥井雅道　日本の近代文学
Asukai Masamichi. *Nihon no kindai bungaku.* San'ichi Shobō, 1961. 258p. (San'ichi raiburari)

Traces the development of literature in relation to political conditions in the Meiji era, e.g. the liberty and popular rights movement; social novels during the Sino-Japanese War; naturalism and romanticism during the Russo-Japanese War, etc. Reference bibliography at the end of each chapter.

F4　近代文学・研究と資料　慶応大学研究会 編
Kindai bungaku: kenkyū to shiryō, ed. by Keio Daigaku Kenkyūkai. Shibundō, 1962. 259p. (Kokubungaku ronsō, no.5)

Contains essays on Taguchi Teiken, Ishibashi Ningetsu, and Uchida Fuchian (Roan) as pioneers of literary criticism in the early Meiji period, reviewed by Yoshida Seiichi; on Shimazaki Tōson's *Hakai*, by Miyoshi Yukio; on beauty and truth in Nagai Kafū's works, by Takada Mizuho; on the diary of Yamada Bimyō from 1891-92, by Shioda Ryōhei; on Masaoka Shiki, by Kiyozaki Toshio; on Izumi Kyōka by Mita Hideaki; Hirose Kazuo, by Sakamoto Ikuo. Includes the letters of Takahashi Taika and a catalog of manuscripts held by the Izumi Kyōka library.

F5　瀬沼茂樹　近代日本文学の構造
Senuma Shigeki. *Kindai Nihon bungaku no kōzō.* Shūeisha, 1963. 2v.

Overview of modern Japanese literature:

V.1 The Meiji period, emphasizing the status of literature during the years of social modernization.

V.2 Intellectual currents and literary criticism of the Taisho and Showa eras.

F6　近代文芸評論集　長谷川　泉 等編
Kindai bungei hyōronshū, ed. by Hasegawa Izumi, et al. Azuma Shuppan, 1965. 238p.

Collection of essays on modern literary cirticism. Consists of two sections: 1) An outline history of modern literary criticism, and 2) Excerpts of criticism by prominent authors, with notes. A text book.

F7 長谷川　泉　近代日本文学評論史
Hasegawa Izumi. *Kindai Nihon bungaku hyōronshi*.
Rev. ed. Yūseidō, 1966. 250p. (Yūseidō sensho)

An outline history of literary criticism from the
Meiji era to the postwar era. Chronology,
1868-1965. Index.

F8 吉田精一　市民の文学
Yoshida Seiichi. *Shimin no bungaku*. Shibundō,
1966-67. 2v. (Nihon no bungaku)

An introduction to modern Japanese literature based
on a series of lectures delivered by the author over
the NHK broadcasting system. Reference bibliography. Index.

F9 現代日本文学の世界　吉田精一 編
Gendai Nihon bungaku no sekai, ed. by Yoshida
Seiichi. Komine Shoten, 1968. 315 p. (Bungaku no
sekai series)

A survey of issues in the study of modern literature,
arranged by topic in historical sequence.

F10 平岡敏夫　日本近代文学史研究
Hiraoka Toshio. *Nihon Kindai bungakushi kenkyū*.
Yūseidō, 1969. 508p.

Modern Japanese literary history. In 4 sections:

-1 Essays on the history of literary research with
   reference to Natsume Sōseki, naturalist literature, and Kobayashi Hideo.
-2 Prevalent ideas in literary history such as the
   young man of the Meiji 40's, watakushi or 'I'
   novels, etc.
-3 Critical studies of authors and their works: Ozaki
   Kōyō, Kōda Rohan, Natsume Sōseki, etc.
-4 Overview of research accomplished in 1960-65.
   Index.

F11 近代文学史　紅野敏郎 等編
Kindai bungakushi, ed. by Kōno Toshirō, et al.
Yūhikaku, 1972. 3v. (Yūhikaku sensho)

Collection of signed articles by specialists. Contains
a reference bibliography. Illustrations. Indexes.

V.1 Meiji literature.
V.2 Taisho literature.
V.3 Showa literature through the postwar period.

F12 土方定一　近代日本文学評論史
Hijikata Teiichi. *Kindai Nihon bungaku hyōronshi*.
Hōsei Daigaku Shuppanbu 1973. 370p.

Reprint of the 1st ed., published in 1948. A pioneer
work on the history of literary criticism in the Meiji
and Taisho eras.

F13 小田切　進　日本近代文学の展開
Odagiri Susumu. *Nihon kindai bungaku no tenkai*.
Yomiuri Shinbunsha. 1974. 317p. (Yomiuri sensho)

Traces the development of modern literature from
the Meiji era to the 1970's. Appended is a collection of wartime articles that appeared in various
literary magazines, p.223-313.

F14 長谷川　泉　近代日本文学の位相
Hasegawa Izumi. *Kindai Nihon bungaku no isō*.
Ōfūsha, 1974. 2v.

A collection of previously published essays on
various aspects of modern literature, grouped by
historical period and topic.

F15 中村新太郎　物語日本近代文学史
Nakamura Shintarō. *Monogatari Nihon kindai bun-
gakushi*. Shin Nihon Shuppansha, 1974-77. 2v.
(Shin Nihon sensho)

A guide to representative writers and their works
from the Meiji through World War II.

F16 近代日本文学史　三好行雄 編
Kindai Nihon bungakushi, ed. by Miyoshi Yukio.
Yūhikaku, 1975. 252p. (Yūhikaku sōsho)

A textbook incorporating postwar research and the
latest interpretations of modern literature with emphasis on poetry, drama and popular literature.
Bibliography and chronology, 1870-1975 included.

F17 小田切秀雄　現 代 文 学 史
Odagiri Hideo. *Gendai bungakushi*. Shūeisha,
1975. 2v.

A history of literature for the years, 1868-1965.

V.1 Discusses *Ukigumo* (The Drifting Cloud) by
    Futabatei Shimei; romanticism; naturalism vs.
    anti-naturalism; the Taisho era and its writers.
V.2 Covers the Showa era tracing the change
    marked by a shift from proletarian to demo-
    cratic literature. Chronology. Index. Kana
    readings are provided.

F18 臼井吉見　近 代 文 学 論 争
Usui Yoshimi. *Kindai bungaku ronsō*. Chikuma
Shobō, 1975. 2v. (Chikuma sōsho)

Collection of 40 serialized articles that appeared in
1954-57, on literary controversies: Tsubouchi Shōyō
vs. Mori Ōgai; naturalism; the Shirakaba (White

birch) school; methodology of criticism, etc., and Takeuchi Yoshimi vs. Itō Sei on national literature.

F19 猪野謙二　日本近代文学の遠近
Ino Kenji. *Nihon kindai bungaku no enkin*. Miraisha, 1977. 2v.

Perspectives on modern literature. V.1 Meiji-Taisho eras. V.2 Showa era writers and their works, including drama. Contains bibliographical references.

F20 村松定孝　新訂近代日本文学の系譜
Muramatsu Sadataka. *Shintei Kindai Nihon bungaku no keifu*. New ed. Shakai Shisōsha, 1977. 304p. (Gendai kyōyō bunko)

Essays on the genealogy of prewar Japanese literature including Mori Ōgai, Ozaki Kōyō, the Ken'yūsha group, etc.

F21 谷沢永一　近代日本文学史の構想
Tanizawa Eiichi. *Kindai Nihon bungakushi no Kōsō*. Shōbunsha, 1977. 306p.

Methodology for the study of the history of modern literature, from 1900 to the postwar period.

F22 伊豆利彦　日本近代文学研究
Izu Toshihiko. *Nihon kindai bungaku kenkyū*. Shin Nihon Shuppansha, 1979. 378p.

Collection of critical essays on proletarian literature; pt.1 Meiji-Taisho eras. Discusses works by Natsume Sōseki, Kunikida Doppo, Shimazaki Tōson, Ishikawa Takuboku, Arishima Takeo, and Akutagawa Ryūnosuke; pt.2 Showa era, Kobayashi Takiji.

F23 紅野敏郎　本の散歩　文学史の森
Kōno Toshirō. *Hon no sanpo: Bungakushi no mori*. Tōjusha, 1979. 331p.

A collection of short essays on books and publishers by members of various literary groups. Contains reproductions of 32 cover designs of first editions.

F24 西田　勝　近代文学の潜勢力
Nishida Masaru. *Kindai bungaku no senseiryoku*. Yagi Shoten, 1979. 275p. (Kindai bungaku kenkyū sōsho)

A collection of essays treating the influence of literature on Meiji era enlightenment and nationalism; on Taisho era democracy; and on the recognition of a proletarian literature.

F25 日本文学史概説　平岡敏夫　等編
Nihon bungakushi gaisetsu. Kindaihen, ed. by Hiraoka Toshio and Tōgō Katsumi. Yūseido, 1979. 247p.

An outline history of modern Japanese literature from Meiji to the present. Contains notes, chronology; divided by genre. Index.

F26 日本現代文学史
Nihon gendai bungakushi. Kōdansha, 1979. 2v. (Nihon gendai bungaku zenshū, suppl. volume)

V.1 History of Meiji literature by Ino Kenji. Traces the history of Meiji-era literature decade-by-decade.

V.2 pt.1 Taisho literature, by Senuma Shigaki; pt.2 consists of topical studies of Showa literature, by Kubota Masabumi. Chronology for the years 1868-1960, ed. by Sōma Yasuo, appended.

F27 磯貝英夫　現代文学史論
Isogai Hideo. *Gendai bungakushiron*. Meiji Shoin, 1980. 302p.

A collection of essays on literary trends from the Taisho to Showa era, such as "I" novels, individualism, interpretation of burai (the decadents), etc.

F28 吉田精一　現代日本文学史
Yoshida Seiichi. *Gendai Nihon bungakushi*. Ōfūsha, 1980. 330p. (Yoshida Seiichi chosakushū, v.21)

A short history of modern Japanese literature from the Meiji to the Showa period. Describes the development of various literary genres in relation to changing currents of thought.

F29 シンポジューム　近代日本文学の軌跡　佐藤泰正　編
Shinpojumu Kindai Nihon bungaku no kiseki, ed. by Satō Yasumasa. Seibunsha, 1980. 274p. (Sōzō sensho)

Report of six symposiums held in 1976-77 on thought in modern literature. Participants were Yoshimoto Takaaki, Ōoka Makoto, Oketani Takao, Kitagawa Tōru, Sako Jun'ichirō, Sasabuchi Tomokazu, Yoshida Hiroo, Byōdō Masanosuke, Suzuki Hideo, Takeda Tomohisa, and Satō Yasumasa.

Symposium 1 The legacy of Kitamura Tōkoku.
Symposium 2 Natsume Sōseki, Shirakaba school, Akutagawa Ryūnosuke.
Symposium 3 Kobayashi Hideo and his circle.
Symposium 4 Dazai Osamu and the Bible.
Symposium 5 The heritage of modern poetry.
Symposium 6 Masamune Hakuchō and naturalism.

Each report contains concluding remarks and reference sources.

F30　近代日本文学　岩崎文人 等編
Kindai Nihon bungaku, ed. by Iwasaki Fumito et al. Hiroshima, Tansuisha, 1981. 355p.

A collection of excerpts sketching the image of women in modern novels. List of materials on the authors and their works given at the end. Excerpts are as follows:

Ukigumo, The drifting cloud, by Futabatei Shimei.
Takekurabe, Growing up, by Higuchi Ichiyō.
Hototogisu, (cuckoo, by Tokutomi Roka.
Gubijinsō, The poppy, by Natsume Sōseki.
Uta andon, A song under lanterns, by Izumi Kyōka.
Tsuchi, The earth, by Nagatsuka Takashi.
Gan, The wild goose, by Mori Ōgai.
Arakure, The wild one, by Tokuda Shūsei.
Aru onna, A certain woman, by Arishima Takeo.
Ku no sekai (world of suffering), by Uno Kōji.
Aru onna no shōgai (the life of a certain woman) by Shimazaki Tōson.
Chijin no ai, A fool's love, by Tanizaki Jun'ichirō.
Nobuko, by Miyamoto Yuriko.
Hanazono no shisō, Ideals of a flower garden, by Yokomitsu Riichi.
Machiko, by Nogami Yaeko.
Hōrōki, A vagabond's story, by Hayashi Fumiko.
Tsuyu no ato saki, Before and after the rains, by Nagai Kafū.
Onna no isshō (the life of a woman), by Yamamoto Yūzō.
Yukiguni, The snow country, by Kawabata Yasunari.
Kurenai, The crimson, by Sata Ineko.
Naoko, by Hori Tatsuo.

F31　岡野他家夫　日本近代文献と書誌
Okano Takeo. *Nihon kindai bunken to shoshi*. Hara Shobō, 1981. 375p.

Reprint of 1967 edition. A collection of essays on modern literature and bibliography. Index.

F32　星野五彦　近代文学とその源流
Hoshino Yukihiko. *Kindai bungaku to sono genryū*. Kyōiku Shuppan Sentā, 1982. 277p. (Ibun sensho)

Folk tales and ethnographic sources of modern literature, presented in 3 parts:

-1 traditional sources.

-2 oral records in setsuwa and folk tales.

-3 modern literature based on classical stories, such as the fiction of Tanizaki Jun'ichirō, Okamoto Kidō, and others.

F33　明治大正文学史集成　平岡敏夫 編
Meiji Taisho bungakushi shūsei, ed. and explained by Hiraoka Toshio. Nihon Tosho Sentā, 1982. 12v.

V.1　日本文学史 I　三上参次・高津桑三郎 共著
History of Japanese literature I, Nara, Heian periods, by Mikami Sanji and Takazu Kuwasaburō, 1890.

V.2　日本文学史 II　三上参次・高津桑三郎 共著
History of Japanese literature II, Kamakura, Muromachi, and Edo periods, by Mikami Sanji and Takazu Kuwasaburō, 1890.

V.3　明治文学史　大和田建樹 著
History of Meiji literature, by Ōwada Tateki, 1894.

V.4　時代文学史　高橋淡水 著
Meiji period literature, by Takahashi Tansui, 1906.

V.5　増補　明治文学史　岩城準太郎 著
History of Meiji literature, rev. and enlarged, by Iwaki Juntarō, 1909.

V.6　明治小説文章変遷史　徳田秋声 著
Changes in the written language of novels in the Meiji period, by Tokuda Shūsei, 1914.
明治小説内容発達史　田山花袋 著
Development of novels in the Meiji period, by Tayama Katai, 1914.
明治文学変遷講話　島村抱月 著
Lectures on the history of Meiji literature, by Shimamura Hōgetsu, 1915.

V.7　近代文芸史論　高須梅渓 著
Discourse on modern literature, by Takasu Baikei, 1921.

V.8　明治大正　新文学史観　小島徳弥 著
New interpretation of the history of modern literature, by Kojima Tokuya.

V.9　明治大正の国文学　岩城準太郎 著
Meiji/Taisho literature, by Iwaki Juntarō, 1925.

V.10　明治大正文学の輪郭　加藤武雄 著
Outline of Meiji/Taisho literature, by Katō Takeo, 1926.

Suppl.1　私の見た明治文壇　野崎左文 著
My view of Meiji literary groups, by Nozaki Samon, 1927.

Suppl.2　自己中心明治文壇史　江見水蔭　著
My view of the history of Meiji literary groups, by Emi Suiin, 1927.

F34　日本の近代文学　同編輯委員会編
Nihon no kindai bungaku, ed. by Nihon no Kindai Bungaku Henshū Iinkai, represented by Wada Shigejirō. Dōhōsha Shuppan, 1982. 258p.

Introductory history of modern literature from Meiji through the postwar period. Contains a bibliography, chronology, 1868-1980. Index.

F35　前田　愛　近代日本の文学空間
Maeda Ai. *Kindai Nihon no bungaku kūkan*. Shin'yōsha, 1983. 496p.

History of language and literature:
1. Origin of Meiji literature, from the Bakumatsu period to Meiji; 2. style; 3. postwar literature and trends in research. Index.

Thought

F36　久山　康　近代日本の文学と宗教
Kuyama Yasushi. *Kindai Nihon no bungaku to shūkyō*. Nishinomiya, Kokusai Nihon Kenkyūjo, 1966. 386p.

Pt.1 religion in the works of Ishikawa Takuboku, Natsume Sōseki, Dazai Osamu, Hori Tatsuo, Shiga Naoya, and Shiina Rinzō; also gives a short description of representative Christian writers: Uemura Masahisa, Uchimura Kanzō, and Kagawa Toyohiko. Pt.2 discusses the changing concepts of tradition during the process of modernization; the emerging identity of Taisho intellectuals; the way of thinking of contemporary Japanese; and the status of Christianity in the history of Japanese thought.

F37　辻橋三郎　近代文学とキリスト教思想
Tsujihashi Saburō. *Kindai bungaku to Kirisutokyō shisō*. Ōfūsha, 1969. 389p. (Kindai no bungaku)

Documents the influence of early Protestant Christian thought on literary men who were members of regional groups such as Kumamoto Bund, Yokohama Bund, or Sapporo Bund. Includes Tokutomi Roka, Iwano Hōmei, Masamune Hakuchō from the Meiji era; Kagawa Toyohiko and Kurata Hyakuzō from the Taisho era; Kobayashi Takiji from the early Showa era. Extensive notes are provided for each chapter. "Kyushu bungaku", no. 31, Jan. 1894, is reprinted as a source material of the founding of Kumamoto Bund.

F38　伊藤一夫　近代日本文学思潮史序説
Itō Kazuo. *Kindai Nihon bungaku shichōshi josetsu*. Ōfūsha, 1969. 367p. (Kindai no bungaku. Suppl. vol.)

Introduction to modern literary thought: romanticism, realism, humanism and existentialism in modern novels. A brief history of drama and poetry is given in a separate chapter. Reproductions of cover designs of first editions of books and magazines, bibliographical references included. A chronology, 1868-1965, includes translations of titles of representative foreign works.

F39　高田瑞穂　近代文学の明暗
Takada Mizuho. *Kindai bungaku no meian*. Shimizu Kōbundō, 1971. 457p.

A discussion of the intellectual conflict between those who held for the Westernization of Japan and those who held for Japanese tradition. Also contains an essay on Kinoshita Mokutarō, p.180-284.

F40　三好行雄　日本文学の近代と反近代
Miyoshi Yukio. *Nihon bungaku no kindai to han-kindai*. Tokyo Daigaku Shuppankai, 1972. 270p. (UP sensho)

Modern and anti-modern thought in Japanese literature. A study of Western enlightenment vs. anti-Western attitudes among Meiji and Taisho writers such as Futabatei Shimei, Mori Ōgai, Natsume Sōseki, Tanizaki Jun'ichiro, Takamura Kōtaro, Saitō Mokichi, Akutagawa Ryūnosuke, and the Shirakaba (White Birch) group.

F41　佐藤泰正　文学・その内なる神
Satō Yasumasa. *Bungaku. Sono uchinaru kami*. Ōfūsha, 1974. 546p.

God in the literature of Natsume Sōseki, Akutagawa Ryūnosuke, Endō Shūsaku and others.

F42　日本現代文学とキリスト教　武田寅雄　等編
Nihon gendai bungaku to Kirisutokyō, ed. by Takeda Torao, et al. Ōfūsha, 1974. 3v.

Christian faith as it is presented in literature. V.1 Meiji-Taisho, V.2 Taisho-Showa, V.3 Showa.

F43　小泉一郎　神と人とのあいだ
Koizumi Ichirō. *Kami to hito to no aida: Kindai Nihon bungakushiron*. Kasama Shoin, 1975. 303p. (Kasama sensho)

Between God and Man: one facet of Meiji and Taisho literary history. Discusses the influence of Protestant Christianity on men of letters, especially Kumamoto Bund; the influence of Puritanism on

Uchimura Kanzō, and Quakerism on Nitobe Inazō; mysticism of Arishima Takeo, Sōseki's search for truth.

F44 近代文学思潮史　堀井哲夫 等編
Kindai bungaku shichōshi, ed. by Horii Tetsuo and Hamakawa Katsuhiko. Ōfūsha, 1976-77. 2v.

A collection of excerpts from literary works. Arranged by date of publication and by topic.

V.1 Works published in the Meiji era. The topics are: enlightenment, neo-classicism, romanticism, naturalism, and anti-naturalism.

V.2 Works published in the Taisho era. The topics are: aesthetic school, humanism, neo-realism, Taisho evaluation of Meiji writers, post-Taisho era.

F45 玉置邦雄　現代日本文芸の成立と展開
Tamaoki Kunio. *Gendai Nihon bungei no seiritsu to tenkai: Kirisutokyō no juyō o chūshin to shite*. Ōfūsha, 1977. 276p.

Christianity and its influence on the development of modern Japanese literature.

F46 朝下　忠　近代日本文芸の研究
Asaka Tadashi. *Kindai Nihon bungei no kenkyū*. Kazama Shobō, 1981. 301p.

A study of modern literature, with emphasis on Christian influence in the work of Tokutomi Roka, Kurata Hyakuzō, Mushakōji Saneatsu, and Kawabata Yasunari.

F47 高田瑞穂　日本近代文学の宿命
Takada Mizuho. *Nihon kindai bungaku no shukumei*. Meiji Shoin, 1982. 201p. (Kokubungaku kenkyū sōsho)

A study of the concept of karma in modern Japanese literature.

F48 千葉　貢　悲しみの文学
Chiba Mitsugi. *Kanashimi no bungaku*. Kōbundō, 1982. 258p.

Sadness (kanashimi) in modern Japanese literature, with emphasis on the work of Nagatsuka Takashi, Ishikawa Takuboku, Akutagawa Ryūnosuke, Dazai Osamu, etc.

proletarian literature

F49 日本のプロレタリア文学　窪川鶴次郎 編
Nihon no puroretaria bungaku, ed. by Kubokawa Tsurujirō, et al. Aoki Shoten, 1956. 245p.

Historical survey and re-examination of Japanese proletarian literature. A collection of essays by Nishida Masaru, Kubokawa Tsurujirō, Odagiri Hideo, Hirano Ken, and others.

F50 日本プロレタリア文学大系　野間　宏 等編
Nihon puroretaria bungaku taikei, ed. by Noma Hiroshi, et al. Kyoto, San'ichi Shobō, 1968-69. (9v.) First ed. 1955.

An outline history of proletarian literature from 1895 to 1945 including novels, criticism, and poetry. Each volume contains a survey of the period and a chronology ed. by Nihon Kindai Bungaku Kenkyūjo. Contents are as follows:

Introductory vol. on the birth of proletarian literature, 1895-1915.

V.1 Rise of the movement: from socialist literature to the publication of *Tane maku hito* (The sower).

V.2 Establishment of the movement: the publication of *Bungei sensen* (Literary front), to the founding of NAPF (the Japanese Proletarian Artists Federation).

V.3 Golden age of the movement: I, the period from the first publication of *Senki* (The battle flag), to the establishment of Bunka Renmei (the Cultural Federation).

V.4 Golden age of the movement: II.

V.5 Golden age of the movement: III.

V.6 Oppression and dissolution: I, the period from the establishment of the Federation to the beginning of the Sino-Japanese war.

V.7 Oppression and dissolution: II.

V.8 Tenkō (conversion) of the communists and resistance against oppression; from the Sino-Japanese War to the defeat of Japan in World War II.

F51 栗原幸夫　プロレタリア文学とその時代
Kurihara Yukio. *Puroretaria bungaku to sono jidai*. Heibonsha, 1971. 272p.

The age of proletarian literature. Discusses works by Nakano Shigeharu, Kurahara Korehito and Kamei Katsuichirō, each of whom represented a different phase of the proletarian movement.

F52 プロレタリア文学　日本文学研究資料刊行会 編
Puroretaria bungaku, ed. by Nihon Bungaku Kenkyū Shiryō Kankōkai. Yūseido, 1971. 309p. (Nihon bungaku kenkyū shiryō sōsho)

A collection of reproductions of critical essays on proletarian writers and their works. Contains a reference bibliography of important monographs.

F53　山田清三郎　プロレタリア文学史
Yamada Seizaburō. *Puroretaria bungakushi.* Rironsha, 1973. 2v. Reprint of 1954 ed.

V.1 traces the beginning of proletarian literature in the new literary movements of the Meiji period, 1868-92; romanticism, naturalism, and socialism 1892-1912; idealism and humanism 1912-20; the publication of *Tane maku hito* (The sower), and the government suppression of the movement at the time of the great earthquake of 1923.

V.2 traces the political struggle of the proletarians from the formation of NAPF (the Japanese Proletarian Artists' Federation) to its dissolution in 1934.

F54　飛鳥井雅道　日本プロレタリア文学史論
Asukai Masamichi. *Nihon puroretaria bungakushi ron.* Yagi Shoten, 1982. 236p. (Kindai bungaku kenkyū sōsho)

A collection of essays describing thirty years of hardship for proletarian writers from the early Taisho era to World War II.

Authors and Their Works

F55　人と作品　現代文学講座　木俣　修　等編
Hito to sakuhin: Gendai bungaku kōza, ed. by Kimata Osamu, et al. Meiji Shoin, 1960-64. 10v.

Lectures on modern literature, writers and their works including criticism, thought, essays, fiction, poetry, and drama. V.1-4 covers Meiji; V.5-7, Taisho; V.8-10, Showa.

F56　伊藤　整　作　家　論
Itō Sei. *Sakkaron.* Chikuma Shobō, 1962. 374p.

Studies of 36 authors, including Mori Ōgai, Natsume Sōseki, Kawabata Yasunari, Ibuse Masuji, Miyoshi Tatsuji, Ishikawa Tatsuzō, and others.

F57　日本の近代文学・人と作品　日本近代文学館 編
Nihon no kindai bungaku: Hito to sakuhin, ed. by Nihon Kindai Bungakkan. Yomiuri Shinbunsha, 1966. 294p.

A collection of lectures by 18 authors on 20 representative works from *Ukigumo* (The drifting cloud) by Futabatei Shimei (1887), to *Ningen shikkaku* (No longer human) by Dazai Osamu (1948). Illustrations

include covers of first editions of books, magazine covers and samples of manuscripts. Author index.

F58　長谷川　泉　近代名作鑑賞
Hasegawa Izumi. *Kindai meisaku kanshō.* New ed. Shibundō, 1967. 1174p.

Guide to the appreciation of modern literature. Consists of excerpts from 35 works by 21 authors, including those of Mori Ōgai, Higuchi Ichiyō, Dazai Osamu and others.

F59　近代日本の文豪　伊藤　整編
Kindai Nihon no bungō, ed. by Itō Sei. Yomiuri Shinbunsha, 1967-68. 3v. Illustrations and portraits.

23 master writers of modern Japan. Reviewed by prominent literary critics.

V.1 Formation of modern literature: Tsubouchi Shōyō, Futabatei Shimei, Mori Ōgai, Ozaki Kōyō, Kōda Rohan, Higuchi Ichiyō, Izumi Kyōka, Masaoka Shiki.

V.2 The development of literature from the late Meiji to the early Taisho period: Shimazaki Tōson, Tokuda Shūsei, Ishikawa Takuboku, Natsume Sōseki, Nagai Kafū, Tanizaki Jun'i-chirō, Hagiwara Sakutarō.

V.3 Maturity: from the late Taisho to the early Showa period: Shiga Naoya, Mushakōji Saneatsu, Arishima Takeo, Akutagawa Ryūnosuke, Saitō Mokichi, Satō Haruo, Yokomitsu Riichi, Kawabata Yasunari. Chronology. Index.

F60　中村光夫　作　家　論　集
Nakamura Mitsuo sakka ronshū. Kōdansha, 1968. 4v.

See no. F120

F61　平野　謙　作　家　論
Hirano Ken. *Sakkaron.* Miraisha, 1970. 431p.

Studies of 23 modern writers, including Hirotsu Kazuo, Miyamoto Yuriko, Yokomitsu Riichi, Ishikawa Shintarō, Kaikō Ken, and Ōe Kensaburō.

F62　現代文学と古典　日本近代文学館 編
Gendai bungaku to koten, ed. by Nihon Kindai Bungakkan. Yomiuri Shinbunsha, 1970. 318p.

A collection of 18 essays on modern literary works that were based on classical literature. A chronology, 1869-1974, with sources in classical literature, appended. Illustrations include portraits of authors, cover designs of first editions, manuscript samples, etc.

F63 三島由紀夫　作　家　論
Mishima Yukio. *Sakkaron*. Chūō Kōronsha, 1971.
249p.

Studies of 15 authors: Mori Ōgai, Ozaki Kōyō,
Izumi Kyōka, Tanizaki Jun'ichirō, Uchida Hyakken,
Inagaki Taruho, Kawabata Yasunari, Ozaki Kazuo,
Tonomura Shigeru, Kanbayashi Akatsuki, Hayashi
Fusao, Takeda Rintarō, Shimaki Kensaku, Enchi
Fumiko.

F64 亀井勝一郎　現 代 作 家 論
Kamei Katsuichirō. *Gendai sakkaron*. Kōdansha,
1972. 560p. (Kamei Katsuichirō zenshū V.5)

Study of 14 authors from Mori Ōgai to Takeda
Taijun, examining each author's position in the
history of thought.

F65 秋山　駿　作　家　論
Akiyama Shun. *Sakkaron*. Daisan Bunmeisha,
1973. 261p.

Study of 18 writers, describing how each discovered
his own style of writing. Contains Ōoka Shōhei,
Abe Kōbō, Mishima Yukio, Mori Ōgai, Natsume
Sōseki, Akutagawa Hiroshi, etc.

F66 石川悌二　近代作家の基礎的研究
Ishikawa Teiji. *Kindai sakka no kisoteki kenkyū*.
Meiji Shoin, 1973. 255p.

Brings to light hitherto unknown biographical data
on writers, including Mori Ōgai, Natsume Sōseki,
Ozaki Kōyō, Izumi Kyōka, Higuchi Ichiyō, and
Tanizaki Jun'ichirō. Refers extensively to the docu-
ment collection held by the Tokyo Municipal
Archives. Illustrated.

F67 小田切秀雄　近代日本の作家たち
Odagiri Hideo. *Kindai Nihon no sakka-tachi*. Rev.
and enlarged edition. Hōsei Daigaku Shuppanbu,
1973. 655p.

Collection of essays on 36 modern authors.

F68 現代作家作品論　瀬沼茂樹 教授
Gendai sakka sakuhinron. Senuma Shigeki koki
kinen ronbunshū, ed. and published by the Kankōkai. Kawade Shobō, 1974. 347p.

Contemporary authors and their works. A festschrift
in honor of Professor Senuma Shigeki. Includes bio-
bibliography.

F69 川副国元　近代文学の評論と作品
Kawazoe Kunimoto. *Kindai bungaku no hyōron to
sakuhin*. Waseda Daigaku Shuppanbu, 1977. 228p.

Literary criticism by Meiji writers, including
Shimamura Hōgetsu, Ozaki Kōyō, Mori Ōgai,
Kunikida Doppo, and others.

F70 久保田正文　作　家　論
Kubota Masafumi. *Sakkaron*. Nagata Shobō, 1977.
534p.

Collection of essays written since the 1920's on 36
authors of the Taisho and Showa eras.

F71 臼井吉見　作家論控え帖
Usui Yoshimi. *Sakkaron hikaechō*. Chikuma Shobō,
1977. 661p.

Notebook of critical essays on 33 authors of the
Taisho and Showa eras.

F72 奥野健男　作　家　論　集
Okuno Takeo. *Sakkaronshū*. Tairyūsha, 1977-78.
5v.

Collection of critical essays on authors from the
Meiji to Showa era.

V.1 Studies of Dazai Osamu and other authors of
the modern period.
V.2 Authors of the Taisho era with emphasis on the
works of Arishima Takeo.
V.3 18 authors of the early Showa era, including
Ishikawa Jun, Itō Sei, etc.
V.4 20 authors of the postwar period, including
Inoue Yasushi, Ōoka Shōhei, etc.
V.5 26 contemporary authors, including Yasuoka
Shōtarō, etc.

F73 日本の近代文学・作家と作品　吉田精一 博士
Nihon no kindai bungaku: sakka to sakuhin.
Yoshida Seiichi Hakushi koki kinen, ed. by the
Kinen Ronshū Kankōkai. Kadokawa Shoten, 1978.
625p.

Modern Japanese literature: authors and works. A
festschrift presented to Professor Yoshida Seiichi.
Includes a bio-bibliography. In 3 sections:

-1 Development of the modern novel.
-2 Modern poetry and poetics.
-3 Various issues in the history of modern Japanese
literature.

F74 中村光夫　近代の文学と文学者
Nakamura Mitsuo. *Kindai no bungaku to bungakusha*. Asahi Shinbunsha, 1978. 391p.

A collection of critical studies of Meiji literature
with emphasis on Kitamura Tōkoku; and of Taisho

literature, with emphasis on Nagai Kafū, Arishima Takeo and Akutagawa Ryūnosuke.

F75　小田切秀雄　明治大正の作家たち
Odagiri Hideo. *Meiji Taisho no sakka tachi*. Daisan Bunmeisha, 1978. 2v. (Regulus library)

Critical study of Meiji and Taisho writers.

V.1 Discusses 17 authors of the Meiji era from Tsubouchi Shōyō to Kinoshita Naoe, etc.

V.2 Discusses 19 authors of the Meiji-Taisho eras from Natsume Sōseki to Miyamoto Yuriko.

F76　小田切秀雄　昭和の作家たち
Odagiri Hideo. *Showa no sakka tachi*. Daisan Bunmeisha, 1979. 2v. (Regulus library)

Showa writers. Companion volume to the above entry. Both together serve as a guide to modern literature.

V.1 Discusses 22 authors from Yoshimitsu Riichi to Koguma Hideo.

V.2 Discusses 27 authors from Dazai Osamu to Itsuki Hiroyuki.

F77　勝本清一郎　近代文学ノート
Katsumoto Seiichirō. *Kindai bungaku nōto*. Misuzu Shobō, 1979-80. 4v.

A collection of previously published notes and essays.

V.1 Contains those of 1934-48, with an essay on Natsume Sōseki and Tokutomi Roka. Explanatory notes by Yamada Hiromitsu.

V.2 Essays on Kitamura Tōkoku, Shimazaki Tōson, Higuchi Ichiyō, with explanatory notes by Ino Kenji.

V.3 Essays on Ozaki Kōyō, Tokutomi Roka, Mori Ōgai, and Izumi Kyōka, with notes by Inagaki Tatsurō.

V.4 Contains miscellaneous notes on literature, books, and publishers, explained by Honda Shūgo. Bibliography of Katsumoto's works appended.

F78　近代日本文学作家研究叢書　笹淵友一　等編
Kindai Nihon bungaku sakka kenkyū sōsho, ed. by Sasabuchi Tomoichi, et al. Yūbun Shoin, 1982. (6v.)

Modern Japanese writers.

V.1 Nakagawa Yoichi.

V.2 Mishima Yukio.

V.3 Nishiwaki Junzaburō.

V.4 Arishima Takeo.

V.5 Takahama Kyoshi.

V.6 Saitō Mokichi.

F79　片岡　懋　近代作家論叢
Kataoka Tsutomu. *Kindai sakka ronsō*. Shintensha, 1983. 613p. (Shintensha kenkyū sōsho)

Collection of previously published essays on the topic of self-discovery, with examples from works of Mori Ōgai in the 1890's, Kitamura Tōkoku, Kunikida Doppo, Shimazaki Tōson, Tayama Katai, Tokuda Shūsei, Takahama Kyoshi, Terada Torahiko, Shiga Naoya, Akutagawa Ryūnosuke, and others.

women writers

F80　馬渡憲三郎　女流文芸研究
Mawatari Kenzaburō. *Joryū bungei kenkyū*. Nansōsha, 1973. 403p.

Studies of twenty-one modern women writers, beginning with Higuchi Ichiyō. Bibliographical references.

F81　奥野健男　女流作家論
Okuno Takeo. *Joryū sakkaron*. Daisan Bunmeisha, 1974. 265p.

Collection of previously published essays on 16 women writers: Nogami Yaeko, Uno Chiyo, Amino Kiku, Mori Mari, Sata Ineko, Kōda Aya, Enchi Fumiko, Hirabayashi Taiko, Tanaka Sumie, Setouchi Harumi, Kōno Taeko, Takenishi Hiroko, Sono Ayako, Kurahashi Yumiko, and Tsushima Yūko. The author questions whether women have innate talent for writing fiction.

F82　巌谷大四　物語女流文壇史
Iwaya Daishi. *Monogatari joryū bundanshi*. Chūō Kōronsha, 1977. 2v.

A narrative history of women writers' groups.

V.1 The Haginoya group of Higuchi Ichiyō, *Jogaku zasshi* (Women's magazine) group, and others from the Meiji to Showa period.

V.2 Showa era, includes postwar writers. Bibliography. Index.

F83　板垣直子　明治大正昭和の女流文学
Itagaki Naoko. *Meiji Taisho Showa no joryū bungaku*. Ōfūsha, 1979. 365p.

Women's literature of the last hundred years, 1868-1967. Describes the literary trends of the Meiji, Taisho, and Showa eras from the works of Higuchi Ichiyō, Yosano Akiko, Tamura Toshiko,

Nogami Yaeko, Yoshiya Nobuko, Miyamoto Yuriko, and others. Contains portraits.

Multiple Sets

F84　新装版　日本文壇史　伊藤　整 等編
Shinsōban Nihon bundanshi. By Itō Sei and Senuma Shigeki. New ed. Kōdansha, 1953-77. 24v.

History of literary circles from Kanagaki Robun in the 1870's to the death of Natsume Sōseki in 1916. Describes writers and the times in which they lived. Senuma Shigeki completed the work after Itō Sei left it unfinished at V.1-18.

V.1 People of the enlightenment period.
V.2 Pioneers of the new literature.
V.3 Disillusioned youth.
V.4 The age of Ichiyō and the Ken'yūsha.
V.5 Poets and revolutionaries.
V.6 Transition period of Meiji literature.
V.7 The end of the Ken'yūsha period.
V.8 Russo-Japanese War.
V.9 New literature of the post Russo-Japanese War period.
V.10 New literary groups.
V.11 Rise of naturalism.
V.12 Naturalism at its peak.
V.13 Decadent writers.
V.14 Anti-naturalist writers.
V.15 Beginnings of the modern drama movement.
V.16 Grand Treason trial.
V.17 Facing the changing times.
V.18 Literary circles at the end of the Meiji era.
V.19 Young writers of the Shirakaba School.
V.20 Disciples of Natsume Sōseki.
V.21 New women writers.
V.22 Afterglow of the literary world of Meiji.
V.23 Rise of Taisho literature.
V.24 Death of Natsume Sōseki.

F85　近代文学研究叢書　昭和女子大学 編
Kindai bungaku kenkyū sōsho, compiled and published by Shōwa Joshi Daigaku Kindai Bungaku Kenkyūshitsu. 1956-(83) (v.55) In progress.

As of 1983, 296 writers and literary scholars active since the year 1868 have been included in the series, with 12 vols. for the Meiji period, 13 vols. for Taisho, and 29 vols. for Showa. Each essay gives a brief biography, a chronological list of works, and a reference bibliography. Each volume contains illustrations and indexes for personal names, titles and subjects.

Alphabetical list of names:
(Names without volume numbers are forthcoming.)

Aeba Kōson, v.21
Akutagawa Ryūnosuke, v.27
Anezaki Chōfū, v.
Aoki Getsuto, v.
Arishima Takeo, v.22
Asada Eiji, v.15
Asano Hyōko, v.41
Baba Kochō, v.46
Ballagh, James Hamilton, v.19
Bettelheim, Bernard James, v.1
Black, John Reddie, v.1
Brinkley, Francis, v.13
Brown, Samuel Robbin, v.1
Chamberlain, Basil Hall, v.38
Chiba Kameo, v.39
Chiba Kikkō, v.43
Chikamatsu Chūkō, v.54
Chino, Masako, v.
Chino Shōshō, v.
Chizuka Reisui, v.49
Clarke, Edward Bramwell, v.37
Cox, W.D., v.8
Cochran, Rev. George, v.5
Dazai Osamu, v.
Dening, Walter, v.14
Dixon, James Main, v.35
Doi Bansui, v.
Doi Shunsho, v.15
Eastlake, Frank Warrington, v.8
Ebara Taizō, v.
Emi Suiin, v.38
Fenollosa, Ernie Fransisco, v.10
Fujii Otoo, v.55
Fujimura Tsukuru, v.
Fujioka Sakutarō, v.11
Fujishino Sojin, v.26
Fukuba Yoshishizu, v.9
Fukuchi Ōchi, v.8
Fukuda Masao, v.
Fukuda Yusaka, v.
Fukui Kyūzō, v.
Fukushi Kōjirō, v.

Takagaki Matsuo, v.47

Takahashi Gorō, v.39

Takasaki Masakaze, v.12

Takasu Baikei, v.

Takata Tamotsu, v.

Takayama Chogyū, v.6

Takayasu Gekkō, v.53

Takazawa Rinsen, v.19

Takenobu Yoshitarō, v.32

Tamura Toshiko, v.55

Taneda Santōka, v.47

Taoka Reiun, v.13

Tayama Katai, v.32

Tazawa Inabune, v.3

Terada Torahiko, v.40

Tobari Chikufū, v.

Togawa Shūkotsu, v.44

Tokai Sanshi, v.21

Tokuda Shūsei, v.52

Tokutomi Roka, v.28

Toyama Masakazu, v.4

Toyoshima Yoshio, v.

Tozawa Koya, v.

Tsubouchi Shōyō, v.38

Tsuchida Kyōson, v.37

Tsuda Umeko, v.30

Tsukahara Shibushien, v.17

Tsunashima Ryōsen, v.9

Tsunoda Chikurei, v.18

Uchida Roan, v.31

Uchimura Kanzō, v.31

Udagawa Bunkai, v.31

Ueda Bin, v.16

Ueda Kazutoshi, v.42

Ueda Seiji, v.23

Uemura Masahisa, v.23

Unakami Tanehira, v.16

Usuda Arō, v.

Utsumi Getsujō, v.40

Verbeck, G.F., v.3

von Koeber, Raphael, v.22

Wakamatsu Shizuko, v.2

Wakayama Bokusui, v.29

Watanabe Katei, v.25

Watanabe Suiha, v.

Williams, Channing Moore, v.12

Wyckoff, Martin Nevius, v.12

Yamada Bimyō, v.11

Yamagishi Kayō, v.55

Yamaguchi Tsuyoshi, v.34

Yamaji Aizan, v.16

Yamakawa Tomiko, v.10

Yamamura Bochō, v.23

Yamagishi Mitsunobu, v.52

Yamazaki Shikō, v.45

Yamagawa Shunyō, v.18

Yano Ryūkei, v.33

Yatabe Ryōkichi, v.4

Yazaki Saganoya, v.

Yoda Gakkai, v.10

Yokomitsu Riichi, v.

Yokose Yau, v.36

Yosano Akiko, v.49

Yosano Hiroshi, v.39

Yoshida Tōdo, v.18

Yoshie Takamatsu, v.46

Yoshizawa Yoshinori, v.

Yuasa Hangetsu, v.50

F86 全集　現代文学の発見　大岡昇平 等編
Zenshū Gendai bungaku no hakken, ed. by Ōoka Shōhei, et al. Gakugei Shoin, 1967-69. 17v.

The development of modern literature. Each volume takes its title from a particular literary theme of the period, e.g. 'politics and literature'. Index to 220 names of authors in v.17 (supp. vol.)

F87 現代日本文学大系
Gendai Nihon bungaku taikei. Chikuma Shobō, 1968-73. 97v.

Compendium of modern Japanese literature. Contains representative works of some 275 men of letters including critics, poets and others.

F88 日本近代文学大系
Nihon kindai bungaku taikei. Kadokawa Shoten, 1969-75. 61v.

Compendium of literature from the Meiji and Taisho eras. Includes important works by 62 authors with commentaries and notes by specialists and 'kana' readings for difficult words. Covers short stories of the Meiji and Taisho eras, modern drama, social novels, socialist literature, translated poetry, modern poetry collections, etc. Criticisms and literary essays are given separate volumes in this set. V.61 consists of indexes to words and subjects, first words of poems, haiku, and titles of poems. General table of contents at the end. Illustrated.

F89 日本現代文学全集　伊藤　整 等編
Nihon gendai bungaku zenshū, ed. by Itō Sei, et al. Kōdansha, 1969-81. 110v.

Complete collection of Japanese literature from the Meiji era to the contemporary period. Includes works by men of letters, poets, and critics. Each volume contains short biographies of the writers, and reference bibliographies. Kana are given for unusual readings and punctuation are supplied for kanbun (Chinese writing).

Supplement:
V.1 A history of the Meiji era, ed. by Ino Kenji.
V.2 A history of the Taisho and Showa eras: Taisho, ed. by Senuma Shigeki, and Showa, ed. by Kubota Masabumi. A chronology, ed. by Sōma Yasurō is appended.

F90 近代文学評論大系
Kindai bungaku hyōron taikei. Kadokawa Shoten, 1971-75. 10 v.

A compendium of critical works on modern literature. Contains portraits and other illustrations, and explanatory notes.

V.1 Meiji era I, ed. by Yoshida Seiichi and Shibui Kiyoshi.
V.2 Meiji era II, ed. by Inagaki Tatsurō and Satō Masaru.
V.3 Meiji era III, ed. by Yoshida Seiichi and Wada Kingo.
V.4 Taisho era I, ed. by Inagaki Tatsurō and Kōno Toshirō.
V.5 Taisho era II, ed. by Endō Yutaka and Sofue Shōji.
V.6 Taisho era III, Showa era I, ed. by Miyoshi Yukio and Sofue Shōji.
V.7 Showa era II, ed. by Takahashi Haruo and Yasumasa Masao.
V.8 Poetic criticism, new poems, tanka and haiku, ed. by Yasuda Yasuo, et al.
V.9 Dramatic criticism, ed. by Nomura Takashi and Fujiki Hiroyuki.
V.10 Chronology of literary criticism, ed. by Yoshida Seiichi. Covers the events from 1868 to 1945. Lists of literary periodicals and pseudonyms appended.

F91 近 代 文 学　三好行雄 等編
Kindai bungaku, ed. by Miyoshi Yukio and Takemori Ten'yū. Yūhikaku, 1977-78. 10v. (Nyūmon. Kiso chishiki hen)

Collection of signed articles. Arranged so as to reflect the chronological development of modern literature.

V.1 Dawn of modern literature.
V.2 Development of Meiji literature.
V.3 Formation of the literary period.
V.4 Phases of Taisho literature.
V.5 Rise of contemporary literature.
V.6 Essence of Showa literature.
V.7 Postwar literature.
V.8 Modern poetry.
V.9 Contemporary poetry.
V.10 Issues and methods in literary research.

F92 筑摩現代文学大系
Chikuma Gendai bungaku taikei. Chikuma Shobō, 1977-79. 97v. Portraits.

Some of the volumes of Meiji literary works in the "Gendai Nihon bungaku taikei" published by Chikuma Shobō, 1968-73, were shortened or replaced with works by contemporary writers, beginning with Tsubouchi Shōyō, 1859-1935, and ending with Tsushima Yūko, 1947-. Each volume contains brief biographies of the writers appearing in that volume. No index.

F93 新批評　近代日本文学の構造
Shin'hihyō Kindai Nihon bungaku no kōzō. Kokusho Kankōkai, 1979-81. 8v.

New critical studies of the structure of modern Japanese literature.

V.1 Writers of modern literature, ed. by Takada Mizuho and Hayashi Keiko.
V.2 Readers of modern literature, ed. by Hasegawa Izumi and Mawatari Kenzaburō.
V.3 The cultural climate of modern literature, ed. by Moriyasu Masafumi and Ariyama Daigo.
V.4 Modern drama, ed. by Muramatsu Sadataka and Takeuchi Kiyomi.
V.5 Modern burai (decadent) literature, ed. by Mawatari Kenzaburō and Takeuchi Kiyomi.
V.6 Modern war literature, ed. by Yasuda Takeshi and Ariyama Daigo.
V.7 New history of modern Japanese literature I, ed. by Moriyasu Masabumi and Ōmori Morikazu.
V.8 New history of modern Japanese literature II, ed. by Moriyasu Masabumi and Ōmori Morikazu.

F94 研究資料　現代日本文学　淺井　清　等編
Kenkyū shiryō gendai Nihon bungaku, ed. by Asai Kiyoshi, et al. Meiji Shoin, 1980-81. 7v.

Sources for research in modern Japanese literature, arranged by genre and writer from the Meiji period to the 1930's. Each writer is given a biography with reviews of representative works.

V.1-2 Fiction and drama.

V.3-4 Criticism and essays.

V.5　Tanka.

V.6　Haiku.

V.7　Poems. Index.

F95 吉田精一　著作集
Yoshida Seiichi chosakushū. Ōfūsha, 1979-82. 27v.

A collection of previously published books, articles, and lecture notes. Ed. by the author.

V.1 Akutagawa Ryūnosuke.

V.2 Akutagawa Ryūnosuke.

V.3 Literary criticism in the Meiji era.

V.4 (Mori) Ōgai and (Natsume) Sōseki.

V.5 Nagai Kafū.

V.6 Shimazaki Tōson.

V.7 Studies in naturalism (Shimamura Hōgetsu, Iwano Hōmei)

V.8 (Tayama) Katai and (Tokuda) Shūsei.

V.9 Studies in romanticism.

V.10 Essays on the aesthetic movement. (Tanbiha)

V.11 Aspects of modern literature.

V.12 Modern poetry I.

V.13 Modern poetry II.

V.14 Appreciation of modern Japanese poetry I.

V.15 Appreciation of modern Japanese poetry II.

V.16 Appreciation and criticism.

V.17 Traditions in poetry.

V.18 Theory of Japanese literature.

V.19 History of Japanese literature.

V.20 History of Meiji and Taisho literature.

V.21 History of contemporary literature.

V.22 Universality of Japanese literature.

V.23 Classics and modern literature.

V.24 Introduction to literature.

V.25 Essay literature (zuihitsu)

Suppl.1 Occasional thoughts.

Suppl.2 Introduction to classical literature.

F96 中村光夫　全集
Nakamura Mitsuo zenshū. Chikuma Shobō, 1971-73. 16v.

V.1 Futabatei Shimei.

V.2 Futabatei Shimei.

V.3 On writers 1, 16 writers including Narushima Ryūhoku, Nakae Chōmin, Fukuzawa Yukichi, Tsubouchi Shōyō, Kitamura Tōkoku and others.

V.4 On writers 2, Nagai Kafū, Tanizaki Jun'ichirō, Satō Haruo, Shiga Naoya.

V.5 On writers 3, 26 writers including Yanagita Kunio, Akutagawa Ryūnosuke, Kikuchi Kan, Satomi Ton, Hirotsu Kazuo, and others.

V.6 On writers 4, Kawabata Yasunari, Kobayashi Hideo, Kawakami Tetsutarō, Kanzai Kiyoshi, Ōoka Shōhei, Mishima Yukio, and miscellaneous reviews.

V.7 On literature 1.

V.8 On literature 2.

V.9 On literature 3.

V.10 Twentieth century novels (foreign literature).

V.11 History of literature: the Meiji, Taisho, and Showa eras; modern and contemporary novels, including genre novels.

V.12 Travels, criticism of civilization.

V.13 Criticism of civilization.

V.14 Miscellaneous essays.

V.15 Drama.

V.16 Novels, 2.

Lecture Series

F97 講座　日本近代文学史　小田切秀雄　編
Kōza Nihon kindai bungakushi, ed. by Odagiri Hideo. Ōtsuki Shoten, 1956-57. 5v.

V.1 Formation of modern Japanese literature: Meiji pt. 1.

V.2 Development and establishment of Meiji literature: pt.2.

V.3 Taisho literature.

V.4 Proletarian literature and the Geijutsuha school: Showa pt.1.

V.5 War-time and postwar literature: Showa pt.2.

Includes bibliographical references. Index in each volume.

F98 近代文学鑑賞講座
Kindai bungaku kanshō kōza. Kadokawa Shoten, 1958-67. 25v.

Lectures on the appreciation of modern literature.

V.1 Futabatei Shimei, ed. by Shimizu Shigeru.

V.2 Kōda Rohan, Ozaki Kōyō, ed. by Fukuda Kiyoto.

V.3 Higuchi Ichiyō, ed. by Wada Yoshie.

V.4 Mori Ōgai, ed. by Inagaki Tatsurō.

V.5 Natsume Sōseki, ed. by Itō Sei.

V.6 Shimazaki Tōson, ed. by Senuma Shigeki.

V.7 Kunikida Doppo, ed. by Nakajima Kenzō.

V.8 Ishikawa Takuboku, ed. by Nakano Shigeharu and Kubokawa Tsurujirō.

V.9 Tanizaki Jun'ichirō, ed. by Yoshida Seiichi.

V.10 Shiga Naoya, ed. by Sudō Matsuo.

V.11 Akutagawa Ryūnosuke, ed. by Yoshida Seiichi.

V.12 Yamamoto Yūzō, ed. by Takahashi Kenji.

V.13 Kawabata Yasunari, ed. by Yamamoto Kenkichi.

V.14 Hori Tatsuo, ed. by Nakamura Shin'ichirō.

V.15 Hagiwara Sakutarō, by ed. by Itō Sei.

V.16 Takamura Kōtarō, Miyazawa Kenji, ed. by Itō Shinkichi.

V.17 Kobayashi Hideo, ed. by Yoshida Hiroo.

V.18 Nakajima Atsushi, Kajii Motojirō, ed. by Fukunaga Takehiko.

V.19 Dazai Osamu, ed. by Kamei Katsuichirō.

V.20 Miyoshi Tatsuji, Kusano Shinpei, ed. by Murakami Kikuichirō.

V.21 Translated literature, ed. by Kawamori Yoshizō.

V.22 Drama, ed. by Tanaka Chikao.

V.23 Modern poetry, ed. by Miyoshi Tatsuji and Itō Shinkichi.

V.24 Haiku and tanka, ed. by Yamamoto Kenkichi.

V.25 Guide to modern literature, ed. by Itō Sei, et al.

Each volume contains bio-bibliographical references.

F99 鑑賞と研究・現代日本文学講座　伊藤　整　等編
Kanshō to kenkyū: Gendai Nihon bungaku kōza, ed. by Itō Sei, et al. Sanseidō, 1962-63. 12v.

Lectures on contemporary Japanese literature: its appreciation and research. Each volume contains a reference bibliography.

Novels

-1 Dawn of modern literature.

-2 Period of naturalism.

-3 Mori Ōgai and Natsume Sōseki.

-4 *Shirakaba* and *Kiseki* literary magazines.

-5 *Mita bungaku* and *Shinshichō* literary magazines.

-6 Proletarian literature and modernist literature.

-7 Contemporary literature.

Criticism and essays

-1 Meiji era.

-2 Taisho era.

-3 Showa era.

Poetry

Tanka, Haiku

F100 現代文学講座　解釈と鑑賞　紅野敏郎　等編
Gendai bungaku kōza: kaishaku to kanshō, ed. by Kōno Toshirō, et al. Shibundō, 1974-75. 8v.

Meiji literature

-1 The beginnings of modern literature.

-2 Nationalism in Meiji literature.

-3 The essence of naturalist literature.

Taisho literature

Natsume Sōseki and Akutagawa Ryūnosuke, etc.

Showa literature

-1 Politics and literature.

-2 Anti-modernism in the *Yoake mae* (Before the dawn) and other essays.

Contemporary poetry.

Issues in the history of literature.

COMPARATIVE LITERATURE

F101 吉武好孝　明治大正の翻訳史
Yoshitake Yoshinori. *Meiji, Taishō no hon'yakushi.* Kenkyūsha, 1959. 262p.

The Japanese assimilation of European literature through English translations in the Meiji-Taisho eras. Contains discussions on translations into classical and colloquial Japanese. Examples are taken from works by Futabatei Shimei, Mori Ōgai, and Kitamura Tōkoku, etc.

F102 木村　毅　日米文学交流史の研究
Kimura Ki. *Nichi-Bei bungaku kōryūshi no kenkyū.* Kōdansha, 1960. 750p. (Reprinted by Kōbunsha, 1982.)

Studies in American and Japanese literary interchange from the beginning of U.S.-Japan relations through the Meiji era. Discusses the American influence on various phases of Japanese social and cultural life.

F103　吉武好孝　飜 訳 事 始 め
Yoshitake Yoshinori. *Hon'yaku koto hajime.* Hayakawa Shobō, 1967. 228p.

On the early years of the translation of foreign literature into Japanese.

F104　日本の英学 100 年史
Nihon no eigaku hyakunenshi, ed. and published by the Editorial Office, 1968-69. 4v. Illustrations.

Collections of essays on 100 years of English studies in Japan. Includes brief biographies of Japanese scholars of English studies, bibliographies, chronology, 1808-1968, a genealogical chart of English periodicals and changes of editors. Index.

F105　安田保雄　比 較 文 学 論 考
Yasuda Yasuo. *Hikaku bungaku ronkō.* Gakuyūsha, 1969, 1974. 2v.

Discusses the influence of foreign literature on modern Japanese literature. Each volume contains 21 previously published essays comparing Japanese fiction and poetry to the fiction and poetry of the West.

F106　日本近代文学の比較文学的研究　吉田精一 編
Nihon kindai bungaku no hikaku bungaku-teki kenkyū, ed. by Yoshida Seiichi. Shimizu Kōbundō, 1971. 562p.

Collection of 21 essays in comparative literature.

- Tsubouchi Shōyō and Shakespeare in *Kiri ichiyō* (The beginning of the end) and Hamlet.
- Turgenev and Futabatei Shimei in *Aibiki* (The rendezvous) and others.
- Sources of *Maihime* (Dancing girl) by Mori Ōgai.
- Mori Ōgai and E.V. Hartmann.
- Ozaki Kōyō, Moliere and E. Brontë in *Konjiki yasha* (Demon gold) and others.
- Influence of Zola in the works of Nagai Kafū.
- Maupassant and his influence on modern literary writers.
- San'yūtei Enchō, Ozaki Kōyō, Tayama Katai, Kunikida Doppo.
- Shimazaki Tōson, Nagai Kafū.
- Natsume Sōseki and his studies in English literature.
- Influence of Hauptmann in Izumi Kyōka's dramas.
- *Subaru* magazine group and the aestheticism of the West.

- Tanizaki Jun'ichirō and Oscar Wilde.
- Tolstoy and the Shirakaba (White Birch) school.
- Akutagawa Ryūnosuke and his works on early Christianity.
- Allegorical meaning of 'time' in Yokomitsu Riichi.
- Kawabata Yasunari and the Bible.
- Mauriac and Hori Tatsuo.
- Nishiwaki Junzaburō and surrealism.
- Itō Sei and James Joyce.
- Inoue Yasushi and Robert Graves.
- Mishima Yukio and ancient Greek stories in *Shishi* (The lion) and the story of Medea.
- Endō Shūsaku and catholicism.

F107　比 較 文 学 講 座　中島健三 等編
Hikaku bungaku kōza, ed. by Nakajima Kenzō, et al. Shimizu Kōbundō, 1971-74. 4v.

Lectures on comparative literature:

V.1 Issues and methodology.
V.2 Modern Japanese poetry.
V.3 Modern Japanese novels.
V.4 Modern Japanese literary criticism.

F108　講座　比較文学　芳賀　徹 等編
Kōza hikaku bungaku, ed. by Haga Tōru, et al. Tokyo Daigaku Shuppankai, 1973-76. 8v.

Lectures in comparative literature:

V.1 The status of Japanese literature in world literature.
V.2 The concern in modern Japanese literature with preserving the Japanese identity in the face of Western influence.
V.3 Thought and art in modern Japan, 1.
V.4 Thought and art in modern Japan, 2.
V.5 The impact of Western culture on Japan.
V.6 Literary thought in the East and the West.
V.7 Various aspects of Western literature.
V.8 Theory and methodology of comparative literature.

F109　吉武好孝　近代文学の中の西欧
Yoshitake Yoshinori. *Kindai bungaku no naka no Sei-ō.* Kyōiku Shuppan Sentā, 1974. 358p. (Hikaku bungaku kenkyū sōsho, no.1)

History of the adaptation of Western literature to the poetry, drama and fiction of the Meiji and Taisho eras. Works by 22 authors, from Yamada Bimyō to Arishima Takeo are examined and compared to the original stories or poems in foreign literature. Kana readings are given for difficult characters.

F110　欧米作家と日本近代文学　福田光治 等編
Ō-Bei sakka to Nihon kindai bungaku, ed. by Fukuda Mitsuharu, et al. Kyōiku Shuppan Sentā, 1974-75. 5v. (Hikaku bungaku series)

European and American literary works in Japanese literature.

V.1 English and American literature I.
V.2 French literature.
V.3 Russian, Northern and Southern European literature.
V.4 German literature.
V.5 English and American literature II.

F111　木村　毅　比較文学新視界
Kimura Ki. *Hikaku bungaku shin-shikai*. Yagi Shoten, 1975. 554p. (Shōin gakujutsu kenkyū sōshō)

Collection of essays in 3 sections:

-1 Comparison of various English translations of Ishikawa Takuboku's poem on the crab.
-2 Translators and translations of occidental literature from ancient to modern times, especially the Bible and works by Goethe, Whitman, and Nietzche.
-3 On the interchange between Meiji literature and occidental literature.

F112　島田謹二　日本における外国文学
Shimada Kinji. *Nihon ni okeru gaikoku bungaku*. Asahi Shinbunsha, 1975-76. 2v.

Studies in comparative literature:

-1 Visitors to Japan: Fernand Baldensperger and Lafcadio Hearn; the Japanese interpretation of foreign literature through the works of Mori Ōgai and Ueda Bin.
-2 Japanese translations of foreign literature.
-3 Adaptation of Western sources in modern Japanese poetry.
-4 Difficulty in adapting foreign culture to Japanese culture.
-5 Interpretation of foreign literature by people of different cultures.

F113　太田三郎　近代作家と西欧
Ōta Saburō. *Kindai sakka to Sei-Ō*. Shimizu Kōbundō, 1977. 348p.

A discussion of foreign sources in the works of modern Japanese writers: Nagai Kafū, Arishima Takeo, Ibuse Masuji, Muroo Saisei, Itō Sei, Tanizaki Jun'ichirō, Kawabata Yasunari, Natsume Sōseki, and Kitahara Hakushū.

F114　佐渡谷重信　日本近代文学の成立
Sadoya Shigenobu. *Nihon kindai bungaku no seiritsu*. Meiji Shoin, 1977. 2v.

Study in comparative literature: the establishment of modern Japanese literature, with special emphasis on the acceptance of American literary thought by the Japanese. Chronologically arranged reference bibliography of essays and monographs, 1866-1926, appended. Illustrated, and extensive notes are given where needed. Index.

F115　ジャンル別比較文学論　日本比較文学会 編
Janru-betsu hikaku bungakuron, ed. by Nihon Hikaku Bungakkai. Karuchā Shuppansha, 1977. 218p.

Collection of essays by the members of the Japan comparative Literature Society in commemoration of the 30th anniversary of its founding. On such topics as psychological novels, the novel of ideas, futuristic novels, etc.

F116　千葉宜一　現代文学の比較文学的研究
Chiba Sen'ichi. *Gendai bungaku no hikaku bungaku-teki kenkyū*. Yagi Shoten, 1978. 327p. (Kindai bungaku kenkyū sōsho)

Collection of 15 essays on comparative literature with emphasis on the acceptance of Western poetry and literary thought by Japanese poets and writers from the Edo period to the postwar period. Subtitled 'dynamic movement of modernism'.

F117　受容の軌跡　ジョゼフ・ローゲンドルフ教授
Juyō no kiseki, ed. by Takayanagi Shun'ichi. Nansōsha, 1979. 366p.

English title: Aspects of cultural reception, Western intellectual trends and modern Japan. A festschrift of 20 essays in honor of Professor Joseph Roggendorf presented by his colleagues at Sophia University. Index.

LANGUAGE

The international explosion of information and the modernization of Japan raised the need for language that could be understood equally well by people in every walk of life. The following three entries by Yamamoto Masahide present vivid pictures of the difficulties the Meiji government and the intellectuals faced in communicating ideas. This resulted in spontaneous movements for 'unity of speech and writing' by literary writers and others, which led to the successful establishment of the modern style of writing.

F118　山本正秀　近代文体発生の史的研究
Yamamoto Masahide. *Kindai buntai hassei no shiteki kenkyū.* Iwanami Shoten, 1965. 853p. Illustrations.

Well documented systematic study of the origins of the modern style of writing. Examines the development of the 'unity of speech and writing' movement from 1866 to 1889.

F119　山本正秀　言文一致の歴史論考
Yamamoto Masahide. *Genbun itchi no rekishi ronkō.* Ōfūsha, 1971. 576p.

History of the movement for 'unity of speech and writing'. Summarizes the above-mentioned work (F118) and expands its thesis with samples from the works of Mori Ōgai, Yamada Bimyō, Ochiai Naobumi, Ozaki Kōyō, Shimamura Hōgetsu, Kōtoku Shūsui, Sakai Kōsen.

F120　近代文体形成史料集成　山本正秀 編
Kindai buntai keisei shiryō shūsei, ed. by Yamamoto Masahide. Ōfūsha, 1978-79. 2v.

Collection of source materials on the formation of the modern style of writing.

V.1 Origins. Contains reproductions of 169 articles published between 1866 and 1899, with bibliographical explanations. Index.

V.2 Establishment. Contains reproductions of 185 articles published between 1899 and 1922. Illustrated. Index.

F121　広田栄太郎　近代訳語考
Hirota Eitarō. *Kindai yakugo kō.* Tokyodō, 1969. 326p.

History of words translated or adapted into Japanese from foreign sources; for example, 'kanojo' (she), 'kisha' or 'kisen' (train or steamship), 'katsudō shashiñ'eiga' (motion pictures), etc.

F122　村松　明　近代の国語
Muramatsu Akira. *Kindai no kokugo: Edo kara gendai e.* Ōfūsha, 1977. 268p.

Traces the history of speech from antiquity to the Edo period, the spread of Edo Japanese as the common tongue for all of Japan, and the change from Edo period Japanese to the contemporary language of Tokyo, which was adopted as the standard language after the Meiji era.

F123　高森邦明　近代国語教育史
Takamori Kuniaki. *Kindai kokugo Kyōikushi.* Hatonomori Shobō, 1979. 503p.

History of modern language education. Reference bibliography. Indexes.

NOVELS

F125　日本近代小説　中島健蔵 等編
Nihon kindai Shōsetsu, ed. by Nakajima Kenzō, et al. Shimizu Kōbundō, 1961. 319p. (Hikaku bungaku kōza v.5)

Historical development of modern novels. A comparison of 13 authors and their works with foreign literature. The authors are Natsume Sōseki, Kunikida Doppo, Arishima Takeo, Akutagawa Ryūnosuke, Nagai Kafū, Tsubouchi Shōyō, Itō Sei, Kobayashi Takiji, Ōoka Shōhei, Masamune Hakuchō, Nakajima Ton, Hori Tatsuo, and Endō Shūsaku.

F126　佐々木一雄　日本近代小説概論
Sasaki Kazuo. *Nihon kindai shōsetsu gairon.* Keiō Daigaku Tsūshinsha, 1965. 495p.

A survey of the development of modern fiction from the gesaku (novels) of the early Meiji era to romantic, naturalist, anti-naturalist, proletarian, and contemporary novels.

F127　山本健吉　私小説作家論
Yamamoto Kenkichi. *Shi shōsetsu sakkaron.* Rev. ed. Shinbisha, 1966. 265p.

Study of 12 'I' novelists, including Kasai Zenzō, Makino Shin'ichi, Kamura Isota, Uno Kōji, Okamoto Kanoko, Hōjō Tamio, Takii Kōsaku, Shiga Naoya, Kajii Motojirō, Kobayashi Akatsuki, Tanaka Hidemitsu, and Hara Tamiki.

F128　日本近代小説の世界　実方　清 編
Nihon kindai shōsetsu no sekai, ed. by Sanekata Kiyoshi. Shimizu Kōbundō. 1969. 364p.

The world of the modern Japanese novel. Essays on 10 authors: Mori Ōgai, Kunikida Doppo, Izumi Kyōka, Shimazaki Tōson, Tayama Katai, Natsume Sōseki, Iwano Hōmei, Arishima Takeo, Akutagawa Ryūnosuke, and Shiga Naoya.

F129 西田正好　私小説再発見
Nishida Masayoshi. *Shi shōsetsu sai-hakken.* Ōfūsha, 1973. 323p.

An interpretation of the 'I' novels as a type of psychological fiction describing the Japanese mind. Traces the origins of the 'I' novel, its growth and decline.

F130 篠田一士　日本の近代小説
Shinoda Hajime. *Nihon no kindai shōsetsu.* Shūei-sha, 1973-75. 2v.

A collection of 12 literary essays on modern Japanese novels. The essays were previously published in *Subaru* magazine in 1971-75.

F131 加賀乙彦　日本の長編小説
Kaga Otohiko. *Nihon no chōhen shōsetsu.* Chikuma Shobō, 1976. 231p.

Analytical studies of ten long novels (over 1,000 pages), their main themes, style of writing, organization, etc. Included are:

Meian, Light and darkness, by Natsume Sōseki.

Aru onna, A certain woman, by Arishima Takeo.

Yoake mae, Before the dawn, by Shimazaki Tōson.

An'ya kōro, Dark night's passing, by Shiga Naoya.

Ryoshū, Travel sadness, by Yokomitsu Riichi.

Sasame yuki, The Makioka sisters, by Tanizaki Jun'ichirō.

Meiro, The labyrinth, by Nogami Yaeko.

Fuji, Mt. Fuji, by Takeda Taijun.

Seinen no wa, The cycle of youth, by Noma Hiroshi.

Shi no shima, The island of death, by Fukunaga Takehiko.

F132 佐伯彰一　日本の「私」を索めて
Saeki Shōichi. *Nihon no 'watakushi' o motomete.* Kawade Shobō Shinsha, 1974. 221p.

The search for 'self' in Japanese fiction.

F133 佐伯彰一　物語芸術論
Saeki Shōichi. *Monogatari geijutsu ron.* Kōdansha, 1979. 256p.

The art of story telling. Discussions of the self in the fiction of Tanizaki Jun'ichirō, Akutagawa Ryūnosuke, and Mishima Yukio.

F134 佐伯彰一　近代日本の自伝
Saeki Shōichi. *Kindai Nihon no jiden.* Kōdansha, 1981. 294p.

A collection of critical essays on literary autobiographies. Included are those of Tokutomi Sohō, Maejima Mitsu, Fukuda Eiko, Ishikawa Sanshirō, Futabatei Shimei, Kinoshita Naoe, Tsubouchi Shōyō, Uchida Roan and others. Personal name index.

Popular Literature

F135 尾崎秀樹　大　衆　文　学
Ozaki Hotsuki. *Taishū bungaku.* Kinokuniya Shoten, 1964. 193p. (Kinokuniya shinsho)

An introductory history of popular literature. Bibliography.

F136 中島河太郎　日本推理小説史
Nakajima Kawatarō. *Nihon suiri shōsetsushi.* Tōgensha, 1964. 308p.

Traces the rise of mystery stories to the translation of "Oranda biseiroku" and the publication of "Shin seinen" (new young man) magazine in the Taisho era.

F137 尾崎秀樹　大　衆　文　学　論
Ozaki Hotsuki. *Taishū bungakuron.* Keisō Shobō, 1965. 417p.

A collection of previously published essays on the development of popular literature including historical novels, rakugo (story telling), etc. Contains a chronology, 1926-45, listing articles in newspapers, magazines, and books.

F138 権田万治　日本探偵作家論
Gonda Manji. *Nihon tantei sakka ron.* Gen'eijō, 1975. 261p. (Gen'eijō hyōron kenkyū sōsho)

Introduction to prewar writers of detective stories, including Edogawa Ranpo, Yokomizo Masashi, and others.

F139 岡　保生　近代文学の異端者
Oka Yasuo. *Kindai bungaku no itansha.* Kadokawa Shoten, 1976. 269p. Portraits and illustrations. (Kadokawa sensho)

Outside of modern literature: an unofficial history of modern Japanese literature. Introduction to 25 little known writers and their works. Includes Sakai Toshihiko (Kosen), Hasegawa Nyozekan, Uchida Hyakken and others. A brief chronology, 1882-1935.

F140　高木健夫　新 聞 小 説 史
Takagi Takeo. *Shinbun shōsetsushi*. Kokusho Kankōkai, 1974-81. 3v. Illustrations.

History of novels serialized in newspapers, also giving a history of the newspaper industry itself. Each volume contains a reference bibliography and an index.
V.1 Meiji era. V.2 Taisho era. V.3 Showa era.

POETRY

Modern Poetry (shi)

F141　寺田　透　近代日本のことばと詩
Terada Tōru. *Kindai Nihon no kotoba to shi*. Shichōsha, 1965. 295p.

A collection of essays on word usage and poetic style, with special reference to the children's literature of Miyazawa Kenji.

F142　鑑 賞 現 代 詩
Kanshō gendaishi. Chikuma Shobō, 1966. 3v.

Appreciation of modern poetry.
V.1 Meiji era, by Yoshida Seiichi. The new poetry written in the colloquial language. Consists of representative poems of 17 poets including Kitamura Tōkoku, Susukida Kyūkin, Kanbara Ariake, Kitahara Hakushū, Miki Rofū, and others.
V.2 Taisho era, by Itō Shinkichi. Thought and expression in proletarian poetry. Consists of works by 22 poets including Takamura Kōtarō, Hagiwara Sakutarō, Miyazawa Kenji, and others.
V.3 Showa era, by Murano Shirō. The new lyricism with examples from the works of 15 representative poets, including Miyoshi Tatsuji, Tachibana Michizō, Nakahara Chūya, Kaneko Mitsuharu, Kusano Shinpei, Murano Shirō, and others.

F143　日 本 の 近 代 詩　日本近代文学館 編
Nihon no kindaishi, ed. by Nihon Kindai Bungakkan, Yomiuri Shinbunsha, 1967. 372p.

Collection of lectures on recent poetry with emphasis on proletarian poetry of Nakano Shigeharu and the poets active since the war. Includes illustrations

of cover designs of poetry books and magazines, chronology, 1868-1966, index of names.

F144　菊地康雄　現代詩の胎動期
Kikuchi Yasuo. *Gendaishi no taidōki*. Revised and enlarged ed. Genbunsha, 1967. 598p.

Traces the development of new forms of poetry in the Taisho and early Showa eras. Includes a bibliographical chronology, 1912-35, consisting of books, review articles, and biographies in periodicals. Author index.

The first edition was published in 1965 under the title: *Aoi kaidan o noboru shijin-tachi* (The age of young poets).

F145　松永伍一　日 本 農 民 詩 史
Matsunaga Goichi. *Nihon nōmin shishi*. Hōsei Daigaku Shuppankyoku, 1967-70. 5v. Illustrations.

100 years of poetry by farmers: a history of thought expressed in poetry.
V.1 Poems and songs on class consciousness in the Meiji and Taisho eras.
V.2 Poems of anarchist and marxist farmers in the prewar Showa era.
V.3 Poems from the war and Occupation period, and the 1960 Anpo Treaty (U.S.-Japan security treaties). Chronology, 1868-1969. No index.

F146　佐藤泰正　日本近代詩とキリスト教
Satō Yasumasa. *Nihon kindaishi to Kirisutokyō*. Shinkyō Shuppansha, 1968. 300p.

A history of the conflict between traditional ideas and Christianity, as expressed by seven poets: Yagi Jūkichi, Kusano Shinpei, Miyazawa Kenji, Kitamura Tōkoku, Shimazaki Tōson, Hagiwara Sakutarō, and Yamamura Bochō.

F147　現 代 詩 人 論　大岡　信 編
Gendai shijin ron, ed. by Ōoka Makoto. Kadokawa Shoten, 1969. 328p.

Surveys half a century of contemporary poetry, 1921-65, with critical reviews of 23 poets and their works, including Kaneko Mitsuharu, Kusano Shinpei, Takamura Kōtarō, Nakahara Chūya, Miyoshi Tatsuji and others.

F148　日本近代詩論の研究　人見円吉 編
Nihon kindai shiron no kenkyū, ed. by Nihon Kindai Shiron Kenkyūkai, Hitomi Enkichi. Kadokawa Shoten, 1972. 965p.

Studies of modern Japanese poetics, based on excerpts from various works by poets and critics since the Meiji era. Grouped by topics. Chronology of poetics, 1871-1926.

F149　中野嘉一　前衛詩運動史の研究
Nakano Kaichi. *Zen'eishi undōshi no kenkyū: modanizumu shi no keifu.* Ōhara Shinseisha, 1975. 480p.

Study of the development of avant garde poetry in 1915 to the period of Showa era surrealism and modernism. Traces the European influence on Japanese poetry. Chronology, 1915-70. Illustrations of magazine covers. Index.

F150　近 代 詩 物 語　分銅準作 等編
Kindaishi monogatari, ed. by Bundō Junsaku and Yoshida Hiroo. Yūhikaku, 1978. 296p. (Yūhikaku books)

An introduction to the new style poetry and poets of the Meiji and Taisho eras, including Shimazaki Tōson, Ishikawa Takuboku, Kitahara Hakushū, Takamura Kōtarō, Hagiwara Sakutarō, and Miyazawa Kenji. Chronology, 1869-1922.

F151　大岡　信　現代の詩人たち
Ōoka Makoto. *Gendai no shijintachi.* Seidōsha, 1981. 2v.

A collection of critical studies of 35 poets from Ishikawa Takuboku to Ishimura Michiko. Index.

F152　江頭彦造　著作集
Egashira Hikozō chosakushū. Sōbunsha, 1982. 3v.

Collected works of Egashira Hikozō:

V.1　Critical essays on lyrical poetry and poets of the Shiki (Four seasons) school.

V.2　Modern poetry and poets.

V.3　Postwar poetry, miscellaneous essays.

F153　日 本 の 詩 歌　伊藤信吉 等編
Nihon no shiika, ed. by Itō Shinkichi, et al. Chūo Kōronsha, 1967-70. 31v.

Chūkō bunko edition, 1974-76. 31v.

Poems and songs of Japan.

V.1　Shimazaki Tōson.

V.2　Doi Bansui, Susukida Kyūkin, Kanbara Ariake, Miki Rofū.

V.3　Masaoka Shiki, Itō Sachio, Nagatsuka Takashi.

V.4　Yosano Tekkan, Yosano Akiko, Wakayama Bokusui, Yoshii Isamu.

V.5　Ishikawa Takuboku.

V.6　Shimaki Akahiko, Koizumi Chikashi, Nakamura Kenkichi, Tsuchiya Bunmei, Oka Fumoto.

V.7　Ōta Mizuho, Maeda Yūgure, Kuwada Jun, Kinoshita Rigen, Ōyama Tokujirō.

V.8　Saitō Mokichi.

V.9　Kitahara Hakushū.

V.10　Takamura Kōtaro.

V.11　Shaku Chōkū, Aizu Yahachi, Kubota Kūho, Toki Zenmaro.

V.12　Kinoshita Mokutaro, Hinatsu Kōnosuke, Noguchi Yonejirō, Nishiwaki Junzaburō.

V.13　Yamamura Bochō, Fukushi Kōjiro, Senke Motomaro, Momota Sōji, Sato Sōnosuke.

V.14　Hagiwara Sakutarō.

V.15　Muro Saisei.

V.16　Satō Haruo.

V.17　Horiguchi Daigaku, Saijō Yaso, Murayama Kaita, Ozaki Kihachi.

V.18　Miyazawa Kenji.

V.19　Iida Dakotsu, Mizuhara Shūōshi, Yamaguchi Seishi, Nakamura Kusatao, Ogiwara Seisensui.

V.20　Nakano Shigeharu, Ono Tōsaburo, Takahashi Shinkichi, Yamanoguchi Baku.

V.21　Kaneko Mitsuharu, Yoshida Issui, Murano Shirō, Kusano Shinpei.

V.22　Miyoshi Tatsuji.

V.23　Nakahara Chūya, Itō Shizuo, Yagi Jukichi.

V.24　Murayama Kaoru, Tanaka Fuyuji, Tachihara Michizō, Tanaka Katsumi, Kurahara Shinjirō.

V.25　Kitagawa Fuyuhiko, Anzai Fuyue, Kitazono Katsue, Haruyama Yukio, Takenaka Iku.

V.26　Collection of representative poems of the Meiji, Taisho and early Showa periods.

V.27　Contemporary poems.

V.28　Collection of Western poems in Japanese translation.

V.29　Collection of tanka.

V.30　Collection of haiku.

V.31　Collection of Japanese songs.

F154　日本現代詩大系
Nihon gendaishi taikei. Kawade Shobō Shinsha, 1974-76. 13v.

Compendium of modern Japanese poetry.

V.1　Rise and development, by Yamamiya Mitsuru.

V.2-3　Period of romanticism, by Hinatsu Kōnosuke.

V.4-5　Modern poetry, 1, 2, by Yano Hōjin.

V.6 Modern poetry, 3, by Miyoshi Tatsuji.

V.7 Modern poetry, 4, by Yano Hōjin.

V.8 Showa era, 1, by Nakano Shigeharu.

V.9 Showa era, 2, by Miyoshi Tatsuji.

V.10 Showa era, 3, by Nakano Shigeharu.

V.11-13 Postwar period, 1, 2, 3, by Ōoka Makoto.

lecture series

F155   現代詩鑑賞講座　伊藤信吉 等編
Gendaishi kanshō kōza, ed. by Itō Shinkichi, et al.
Kadokawa Shoten, 1968-69. 12v.

A lecture series on the appreciation of modern poetry.

V.1 A symposium on poetry.

V.2 Modern poetry 1. The new style. Discusses 8 Meiji poets.

V.3 Modern poetry 2. Poets of the aesthetic movement. Discusses 8 poets, including Kanbara Ariake, etc.

V.4 Modern poetry 3. Songs of life. Discusses 8 poets, including Kawaji Ryūkō, Ishikawa Takuboku, etc.

V.5 Modern poetry 4. The new lyricism. Discusses 10 poets, including Hagiwara Sakutarō, Satō Haruo, etc.

V.6 Modern poetry 5. Humanism. Discusses 10 poets, including Senke Motomaro, Ikuta Shungetsu, etc.

V.7 Contemporary poetry 1. Poetry of nihilism; songs of thought. Discusses 9 poets, including Kaneko Mitsuharu, Nakano Shigeharu, etc.

V.8 Contemporary poetry 2. The Rekitei group of poets. Discusses 11 poets, including Kusano Shinpei, Takahashi Shinkichi (dadaist), Yagi Jūkichi, etc.

V.9 Contemporary poetry 3. The standard of modernism. Discusses 9 poets, including Nishiwaki Junzaburō, Kitagawa Fuyuhiko, etc.

V.10 Contemporary poetry 4. Lyricism in contemporary poetry. Discusses 9 poets, including Miyoshi Tatsuji, Itō Sei, etc.

V.11 Contemporary poetry 5. An introduction to the work of 71 poets.

V.12 A history of Meiji poetry, by Suzuki Tōru; A history of Taisho poetry, by Anzai Hitoshi; A history of Showa poetry 1, by Ōoka Makoto; A history of Showa poetry 2, by Kuritsu Norio.

Each volume contains a bibliography, a chronology. Index.

F156   講座　日本現代詩史　村野四郎 等編
Kōza Nihon gendaishishi, ed. by Murano Shirō, et al. Yūbun Shoin, 1973. 4v.

Lectures on the history of modern Japanese poetry.

V.1 Meiji era.

V.2 Taisho era.

V.3 Early Showa era.

V.4 Postwar period.

Tanka (waka)

F157   近 代 短 歌 史　窪田空穂 等編
Kindai tankashi, ed. by Kubota Utsubo, et al. Shunjūsha, 1958. 3v.

Lectures on modern tanka.

V.1 Meiji era, by Katagiri Kenchi, et al.

V.2 Taisho era, by Gomi Yasuyoshi, et al.

V.3 Showa era, by Watanabe Junzō, et al.

F158   渡辺順三　定本近代短歌史
Watanabe Junzō. *Teihon Kindai tankashi*. Shunjūsha, 1963. 2v.

History of the proletarian tanka movement.

V.1 Meiji era, arranged by group including Shinpa (the new school), romantics, naturalists, and modernists, to the rise of the Araragi school.

V.2 Taisho era, the new-movement of socialists and proletarians, and the Tanka schools of the Showa era. Indexes.

F159   木俣　修　近代短歌の史的展開
Kimata Osamu. *Kindai tanka no shiteki tenkai*. Meiji Shoin, 1965. 445p.

A survey history of modern tanka. Covers the new revisionists group of the Meiji era, the rise of the Araragi school in the Taisho era, the modernist group of the early Showa era, wartime patriotic tanka, and the postwar revival of literary tanka. A chronology, 1868-1950. Indexes. Illustrations give first editions of magazines and portraits.

F160   斉藤茂吉　明治大正短歌史
Saitō Mokichi. *Meiji Taisho tankashi*. Chūō Kōronsha, 1970-71. 2v.

Reprint of 1950 ed.

V.1 Historical survey of tanka from the Meiji-Taisho eras.

V.2 25 years of the poetry magazine *Araragi*.

Index in each volume.

F161　木俣　修　評論明治大正の歌人たち
Kimata Osamu. *Hyōron Meiji Taisho no kajintachi.*
Meiji Shoin, 1971. 635p.

Collection of essays on 15 poets active from the
Meiji to the Shōwa era, including Sasaki Nobutsu-
na, Yosano Akiko, Ishikawa Takuboku, Saitō
Mokichi, Kubota Utsubo, Toki Zenmaro, Ōta
Mizuho, etc.

F162　篠　　弘　近代短歌史・無名者の世紀
Shino Hiroshi. *Kindai tankashi: Mumeisha no seiki.*
San'ichi Shobō, 1974. 282p.

History of contributors of poems to the Tanka
section of newspapers from the turn of the century
to 1955.

F163　篠　　弘　近代短歌論争史
Shino Hiroshi. *Kindai tanka ronsōshi.* Kadokawa
Shoten, 1976, 1981. 2v.

Meiji-Taisho hen, 1976. 544p.
Showa hen, 1981. 592p.

A history of disputes over modern tanka, from the
1900's to the early Showa era. Sources are listed for
each topic discussed.

F164　現代短歌全集　上田三四二　等編
Gendai tanka zenshū, ed. by Ueda Miyoji, et al.
Chikuma Shobō, 1980. 15v.

A complete collection of modern tanka anthologies.
Arranged by periods: pre-1909, and 1910-70, with
comments by specialists.

F165　短歌シリーズ　人と作品
Tanka shiriizu: Hito to sakuhin. Ōfūsha, 1980-82.
24v.

Contains anthologies of 20 major poets from Masaoka Shiki to Kondō Yoshimi. V.22 is on
contemporary tanka poets; V.23 is on an appreciation of outstanding modern tanka; V.24 is a history
of tanka by Abe Masamichi.

F166　薄井忠男　近代短歌史論考
Usui Tadao. *Kindai tankashi ronkō.* Ōfūsha, 1981.
650p.

Posthumous collection of essays on modern tanka
history, including the poetry salons surrounding
such writers as Masaoka Shiki, Itō Sachio, Shimaki
Akahiko, etc.

F167　簗瀬一雄　近代短歌研究
Yanase Kazuo. *Kindai tanka kenkyū.* Katō
Chūdōkan, 1982. 433p. (Yanase Kazuo chosakushū
V.6)

A study of modern tanka, with emphasis on the
work of Kubota Utsubo, Uematsu Hisaki, Handa
Ryōhei, etc.

Haiku

F168　伊沢元美　現代俳句の流れ
Izawa Motoyoshi. *Gendai haiku no nagare.* Kawade
Shobō Shinsha, 1956. 177p. (Kawade shinsho)

An introductory history of modern haiku. Discusses
21 haiku poets from Masaoka Shiki to Ishida
Hakyō.

F169　近　代　俳　句　神田秀夫　等著
Kindai haiku, by Kanda Hideo and Kusumoto Kenkichi. Yūseidō, 1965. 366p. (Kindai bungaku
chūshaku taikei, no.1 series)

Works by 232 haiku poets are arranged by period:
Meiji, Taisho, Showa, and contemporary. Readings
and explanations are given for each entry. Contains
a brief history of haiku, reference bibliographies
and a chronology, 1869-1944.

F170　松井利彦　近　代　俳　論　史
Matsui Toshihiko. *Kindai haironshi.* Ōfūsha, 1965.
563p. (Haiku shiriizu: Hito to sakuhin, 1965.
Suppl.1)

A study of stylistic change in haiku from the Meiji
to postwar period. Illustrations.

F171　山本健吉　現　代　俳　句
Yamamoto Kenkichi. *Gendai haiku.* Revised ed.
Kadokawa Shoten, 1971. 2v. (Kadokawa shinsho)

A study of 38 modern haiku poets and their works.
Indexes to names of poets.

F172　新訂　俳句シリーズ　人と作品
Shintei haiku shiriizu: hito to sakuhin. Ōfūsha,
1973. 20v.

A guide to 17 haiku poets and their works, including Matsuo Bashō, Yosa Buson, Kobayashi Issa,
Masaoka Shiki, Takahama Kyoshi, Mizuhara Shūōshi, and others. V.18 is a survey of early modern
haiku; V.19, a survey of modern haiku; and V.20, a
survey of contemporary haiku.

F173　村山古郷　明治大正俳句史話
Murayama Kokyō. *Meiji Taisho haikushiwa.* Kadokawa Shoten, 1982. 291p.

A collection of essays on haiku and haiku circles from the Meiji era to the new reform movement. Includes essays on haiku by Ozaki Kōyō, Masaoka Shiki, Natsume Sōseki, Hekigodō, etc.

PERFORMING ARTS

F174　秋庭太郎　日 本 新 劇 史
Akiba Tarō. *Nihon shingekishi.* Risōsha, 1955-56. 2v.

History of the new drama of the Meiji era and the proletarian drama of the Showa era. Contains sources of information on playwrights and their works, theaters and theater groups. A bibliography, illustrations, index.

F175　田中栄三　明治大正新劇史資料
Tanaka Eizō. *Meiji Taisho shingekishi shiryō.* Engeki Shuppansha, 1964. 256p.

An outline history of the new theater movement from the latter part of the Meiji period to the establishment of the Tsukiji Little Theater in the late Taisho period. The major part of the book is devoted to a listing of programs of public performances and source material of 103 new theater groups.

F176　松本克平　日 本 新 劇 史
Matsumoto Kappei. *Nihon shingekishi.* Chikuma Shobō, 1966. 658p.

Japanese new drama, as seen in the movement of small theatrical companies that searched for the identity of modern man. Traces the beginnings of the movement to the Jiyū Gekijō (Free theater) of the Meiji era and its development in the Tsukiji Little theater. Illustrations include group photographs, stage scenes, etc. Indexed.

F177　大山　功　近代日本戯曲史
Ōyama Isao. *Kindai Nihon gikyokushi.* Yamagata, Kindai Nihon Gikyokushi Kankōkai, 1968-73. 4v.

Historical discourse on the development of drama and on individual playwrights and their works. V.1 Meiji era. V.2 Taisho era. V.3 Showa era. Indexes for author's names, titles, drama companies, and theaters in each volume. Illustrations.

F178　越智治雄　明治大正の劇文学
Ochi Haruo. *Meiji Taisho no geki bungaku.* Hanawa Shobō, 1971. 525p.

Study of modern dramatic literature from the Meiji and Taisho eras. Contains a bibliographical guide, p.495-572. Author/title index.

F179　吉田謙吉　築地小劇場の時代
Yoshida Kenkichi. *Tsukiji shōgekijō no jidai.* Yaedake Shobō, 1971. 272p.

English title: Age of Tsukiji Little Theater. Based on the diary of the author. Describes the struggles of this theater, and its resistance to censorship, etc.

F180　現代日本戯曲大系
Gendai Nihon gikyoku taikei. San'ichi Shobō, 1971-72. 8v.

A systematic collection of representative plays from the years 1946-71, arranged by publishing dates. Each volume contains comments, bibliographical notes for each play and a chronological table.

F181　永平和大　近代戯曲の世界
Nagahira Kazuo. *Kindai gikyoku no sekai.* Tokyo Daigaku Shuppankai, 1972. 281p.

The world of modern drama. A historical account based on the works of Tsubouchi Shōyō, Mori Ōgai, Okamoto Kidō, Osanai Kaoru, Shirakaba School playwrights, Taisho drama, Kishida Kokushi, Kubo Sakae, Mabune Yutaka, and Miyoshi Jūrō.

F182　松本克平　日本社会主義演劇史
Matsumoto Kappei. *Nihon shakaishugi engekishi.* Chikuma Shobō, 1975. 880p.

A history of Japanese socialist drama of the Meiji and Taisho eras. Continuation of "Nihon shingekishi" (F176). Author-subject index. Illustrations include portraits, etc.

F183　富士田元彦　日本映画現代史
Fujita Motohiko. *Nihon eiga gendaishi.* Kashinsha, 1977. 2v.

A history of Japanese film. Gives critical reviews of representative directors and their films. Each volume contains a chronology.

V.1 The wartime film industry.

V.2 The postwar period.

F184　向井爽也　にっぽん民衆演劇史
Mukai Sōya. *Nippon minshū engekishi.* Nippon Hōsō Shuppan Kyōkai, 1977. 333p.

A history of Japanese popular theater, covering revue shows, light theatricals, and samurai plays. Brief bibliography. Illustrations.

F185 田中千禾夫　劇的文体論序説
Tanaka Chikao. *Gekiteki buntairon josetsu.* Hakusuisha, 1977-78. 2v.

Introduction to dramaturgy. Discusses the style of monogatari (narrative literature) in the works of modern novelists, and the recognition of drama as literature by later playwrights, such as Kishida Kokushi and others. Also gives an analysis of various modern drama. Each volume contains an author/title index.

F186 佐怒賀三夫　テレビドラマ史・人と映像
Sanuka Mitsuo. *Terebi doramashi: hito to eizō.* Nippon Hōsō Shuppan Kyōkai, 1978. 302p.

History of television drama: people and images. Contains a reference bibliography, a chronology of dramas, 1953-77. Author, title indexes.

F187 吉田智恵男　もう一つの映画史
Yoshida Chieo. *Mō hitotsu no eigashi.* Jiji Tsūshinsha,1978. 278p.

The age of the silent film reciters such as Tokugawa Musei, etc. Source materials include a list of movie theaters and a chronological table. Author/title index. Illustrations.

F188 暉峻康隆　落語の年輪
Teruoka Yasutaka. *Rakugo no nenrin.* Kōdansha, 1978. 518p.

A history of rakugo in Tokyo and the Kyoto/Osaka area from the Edo period to the present. Chronological listing of reference sources appended.

F189 日本流行歌史　古茂田信男　等著
Nihon ryūkōkashi, by Komota Nobuo, et al. Shakai Shisōsha, 1980. 2v.

A history of Japanese popular song. Arranged by period: V.1 prewar period; V.2 postwar period. Each volume contains a year by year summary of the trends in popular song and the lyrics of representative songs. Chronological tables (1869-1945, 1946-79). Indexes for authors, subjects, and titles of songs.

F190 河竹登志夫　近代演劇の展開
Kawatake Toshio. *Kindai engeki no tenkai.* Nihon Hōsō Shuppan Kyōkai, 1982. 236p. (Shin NHK Shimin Daigaku sōsho)

Survey of the development of modern drama, its language and techniques, in 3 parts:

-1 The modernization of Kabuki; the rise of Shinpa, the new school for adaptation of Western drama; the establishment of shingeki, the new drama.
-2 The establishment of the Tsukiji Little Theater and its closing during World War II.
-3 Postwar developments in drama.

LIFE AND CULTURE

F191 明 治 文 化 史　開国百年記念文化事業会 編
Meiji bunkashi, ed. by Kaikoku Hyakunen Kinen Bunka Jigyōkai. Yōyōsha, 1953-57. (14v.)

V.12 Daily life, ed. by Shibusawa Keizō, 1955. Descriptions of living conditions based on product consumption and changes caused by the influence of Western goods.
V.13 Manners and customs, ed. by Yanagita Kunio, 1954. Includes essays on clothing, food, dwellings, travel, weddings and funerals, annual festivals, religion, language, etc.

A chronological table in both volumes.

F192 小野忠重　版画・日本の自我像
Ono Tadashige. *Hanga: Nihon no jigazō.* Iwanami Shoten, 1961. 261p. (Iwanami shinsho)

The portrait of modern Japan in Hanga. A collection of essays on the popular woodblock prints, covering the years from the end of the Edo period through Showa. Contains a chronology of prints, 1860-1955. Illustrations. Index.

F193 近代日本風俗史　日本風俗史学会 編
Kindai Nihon fūzokushi, ed. by Nihon Fūzokushi Gakkai. Yūzankaku, 1968. 7v.

A collection of essays by specialists. Illustrated. .
V.1 Fashion, clothing, and accessories.
V.2 Industry and transportation.
V.3 Clothing and accessories.
V.4 Houses and furniture.
V.5 Meals and food products.
V.6 Sports and entertainment.
V.7 Speech and mass communication.

F194 食生活近代史　大塚　力 編
Shoku seikatsu kindaishi, ed. by Ōtsuka Tsutomu. Yūzankaku, 1969. 296p.

History of the introduction of new foods and dining customs to Japan. Illustrated.

F195　近代日本食物史　昭和女子大学 編
Kindai Nihon shokumotsushi. by Showa Joshi Daigaku, Shokumotsugaku Kenkyūshitsu. Kindai Bunka Kenkyūjo, 1971. 899p.

Modern Japanese cuisine is traced to the industrial modernization of food preparation and subsequent changes in the national diet, brought about by the introduction of Western foods and dietetic research, in the early Meiji and Taisho periods. Appended are a chronology, 1859-1926, and a bibliography of books, magazines and newspapers. Illustrations.

F196　加藤秀俊　明治大正昭和食生活世相史
Katō Hidetoshi. *Meiji Taisho Showa shoku seikatsu sesōshi*. Shibata Shoten, 1977. 220p. (Shiriizu Shoku seikatsu bunka no hakken)

A study of the changes in eating habits and the food industry in relation to advances in modern transportation. Reference bibliography, indexes.

F197　矢木明夫　生 活 経 済 史
Yagi Haruo. *Seikatsu keizaishi*. Hyōronsha, 1978. 313p. (Kyōyō sosho)

History of living conditions in the Taisho and Showa periods. Contains a bibliography.

F198　匠　秀夫　近代日本の美術と文学
Takumi Hideo. *Kindai Nihon no bijutsu to bungaku*. Mokujisha, 1969. 379p.

A study of the relationship between art and literature in the modern age, focusing on book illustrations of the Meiji, Taishō, and Shōwa periods. Includes discussions of the literary magazine *Myōjō* (Morning Star), the haiku magazine *Hototogisu*, and modern novels. Illustrations.

F199　匠　秀夫　近代日本洋画の展開
Takumi Hideo, *Kindai Nihon yōga no tenkai*. Revised ed., Akimorisha, 1977. 436p.

Analyzes the evolution of Western-style painting in the Meiji and Taishō eras. Considers art from the perspectives of culture and literature. Illustrations. Bibliographical references. Index.

F200　近代日本絵画史　河北倫明 等著
Kindai Nihon kaigashi, by Kawakita Michiaki and Takashina Shūji. Chūō Kōronsha, 1978. 374p.

Collection of essays previously published in *Nihon no meiga*, analyzing the development of Western-influenced Japanese painting from the late Edo to postwar Showa period. 32 color plates. List of drawings. Bibliographical references. Index.

F201　飯沢　匡　現代漫画家列伝
Iizawa Tadasu. *Gendai mangaka retsuden*. Sōjusha, 1978. 306p.

Biographies of cartoonists in the last century. Illustrations.

F202　石子　順　日 本 漫 画 史
Ishiko Jun. *Nihon mangashi*. Ōtsuki Shoten, 1979. 2v.

History of Japanese cartoons, their origins in the 1870's to their development, decline, and revival in the post-war Shōwa period. Illustrations. Bibliographical references.

F203　村松貞次郎　日本近代建築史ノート
Muramatsu Teijirō, *Nihon kindai kenchikushi nōto*. Sekai Shoin, 1965. 349p.

Collection of previously published essays on the history of Japanese architecture in the modern age with emphasis on the pioneering architects who built the *seiyōkan* (Western-style buildings) of the Meiji era. Biographical notes. Photographs.

F204　岡野他家夫　日本出版文化史
Okano Takeo. *Nihon shuppan bunkashi*. Shunpodō, 1959. 663p.

A history of Japanese publishing, from Edo to the postwar period, with emphasis on the establishment of the publishing industry and the rise of the large book stores in the mid-Meiji period. Index.

BY PERIOD
MEIJI ERA, 1868-1912

General

F205　興津　要　轉 換 期 の 文学
Okitsu Kaname. *Tenkanki no bungaku: Edo kara Meiji e*. Waseda Daigaku Shuppanbu, 1960. 381p.

Study of gesaku writers active from the end of the Edo period to the early Meiji period: Mantei Ōga, Baitei Kinga, Nisei Shunsui (Somezaki Nobufusa), Kanagaki Robun, Sansei Tanehiko (Takabatake Ransen), and Sansantei Yujin (Saigiku Sanjin). Chronology, 1844-1884. Title index, with readings.

F206　柳田　泉　明治文学研究
Yanagida Izumi. *Meiji bungaku kenkyū*. Revised and enlarged ed. Shunjūsha, 1960-68. 11v.

Studies in early Meiji literature.

V.1 The early years of Tsubouchi Shōyō.

V.2 *Shōsetsu shinzui* (The essence of the novel).

V.3 Gesaku literature (Edo period popular fiction) in the early Meiji period.

V.4 Literary thought, 1.

V.5 Translations of foreign literature.

V.6 Literary thought, 2.

V.7 Importation of Western literature.

V.8-10 On political novels, 1,2,3.

V.11 Studies of Futabatei Shimei.

F207 柳田　泉　明治初期の翻訳文学の研究
Yanagida Izumi. *Meiji shoki no hon'yaku bungaku no kenkyū*. Newly rev. and enlarged ed. Shunjūsha, 1961. 509p. (The author's Meiji bungaku kenkyū v.5)

History of translated literature and its influence on Japanese literature. Includes biographies of translators, and a chronology, 1868-1922. Author and title indexes.

F208 座談会　明治文学史　柳田　泉　等編
Zadankai Meiji bungakushi, ed. by Yanagida Izumi and Katsumoto Seiichirō. Iwanami Shoten, 1961. 570p.

A monograph edition of the report of the round table discussion on Meiji literature chaired by Ino Kenji.

F209 中村光夫　明治文学史
Nakamura Mitsuo. *Meiji bungakushi*. Chikuma Shobō, 1963. 285p. (Chikuma sōsho)

Introduction to Meiji literary history. Divided into three periods: early, middle, and late, with emphasis on novels, including those of Natsume Sōseki, Mori Ōgai, Nagai Kafū, and Tanizaki Jun'ichirō.

F210 明治文学全集
Meiji bungaku zenshū. Chikuma Shobō, 1965-83. (99v.)

V.1-2 A collection of early Meiji literature, 1,2, ed. by Ōkubo Toshiaki.

V.3 Meiji enlightenment literature, ed. by Ōkubo Toshiaki.

V.4 Works of Narushima Ryūhoku, Hattori Bushō, Kurimoto Joun, ed. by Shioda Ryōhei.

V.5-6 Meiji political novels, 1,2, ed. by Yanagida Izumi.

V.7 Collection of Meiji translated literature, ed. by Kimura Ki. Reprinted by Chikuma Shobō in 1972. 435p.

V.8 Works of Fukuzawa Yukichi, ed. by Tomita Masabumi.

V.9 Collected works of Kawatake Mokuami, ed. by Kawatake Toshio.

V.10 Collected works of San'yūtei Enchō, ed. by Okitsu Kaname.

V.11 Collected works of Fukuchi Ōchi, ed. by Yanagida Izumi.

V.12 Works of Ōi Kentaro, Ueki Emori, Baba Tatsuo, and Ono Azusa, ed. by Ienaga Saburō.

V.13 Collected works of Nakae Chōmin, ed. by Hayashi Shigeru.

V.14 Collected works of Taguchi Teiken (Ukichi), ed. by Ōkubo Toshiaki.

V.15 Collected works of Yano Ryūkei, ed. by Ochi Haruo.

V.16 Collected works of Tsubouchi Shōyō, ed. by Inagaki Tatsurō.

V.17 Futabatei Shimei, Saganoya Omuro, ed. by Nakamura Mitsuo.

V.18 Collected works of Ozaki Kōyō, ed. by Fukuda Kiyohito.

V.19 Collected works of Hirotsu Ryūrō, ed. by Hirotsu Kazuo.

V.20 Works of Kawakami Bizan, and Iwaya Sazanami, ed. by Senuma Shigeki.

V.21 Collected works of Izumi Kyōka, ed. by Naruse Masakatsu.

V.22 Collection of Ken'yūsha literature, ed. by Fukuda Kiyohito.

V.23 Works of Yamada Bimyō, Ishibashi Ningetsu, Takase Bun'en, ed. by Fukuda Kiyohito.

V.24 Collected works of Uchida Roan, ed. by Inagaki Tatsurō.

V.25 Collected works of Kōda Rohan, ed. by Yanagida Izumi.

V.26 Collected works of the Negishi literature group, ed. by Inagaki Tatsurō.

V.27 Collected works of Mori Ōgai, ed. by Karaki Junzō.

V.28 Collected works of Saitō Ryokuu, ed. by Inagaki Tatsurō.

V.29 Collected works of Kitamura Tōkoku, ed. by Odagiri Hideo.

V.30 Collected works of Higuchi Ichiyō, ed. by Wada Yoshie.

V.31 Collected works of Ueda Bin, ed. by Yano Hōjin.

V.32 Jogaku zasshi, Bungakkai literature, ed. by Iwamoto Yoshinari.

V.33 Collected works of Miyake Setsurei, ed. by Yanagida Izumi.

V.34 Collected works of Tokutomi Sohō, ed. by Uete Michiari.

V.35 Collected works of Yamaji Aizan, ed. by Ōkubo Toshiaki.

V.36 Collection of Min'yūsha literature, ed. by Yanagida Izumi.

V.37 Collection of Seikyōsha literature.

V.38 Collected works of Okakura Tenshin, ed. by Kamei Katsuichirō and Miyakawa Torao.

V.39 Collected works of Uchimura Kanzō, ed. by Kawakami Tetsutarō.

V.40 Takayama Chogyū, Saitō Nonohito, Anezaki Chōfū, Tobari Chikufū, ed. by Senuma Shigeki.

V.41 Shioi Ukō, Takeshima Hagoromo, Ōmachi Keigetsu, Kubo Tenzui, Sasakawa Rinpū, Higuchi Ryūkyō.

V.42 Collected works of Tokutomi Roka, ed. by Kanzaki Kiyoshi.

V.43 Works of Shimamura Hōgetsu, Katakami Tengen, Hasegawa Tenkei, Sōma Gyofū, ed. by Kawazoe Kunimoto.

V.44 Works of Ochiai Naobumi, Ueda Mannen, Haga Yaichi, Fujioka Sakutarō, ed. by Hisamatsu Sen'ichi.

V.45 Collected works of Kinoshita Naoe, ed. by Yamagiwa Keishi.

V.46 Works of Niijima Yuzuru, Uemura Masahisa, Kiyosawa Mitsuyuki, Tsunajima Ryōsen, ed. by Takeda Kiyoko and Yoshida Hisakazu.

V.47 Collected works of Kuroiwa Ruikō, ed. by Kimura Ki.

V.48 Collected works of Koizumi Yagumo, ed. by Nakano Yoshio.

V.49 Works of Erwin von Baelz, Edward S. Morse, Wenceslao de Moraes, Engelbert Kaempfer, Stanley Washburn, ed. by Karaki Junzō.

V.50 Works of Kaneko Chikusui, Tanaka Gyokudō, Katayama Koson, Nakazawa Rinsen, Uozumi Setsuro, ed. by Inagaki Tatsurō.

V.51 Works of Yosano Tekkan, Yosano Akiko, ed. by Noda Utarō.

V.52 Collected works of Ishikawa Takuboku, ed. by Odagiri Hideo.

V.53 Collected works of Masaoka Shiki, ed. by Kubota Masabumi.

V.54 Works of Itō Sachio, Nagatsuka Takashi, ed. by Honbayashi Katsuo.

V.55 Collected works of Natsume Sōseki, ed. by Ino Kenji.

V.56 Works of Takahama Kyoshi, Kawahigashi Hekigodō, ed. by Yamamoto Kenkichi.

V.57 Meiji period haiku, ed. by Yamamoto Kenkichi.

V.58 Works of Doi Bansui, Susukida Kyūkin, Kanbara Ariake, ed. by Yano Hōjin.

V.59 Works of Kawai Suimei, Yokose Yau, Irako Seihaku, Miki Rofū, ed. by Yano Hōjin.

V.60-61 Meiji poems, 1,2.

V.62 Collection of Meiji period Chinese prose and poetry, ed. by Kanda Kiichirō.

V.63 Works of Sasaki Nobutsuna, Kaneko Kun'en, Onoe Saishū, Ōta Mizuho, Kubota Utsubo, Wakayama Bokusui, ed. by Yamazaki Toshio.

V.64 Anthology of Meiji tanka, ed. by Yamazaki Toshio.

V.65 Works of Kosugi Tengai, Oguri Fūyō, Gotō Chūgai, ed. by Itō Sei.

V.66 Collected works of Kunikida Doppo, ed. by Nakajima Kenzō.

V.67 Collected works of Tayama Katai, ed. by Yoshida Seiichi.

V.68 Collected works of Tokuda Shūsei, ed. by Yoshida Seiichi.

V.69 Collected works of Shimazaki Tōson, ed. by Sasabuchi Tomokazu.

V.70 Works of Mayama Seika, Chikamatsu Shūkō, ed. by Hirano Ken.

V.71 Collected works of Iwano Hōmei, ed. by Yoshida Seiichi.

V.72 Works of Mizuno Habune, Nakamura Seiko, Mishima Sōsen, Kamitsukasa Shōken, ed. by Yoshida Seiichi.

V.73 Collected works of Nagai Kafū, ed. by Naruse Masakatsu.

V.74 Collection of the Han-shizenha (anti-naturalist) group 1, ed. by Noda Utarō.

V.75 Collection of the Han-shizenha (anti-naturalist) group 2, ed. by Naruse Masakatsu.

V.76 Early Shirakabaha literature, ed. by Honda Shūgo.

V.77-78 Essays on Meiji period history, 1,2, ed. by Matsushima Eiichi.

V.79 Collection of Meiji aesthetic literature, ed. by Hijikata Sadakazu.

V.80 Meiji philosophy and thought, ed. by Senuma Shigeki.

V.81-82 Meiji women's literature, 1,2, ed. by Odagiri Susumu.

V.83-84 Meiji socialist literature, 1,2, ed. by Odagiri Susumu.

V.85 Meiji historical drama, ed. by Tozaka Kōji.

V.86 Contemporary Meiji drama, ed. by Akiba Tarō.

V.87 Collection of Meiji religious literature, 1, ed. by Yoshida Kyūichi.

V.88 Collection of Meiji religious literature, 2, ed. by Takeda Seiko.

V.89 Collection of Meiji historical literature, 1, ed. by Inagaki Tatsurō.

V.90 Collection of Meiji historical literature, 2, ed. by Senuma Shigeki.

V.91 Collection of literature written by Meiji period journalists, by Yano Ryūkei, et al.

V.92 A Who's Who of the Meiji period, ed. by Kimura Ki.

V.93 Meiji family novels, ed. by Senuma Shigeki.

V.94 Collection of Meiji travel literature, ed. by Fukuda Kiyoto.

V.95 Collection of Meiji juvenile literature, ed. by Fukuda Kiyoto.

V.96 Collection of Meiji documentary literature, ed. by Kanzaki Kiyoshi.

V.97 Collection of Meiji war literature, ed. by Kimura Ki.

V.98-99 Collection of Meiji literary memoirs, 1,2, ed. by Usui Yoshimi.

F211　西田長寿　明治時代の新聞と雑誌
Nishida Taketoshi. *Meiji jidai no shinbun to zasshi.* Enlarged ed. Shibundō, 1966. 277p. (Nihon rekishi sensho)

Traces the role of newspapers and magazines as instruments for influencing the masses, first by supporting the 'freedom and people's right movement' through political opinion and party politics, and later by promoting nationalism and imperialism.

F212　興津　要　明治開化期文学の研究
Okitsu Kaname. *Meiji kaikaki bungaku no kenkyū.* Ōfūsha, 1968. 284p.

A study of early Meiji period small newspapers as a source of information and enlightenment for the masses. Contains a chapter on the readership of this period. Illustrations.

F213　塩田良平　明治文化論考
Shioda Ryōhei. *Meiji bunka ronkō.* Ōfūsha, 1970. 806p. (Kindai bungaku kenkyū sōsho)

A collection of previously published essays on Meiji culture. In 3 sections: research, sources, and classics in modern literature. Contains a contemporary bibliographical study of Heian literary history, p.635-803.

F214　谷沢永一　明治期の文芸評論
Tanizawa Eiichi. *Meijiki no bungei hyōron.* Yagi Shoten, 1971. 373 p. (Kindai bungaku kenkyū sōsho)

A collection of essays on literary criticism in the Meiji era. Includes the work of Tsubouchi Shōyō, Mori Ōgai, Ishibashi Ningetsu, Masaoka Shiki, Mushakōji Saneatsu, Iwano Hōmei, Takamura Kōtarō, Saitō Mokichi. Also contains extensive bibliographical notes on the study of *Shōsetsu shinzui* (the essence of the novel) and critical works on anti-idealism and naturalism.

Continued in *Taishōki no bungei hyōron* (F251)

F215　飛鳥井雅道　日本近代の出発
Asukai Masamichi. *Nihon kindai no shuppatsu.* Hanawa Shobō, 1973. 405p.

Discusses society, thought, and culture in political novels of the Meiji era, with emphasis on the work of Nakae Chōmin and Hirotsu Ryūrō.

F216　平岡敏夫　日本近代文学の出発
Hiraoka Toshio. *Nihon kindai bungaku no shuppatsu.* Kinokuniya 1973. 211p. (Kinokuniya shinsho)

The first 20 years of the Meiji era as the beginnings of modern literature.

F217　小田切秀雄　明治文学史
Odagiri Hideo. *Meiji bungakushi.* Ushio Shuppansha, 1973. 418p. (Ushio bunko)

Survey of literature from the Meiji enlightenment to the formation of the literary movements of the Russo-Japanese war period. Chronology, 1868-1912. Index.

F218　越智治雄　近代文学の誕生
Ochi Haruo. *Kindai bungaku no tanjō.* Kōdansha, 1975. 222p. (Nihon no koten 5. Kōdansha shinsho)

Sees modern literature emerging from the conflicting ideas of the Meiji period: Westernization vs. revival of traditional culture.

F219　吉田精一　近代文芸評論史
Yoshida Seiichi. *Kindai bungei hyōronshi*. Mei-jihen. Shibundo, 1975. 1043p.

Traces the history of modern criticism. Arranged by topic: translations of Western literary criticism, professional critics, theory of literature, romantics, nationalism, pragmatic criticism, etc.

F220　日本文学全史　巻五　近代　三好行雄　編
Nihon bungaku zenshi, v.5 Kindai, ed. by Miyoshi Yukio. Gakutosho, 1978. 679p.

Traces the history of literature from the modernization movement of the early Meiji period to the novels, popular literature, drama, and new style poetry of the Taisho period. Extensive chapter by chapter reference bibliography appended. Index.

F221　明 治 の 文 学　日本文学研究資料刊行会　編
Meiji no bungaku, ed. by Nihon Bungaku Kenkyū Shiryō Kankōkai. Yūseidō, 1981. 311p. (Nihon bungaku kenkyū shiryō sōsho)

A collection of essays on literature in the middle decades of the Meiji period. Reference bibliography.

F222　木村　毅　明治文学展望
Kimura Ki. *Meiji bungaku tenbō*. Kōbunsha, 1982. 301p.

Reprint of the 1928 ed. published by Kaizōsha. A collection of 17 essays on various aspects of Meiji literature and culture.

F223　木村　毅　明治文学を語る
Kimura Ki. *Meiji bungaku o kataru*. Kōbunsha, 1982. 209p.

Reprint of the 1934 ed. published by Rakurō Shoin. A collection of essays on various aspects of Meiji literature and culture. A continuation of the above entry.

F224　日本近代文学の書誌　日本文学研究資料刊行会　編
Nihon kindai bungaku no shoshi. Meijihen, ed. by Nihon Bungaku Kenkyū Shiryō Kankōkai. Yūseido, 1982. 314p. (Nihon bungaku kenkyū shiryō sōsho)

Lists the contents of Meiji era magazines and newspapers. Contains a chronology of gesaku fiction written in the early Meiji era, the contents of *Garakuta bunko*, *Bunshō sekai*, and *Shishi* (poetry), and a chronology of fiction which appeared in the Asahi, Mainichi, and Yomiuri newspapers. Reference bibliography.

F225　小川和夫　明治文学と近代自我
Ogawa Kazuo. *Meiji bungaku to kindai jiga*. Nan'undō, 1982. 375p.

A study of Meiji literature as it was influenced by modern European concepts of the self.

Thought

F226　吉田精一　自然主義の研究
Yoshida Seiichi. *Shizenshugi no kenkyū*. Tokyodō, 1955-58. 2v.

Attributes the rise and decline of naturalism to the works of the enlightenment period: Tayama Katai, Shimazaki Tōson, Kunikida Doppo, Iwano Hōmei, Tokuda Shūsei, and Masamune Hakuchō; and critics, including Kitamura Hōgetsu and others. Index.

F227　西田　勝　日本革命文学の展望
Nishida Masaru. *Nihon kakumei bungaku no tenbō*. Seishin Shobō, 1958. 277p.

Survey of Japanese revolutionary literature. Includes ten essays on anti-war activism, and on Meiji period socialist and proletarian literature.

F228　笹渕友一　文学界とその時代
Sasabuchi Tomoichi. *Bungakkai to sono jidai*. Meiji shoin, 1959-60. 2v.

Analyses the Bungakkai movement and its times, especially the early romantic movement within the coterie of the Bungakkai, with emphasis on Kitamura Tōkoku and Shimazaki Tōson.

F229　伊狩　章　硯友社の文学
Ikari Akira. *Ken'yūsha no bungaku*. Hanawa Shobō, 1961. 290p.

A study of the Ken'yūsha (The society of friends of the inkstone), a literary reform movement organized in 1885 under the leadership of Ozaki Kōyō and Yamada Bimyō, and their organ, *Garakuta bunko*. Bibliographic notes and references are added where necessary. Illustrations. Index.

In 1957, the author published a book, titled: *Kōki Ken'yūsha bungaku no kenkyū* from Yajima Shobō. It analyzed both well-known and obscure writers of the Ken'yūsha group of the 1890's.

F230　笹渕友一　浪漫主義文学の誕生
Sasabuchi Tomoichi. *Romanshugi bungaku no tanjō*. Meiji Shoin, 1962. 899p. (2nd printing)

Study of the birth of early romantic literature in the *Bungakkai* (The world of literature) magazine. Centers on the works of Tokutomi Sohō, Yazaki

Saganoya, Kōda Rohan, Mori Ōgai, Miyazaki Koshoshi (Yaokichi) and others. Illustrations. Index.

F231　柳田　泉　明治初期の文学思想
Yanagida Izumi. *Meiji shoki no bungaku shisō*. Shunjūsha,1965. 2v. (The author's Meiji bungaku kenkyū v.4,6)

Discusses the development of literary thought, criticism, aestheticism, poetics, etc. in the early Meiji period as expressed in the work of Fukuzawa Yukichi, Nakamura Keiu, Inoue Tetsujiro, Fukuchi Ōchi and others.

F232　和田謹吾　自然主義文学
Wada Kingo. *Shizenshugi bungaku*. Shibundō, 1966. 419p.

A history of naturalist literature. In three parts:

-1　The founding of the naturalist movement by members of the Ryūdo club.

-2　An analysis of the works of Kawakami Bizan, Kunikida Doppo, Shimazaki Tōson, Tayama Katai, Iwano Hōmei, Tokuda Shūsei, and Masamune Hakuchō.

-3　The influence of naturalism on Taisho literature; post-war studies of naturalism. Index.

F233　柳田　泉　政治小説研究
Yanagida Izumi. *Seiji shōsetsu kenkyū*. Revised and enlarged ed. Shunjūsha, 1967-68. 3v. (The author's Meiji bungaku kenkyū v.8-10)

Political novels prospered as men of letters supported the political movement for liberty and people's rights during 1878-98, when the Jiyūtō (the liberal Party) and the later Kaishintō (the Progressive Party) came into existence. Authors supporting these parties declared their political ideology through novels. But the popularity of these novels waned when the concerns of modern industrialization captured the attention of the reading public. This study gives detailed and documented introductions to writers and their works.

F234　片岡良一　日本浪漫主義文学研究
Kataoka Yoshikazu. *Nihon romanshugi bungaku kenkyu*. Rev. and enlarged, Hōsei Daigaku Shuppankyoku, 1967. 398p.

A textbook on Japanese romantic literature of the 1890's. Examines the literary climate of the early period by treating Ozaki Kōyō and Kōda Rohan as leaders of the Romantic movement. Also discusses the work of Takayama Chogyū and Izumi Kyōka.

F235　安住誠悦　浪漫主義文学
Azumi Seietsu. *Romanshugi bungaku*. Sapporo, Kita Shobō, 1969. 344p.

The place of romantic literature in the history of modern literature. A posthumous collection of essays on Kitamura Tōkoku, Kunikida Doppo, Takayama Chogyū and others.

F236　亀井俊介　ナショナリズムの文学
Kamei Shunsuke. *Nationalism no bungaku*. Kenkyūsha, 1971. 220p. (Kenkyūsha sōsho)

The spirit of the Meiji era in nationalist literature. Discusses the work of Fukuzawa Yukichi, Tokutomi Sohō, Kitamura Tōkoku, Shiga Shigetaka, Uchimura Kanzō, and Noguchi Yone. Index.

F237　平川祐弘　和魂洋才の系譜
Hirakawa Sukehiro. *Wakon yōsai no keifu*. Kawade Shobō Shinsha, 1972. 429p.

The Japanese spirit under the influence of the West: cultural, psychological, and racial problems during the Meiji period. Reference sources drawn mainly from the work of Mori Ōgai.

F238　和田繁二郎　近代文学創成期の研究
Wada Shigejirō. *Kindai bungaku sōseiki no kenkyū*. Ōfūsha, 1973. 619p.

Analyzes the formation of 'realism' in the creative period of modern literature, and explains the theory of realism as expressed in the works of Tsubouchi Shōyō and Futabatei Shimei.

F239　相馬庸郎　日本自然主義再考
Sōma Tsuneo. *Nihon shizenshugi saikō*. Yagi Shoten, 1981. 359p. (Kindai bungaku kenkyū sōsho)

Analysis of works of the Japanese naturalist school including Shimamura Hōgetsu, Hasegawa Tenkei, Iwano Hōmei, Tayama Katai, Shimazaki Tōson, Tokuda Shūsei, Masamune Hakuchō, Ishikawa Takuboku, Mori Ōgai, and Natsume Sōseki. Index.

Authors

F240　塩田良平　明治女流作家論
Shioda Ryōhei. *Meiji joryū sakkaron*. Nara Shobō, 1965. 405p.

Contains biographies and works of 22 women writers active in the Meiji and Taisho eras. Chronology of works, 1868-1913.

F241　猪野謙二　明治の作家
Ino Kenji. *Meiji no sakka*. Iwanami Shoten, 1966. 674p.

Discusses Natsume Sōseki, Kunikida Doppo, Ishikawa Takuboku, Shimazaki Tōson, and other naturalist writers. Also surveys political and social literature of the time and literary developments from the Meiji era to the Taisho era. A bibliographical survey is appended. Index.

F242　中村真一郎　明治作家論
Nakamura Shin'ichirō. *Meiji sakkaron*. Kōsōsha, 1978. 226p.

Study of the Meiji writers Tsubouchi Shōyō, Kosugi Tengai, Kanbara Ariake, Masamune Hakuchō, Mori Ōgai, Natsume Sōseki, and Nagai Kafū.

See also *Taisho sakkaron* (F265) and *Showa sakkaron* (F303)

Language

F243　近代語の成立　森岡健二　編
Kindaigo no seiritsu. Meiji goi-hen, ed. by Morioka Kenji. Meiji Shoin, 1969. 441p.

Collection of essays on the creation of a modern vocabulary during the Meiji era, with examples drawn from the Japanese translation of the Bible.

F244　進藤咲子　明治時代語の研究
Shindō Sakiko. *Meiji jidaigo no kenkyū*. Meiji Shoin, 1981. 453p.

Linguistic study of Meiji era vocabulary and sentence structure. Index.

Poetry (Tanka, haiku, shi)

F245　小泉苳三　近代短歌史
Koizumi Tōzō. *Kindai tankashi*. Meiji-hen. Hakuyōsha, 1955. 858p.

Traces the development of tanka from the early modern period to the birth of modern style waka, 1893-99; idealistic tanka, 1900-1908; and realistic tanka of the Negishi Tankakai. A genealogy of tanka groups, appended. Indexes.

F246　村山古郷　明治俳壇史
Murayama Kokyō. *Meiji haidanshi*. Kadokawa Shoten, 1978.

A history of haiku poetry circles during the Meiji era. Bibliography, author-title index at the end.

F247　近代詩の成立と展開
Kindaishi no seiritsu to tenkai. Supervisory editors: Nakajima Kenzō and Yano Hōjin. Yūseidō, 1969. 254p.

A revised and enlarged edition of "Hikaku bungaku kenkyū no. 2". Surveys the history of modern poetry by comparing translations in the *Shintaishi shō* (Selection of poetry in the new style) and these other collections of translated poems: *Omokage* (Vestiges), *Kaishōon* (Sound of the tide) and *Sangoshū* (Corals). Contains a reference bibliography.

F248　人見円吉　口語詩の史的研究
Hitomi Enkichi. *Kōgoshi no shiteki kenkyū*. Ōfūsha, 1975. 748p.

Traces the origins of poetry written in the colloquial language to the movement for the unity of speech and writing and the publication of *Fūkin shirabe no hitofushi* by Yamada Bimyō in 1888. Contains many samples of poetry and illustrations of magazine covers. Index.

Performing Arts

F249　松本伸子　明治前期演劇論史
Matsumoto Shinko. *Meiji zenki engekironshi*. Engeki Shuppansha, 1974. 405p.

Study of the first 20 years of Meiji theater. Extensively documented. Index.

F250　松本伸子　明治演劇論史
Matsumoto Shinko. *Meiji engekironshi*. Engeki Shuppansha, 1980. 1102p.

Continuation of the above entry, taking up the period from 1887 to 1912. Discusses the rise of the new drama, plays by Tsubouchi Shōyō, the establishment of 'shinpa', the rise of new theatre groups, etc. Index.

TAISHO ERA, 1912-26

General

F251　谷沢永一　大正期の文芸評論
Tanizawa Eiichi. *Taishōki no bungei hyōron*. Hanawa Shobō, 1962. 338p. (Hanawa sensho)

Study of representative criticism from the Taisho era, including Katayama Shin and Sōma Gyofū on naturalism; and Ikuta Nagae, Akagi Kōhei, Hirotsu Kazuo, and Satō Haruo on general literary trends. Contains bibliographical notes on source materials.

F252　臼井吉見　大 正 文 学 史
Usui Yoshimi. *Taisho bungakushi*. Chikuma Shobō, 1963. 275p. (Chikuma sōsho)

A monograph edition excerpted from "Gendai Nihon bungaku zenshū", suppl.1.

A literary history of the Taisho period. Divided into 2 periods: 1910-18: the naturalist movement and the Shirakaba (White birch) group; 1919-27: the development of psychological and popular novels, and the proletarian movement. Chronology, 1910-22. Illustrations. Index.

F253　座談会　大正文学史　柳田　泉 等編
Zadankai Taisho bungakushi, ed. by Yanagida Izumi and Katsumoto Seiichirō. Iwanami Shoten, 1965. 757p.

A round table discussion on Taisho literature. Continuation of the "Zadankai Meiji bungakushi" (F208). Discusses thought and literature in various literary genres of the period, including the works of Arishima Takeo, Mushakōji Saneatsu, Nagai Kafū, Tanizaki Jun'ichirō, Kikuchi Kan, Akutagawa Ryūnosuke, etc.

F254　大正文学の比較文学的研究　成瀬正勝 編
Taisho bungaku no hikaku bungakuteki kenkyū, ed. by Naruse Masakatsu. Meiji Shoin, 1968. 364p.

Consists of 12 essays on comparative studies in Taisho literature and Western literature, e.g. Dostoevski and Natsume Sōseki and Morita Sōhei; Akutagawa Ryūnosuke and Anatole France, Satō Haruo and Oscar Wilde, etc.

F255　文学 1910 年代　川副国基 編
Bungaku 1910 nendai, ed. by Kawazoe Kunimoto. Meiji Shoin, 1979. 373p.

Collection of 27 essays on various aspects of literature written bétween 1910 and 1920, including the rise and fall of the naturalism movement, the beginnings of children's literature, etc.

F256　吉田精一　近代文芸評論史
Yoshida Seiichi. *Kindai bungei hyōronshi. Taishōhen*. Shibundō, 1980. 794p.

Companion volume to "Kindai bungei hyōronshi. Meiji hen". (F219) A collection of critical essays on Taisho literature.

F257　大 正 文 学 論　高田瑞穂 編
Taisho bungaku ron, ed. by Takada Mizuho. Yūseidō, 1981. 426p.

A festschrift in honor of Takada Mizuho. Contains 28 essays on Taisho literature contributed by his colleagues and friends.

F258　大 正 の 文 学　日本文学研究資料刊行会 編
Taisho no bungaku, ed. by Nihon Bungaku Kenkyū Shiryō Kankōkai. Yūseidō, 1981. 311p. (Nihon bungaku kenkyū shiryō sōsho)

A collection of critical essays on the leading writers of Taisho literature. Reference bibliography.

F259　大西　貢　近代日本文学の分水嶺
Ōnishi Mitsugi. *Kindai Nihon bungaku no bunsuirei*. Meiji Shoin, 1982. 324p. (Kokubungaku kenkyū sōsho)

Collection of essays discussing the artistic distinctions between Meiji and Taisho literature. The writers of the essays include Hirotsu Kazuo, Kikuchi Kan, Kume Masao, etc.

Thought

F260　高田瑞穂　近 代 耽 美 派
Takada Mizuho. *Kindai tanbiha*. Hanawa Shobō, 1967. 218p. (Hanawa sensho)

A collection of essays on the advocates of the aesthetic movement (Tanbiha). Discusses the philosophy expressed in the works of Mori Ōgai, Ueda Bin, Nagai Kafū, Tanizaki Jun'ichirō, etc.

F261　森山重雄　実 行 と 芸 術
Moriyama Shigeo. *Jikkō to geijutsu*. Hanawa Shobō, 1969. 496p.

Anarchism and its literary expression. Analyzed on the basis of 'action and art' as exemplified in the works of Kitamura Tōkoku, Ōsugi Sakae, Arishima Takeo and other writers.

F262　森山重雄　序説轉換期の文学
Moriyama Shigeo. *Josetsu Tenkanki no bungaku*. San'ichi Shobō, 1974. 316p.

Continuation of the above entry. This introduction to 'literature of the transitional period' consists of 2 parts:

-1 Contains articles on the' time of the magazine, *Tane maku hito* (The sower); the second phase of proletarian literature; changes in the proletarian literary movement; establishment of the NAPF (Japanese Proletarian Artists' Federation) and its literary theory; the controversy over 'art for the masses'; disputes over formalism in literature; and art and the masses.

-2 Contains articles on contributors to the magazines: *Kokuen* (Black smoke), *Tane maku hito* (The sower).

F263　秋山　清　アナキズム文学史
Akiyama Kiyoshi. *Anakizumu bungakushi*. Chikuma Shobō, 1975.

History of anarchist literature between 1912-35. Describes various anarchist magazines. Chronology, 1912-1936.

Authors

F264　巌谷大四　物語大正文壇史
Iwaya Daishi. *Monogatari Taisho bundanshi*. Bungei Shunjūsha, 1976. 275p.

A narrative history of the Taisho literary world.

F265　中村真一郎　大　正　作　家　論
Nakamura Shin'ichirō. *Taisho sakkaron*. Kōsōsha, 1977. 310p.

Collection of previously published essays on Tanizaki Jun'ichirō, Nagayo Yoshirō, Toyoshima Yoshio, Akutagawa Ryūnosuke, Satō Haruo, and the poets Kitahara Hakushū and Hagiwara Sakutarō.

Poetry (tanka, haiku, shi)

F266　木俣　修　大　正　短　歌　史
Kimata Osamu. *Taishō tankashi*. Meiji Shoin, 1971. 1099p.

A history of Taishō era tanka, which reflected the political changes of the times. A chronological table, 1912-26. Index.

F267　村山古郷　大　正　俳　壇　史
Murayama Kokyō. *Taishō haidanshi*. Kadokawa Shoten, 1980. 302p.

A history of haiku during the Taisho era, giving a record of haiku poets and their reactions to events of the period, including the great earthquake of 1923. Bibliography, author/title index.

F268　矢本貞幹　日本近代詩の青春
Yamoto Tadayoshi. *Nihon kindaishi no seishun*. Kobian Shobō, 1981. 353p.

An analysis of the work of Kinoshita Mokutarō, Kitahara Hakushū, Tamura Kōtarō. amd Hagiwara Sakutarō.

SHŌWA ERA, 1926-

General

F269　昭 和 文 学 史　荒　正人　等編
Showa bungakushi, ed. by Ara Masato, et al. Kadokawa Shoten, 1956. 2v. (Kadokawa bunko)

A concise introduction to Showa literary history.

V.1 The rise and decline of proletarianism and modernism, the period of 'tenko' (conversion), and wartime literature.

V.2 A survey of postwar literature and poetry. Chronology, 1926-54. Illustrations. Index.

F270　高見　順　昭和文学盛衰史
Takami Jun. *Showa bungaku seisuishi*. Bungei Shunjūsha, 1958. 2v.

A personal account of the rise and decline of literature in the prewar Showa era. Documented with excerpts from many sources.

F271　昭 和 文 学 史　吉田精一　等著
Showa bungakushi, by Yoshida Seiichi, et al. Shibundō, 1959. 381p.

Consists of chapters on the proletarian movement, 1924-34; modernist literature; traditional literature; age of renaissance and 'tenko' wartime literature; and postwar literature, 1945-57. Appended are a chronology, 1926-57, and the table of contents for each issue of the following magazines: *Bungei sensen* (Literary front), *Bunsen* (Literary war), *Bungei jidai* (Literary age), and *Senki* (Battle flag). Author index.

F272　平野　謙　昭 和 文 学 史
Hirano Ken. *Showa bungakushi*. Chikuma Shobō, 1963. 332p. (Chikuma sōsho)

Introduction to Showa literature, 1925-55. Deals with the suicide of Akutagawa Ryūnosuke, the rise and fall of marxist literature, wartime and postwar literature. Chronology. Illustrations. Index.

F273　小田切　進　昭和文学の成立
Odagiri Susumu. *Showa bungaku no seiritsu*. Keisō Shobō, 1965. 326p.

Topical introduction to Showa literature from the publication of *Tane maku hito* (The sower) to the development of modernism. Appended are a chronology, 1921-45, and a list of major literary magazines. Illustrations include cover designs of books and magazines.

F274　昭和文学十四講　成瀬正勝 編
Showa bungaku 14-kō, ed. by Naruse Masakatsu. Yūbun Shoin, 1966. 712p.

Introduction to Showa literature in 14 lectures.

1. Survey of Showa literature, by Naruse Masakatsu.
2. Proletarian literature, by Asukai Masamichi.
3. Literature of the Artists group (Geijutsuha), by Harao Shūji.
4. Literature by established writers, by Muramatsu Sadanori.
5. Literary renaissance, by Isogai Hideo.
6. Wartime literature, by Shindō Sumitaka.
7. Postwar literature, by Hayakawa Tōzō.
8. Literary criticism,
   -1 The heart of Showa literary criticism, by Isoda Kōichi.
   -2 Origins of modern literary criticism, by Hinuma Rintarō.
9. Showa period children's literature, by Furuta Ashibi.
10. Showa poetry, by Ema Akiko.
11. Tanka and haiku, by Saitō Kiyoe.
12. Performing arts, by Iwabuchi Tatsuji.
13. Comparison with European and American literature, by Kobayashi Tadashi and Kodama Kōichi.
14. Showa literary trends by Hasegawa Izumi.

Chronology, 1926-65. Author index at the end.

F275　大岡昇平　昭和文学への証言
Ōoka Shōhei. *Showa bungaku e no shōgen*. Bungei Shunjū, 1969. 284p.

Essays on Kobayashi Hideo and other writers of the Meiji/Taisho period. List of sources appended.

F276　小笠原　克　昭和文学史論
Ogasawara Masaru. *Showa bungakushi ron*. Yagi Shoten, 1970. 320p. (Kindai bungaku kenkyū sōsho)

Studies in the history of Showa literature, specifically the work of Kobayashi Hideo, Nakano Shigeharu, etc.

F277　橋川文三　政治と文学の辺境
Hashikawa Bunzo. *Seiji to bungaku no henkyō*. Tōjusha, 1971. 332p.

Contains essays on propaganda and literature in the works of Shimaki Kensaku, Dazai Osamu, Itō Sei, Mishima Yukio, Takami Jun, and others.

F278　大久保典夫　昭和文学史の構想と分析
Ōkubo Tsuneo. *Showa bungakushi no kōsō to bunseki*. Kōbundō, 19711. 531p.

Analysis of the structure of Showa literature. Consists of discussions of the revolutionary movement during the Showa era, romanticism in relation to the War, literary issues of the postwar period, and literary criticism on Dazai Osamu, Mishima Yukio, Abe Kōbō, etc.

F279　平野　謙　文学・昭和10年前後
Hirano Ken. *Bungaku: Showa 10-nen zengo*. Bungei Shunjūsha, 1972. 277p.

The literature of the 1930's. A collection of essays serialized in *Bungakkai* (the World of literature) in 1960-63.

F280　窪川鶴次郎　昭和十年代文学の立場
Kubokawa Tsurujirō. *Showa 10-nendai bungaku no tachiba*. Kawade Shobō Shinsha, 1973. 377p.

Collection of essays written by the critic. Selected by Odagiri Hideo.

F281　大久保典夫　昭和文学の宿命
Ōkubo Tsuneo. *Showa bungaku no shukumei*. Tōjusha, 1975. 305p.

Describes the development of Showa literature as influenced by the suicides of Akutagawa Ryūnosuke and Dazai Osamu; by the return to romanticism of Hagiwara Sakutarō and Yasuda Yojūrō; by the buraiha (decadents) literature of Hayashi Fumiko, Hirabayashi Taiko and Nozaka Shōjo; and by wartime and postwar period tenkō (conversion) literature.

F282　饗庭孝男　昭和文学私論
Aeba Takao. *Showa bungaku shiron*. Ozawa Shoten, 1976. 275p.

Discusses the expression of self consciousness in writers of the early Showa period: Kobayashi Hideo, Nakajima Atsushi, Kajii Motojirō, Makino Shinkichi, Hōjō Tamio, Kanbayashi Akatsuki, Kitahara Takeo, Itō Sei, Sakaguchi Ango, Dazai Osamu, and Mishima Yukio.

F283　瀬沼茂樹　完本　昭和の文学
Senuma Shigeki. *Kanpon Showa no bungaku*. Tōjusha, 1976. 679p.

Complete collection of previously published works on Showa literature. In 3 parts:

-1 A revised and enlarged edition of the title: 'Showa no bungaku' 1954.

-2 A collection of essays on Showa literature.

-3 A review of 13 writers: Shimazaki Tōson, Masamune Hakuchō, Nogami Yaeko, Tanizaki Jun'ichirō, Arishima Takeo, Aono Suekichi, Yokomitsu Riichi, Hayashi Fusao, Takeda Rintarō, Serizawa Kōjirō, Tanikawa Tetsuzō, Itō Sei, and Ishikawa Yōjirō. Includes bibliographical notes and comments. Illustrations. Index.

F284 平野　謙　昭和文学私論
Hirano Ken. *Showa bungaku shiron*. Mainichi Shinbunsha, 1977. 493p.

A collection of articles serialized in the Mainichi Evening News from 1969 to 1975 documenting wartime literature and thought. Discusses the efforts writers made to prevent their work from being suppressed.

F285 佐伯彰一　物語芸術論
Saeki Shōichi. *Monogatari geijutsu ron*. Kōdansha, 1979. 253p.

A study of the self as expressed in novels by Tanizaki Jun'ichiro, Akutagawa Ryūnosuke, and Mishima Yukio.

F286 昭和文学の諸問題　昭和文学研究会　編
Showa bungaku no shomondai, ed. by Showa Bungaku Kenkyūkai. Kasama Shoin, 1979. 255p. (Showa bungaku kenkyū sōsho)

Issues in Showa literature.

-1 Akutagawa Ryūnosuke, by Kikuchi Hiroshi.

-2 The new sensationalist school, by Yakushiji Noriaki.

-3 Notes on proletarian literature, by Shimada Akio.

-4 Freud and his influence on literature, by Sono Hiroyoshi.

-5 The meaning of the self to Kobayashi Hideo, by Morota Kazuharu.

-6 On Hirotsu Kazuo, by Kori Tsuguo.

-7 One phase of tenkō (conversion) literature: The background of *Saiken* (Reconstruction) magazine, ed. by Shimaki Kensaku, discussed by Takahashi Haruo.

-8 The Japanese romantic movement, by Ōkubo Tsuneo.

-9 Buraiha (decadent) literature, by Tsukakoshi Kazuo.

-10 Postwar writers, by Matsumoto Tetsu.

-11 The new generation, by Ōkōchi Shōji.

-12 Abe Kōbō and Mishima Yukio, by Kubota Yoshitarō.

F287 昭和の文学　日本文学研究資料刊行会　編
Showa no bungaku, ed. by Nihon Bungaku Kenkyū Shiryō Kankōkai. Yūseido, 1981. 318p. (Nihon bungaku kenkyū shiryō sōsho)

A collection of previously published essays on Showa literature, including the wartime and postwar periods. Reference bibliography.

multiple sets

F288 新鋭文学叢書
Shin'ei bungaku sōsho. Kasama Shobō, 1960-61. 12v.

Collected works of 12 contemporary writers: Agawa Hiroyuki, Kojima Nobuo, Yasuoka Shōtarō, Yoshiwara Junnosuke, Endō Shūsaku, Kikumura Itaru, Kaikō Ken, and Ōe Kensaburō. Each volume includes a biographical note and critical comments.

F289 新潮現代文学
Shinchō gendai bungaku. Shinchōsha, 1977-80. 78v.

Collection of contemporary popular novels.

F290 昭和批評大系　村松　剛　等編
Showa hihyō taikei, ed. by Muramatsu Takeshi, et al. Banchō Shobō, 1978. 5v.

Compendium of literary criticism from the Showa era. Each volume consists of reprints of critical essays and documents with explanatory notes. Illustrations and a chronology.

F291 増補　昭和国民文学全集
Zōho Showa Kokumin bungaku zenshū. Chikuma Shobō, 1978-79. 35v.

Enlarged collection of popular literature from the Showa era. Each volume contains representative works by one or more writers of popular fiction with short biographical and explanatory notes.

Thought

tenkō (conversion)

F292 共同研究轉向　思想の科学研究会　編
Kyodō kenkyū tenkō, ed. by Shisō no Kagaku Kenkyūkai. Heibonsha, 1959-62. 3v.

A collection of essays on tenkō, or the 'conversion' of intellectuals and critics, from the prewar period through the postwar period.

F293　本多秋五　轉向文学論
Honda Shūgo. *Tenkō bungaku ron.* Enlarged ed. Miraisha, 1964. 291p.

A pioneer work on tenkō literature, consisting of chapters on Kobayashi Hideo, Kurahara Koreto, Miyamoto Yuriko, and chapters on the meaning and value of tenkō literature.

F294　大久保典夫　轉向と浪漫主義
Ōkubo Tsuneo. *Tenkō to romanshugi.* Shinbisha, 1967. 251p.

Collection of critical essays on the tenkō movement and romanticism in the context of Showa literature.

F295　後藤宏行　轉向と伝統思想
Gotō Hiroyuki. *Tenkō to dentō shisō.* Shisō no Kagakusha, 1977. 351p.

Examines Shinran's religious thought and Saikaku's rhetoric as these appear in the works of Showa tenkō writers and literary critics: Aono Suekichi, Kamei Katsuichirō, Miki Kiyoshi, Takeda Rintarō, and Dazai Osamu. Index.

buraiha (The decadents)

F296　無頼文学研究　森安理文 編
Burai bungaku kenkyū, ed. by Moriyasu Masafumi. Miyai Shoten, 1972. 431p. (Sōsho Kindai bungaku kenkyū)

Collection of essays. Discusses the meaning and history of burai (decadent) thought as it appears in Japanese literature from antiquity to the present. Studies of individual writers include Tanizaki Jun'ichirō, Sakaguchi Ango, Nagai Kafū, Ishikawa Jun, Narushima Ryūhoku, Tsuji Jun, Origuchi Shinobu, Ishihara Jun, and Iwano Hōmei. Bibliography, p. 403-424.

F297　無頼派の文学　無頼派文学研究会 編
Buraiha no bungaku, ed. by Buraiha Bungaku Kenkyūkai. Kyōiku Shuppan Sentā, 1974. 341p. (Ibun sensho)

Collection of essays on buraiha literature. Contains a general introduction, followed by studies of individual writers and their works, Dazai Osamu, Sakaguchi Ango, Oda Sakunosuke, Tanaka Hidemitsu, Ishikawa Jun, Itō Sei, Takami Jun, Isonokami Gen'ichirō, Dan Kazuo, Matsuo Kazumitsu, etc.

Appendix: *Buraiha bungaku jiten,* a dictionary, ed. by the same study group, p.223-239, with a reference bibliography for each topic.

Authors

F298　磯貝英夫　昭和文学作家研究
Isogai Hideo. *Showa bungaku sakka kenkyū.* Kyoto, Yanagiwara Shoten, 1055. 300p.

Issues in literary history from the Taisho to the prewar Showa era. Discusses the works of 10 writers: Makino Shin'ichi, Ibuse Masuji, Yokomitsu Riichi, Kobayashi Hideo, Nakano Shigeharu, Kawabata Yasunari, Takeda Rintarō, Takami Jun, Ishikawa Jun, and Itō Sei. A study of Mori Ōgai is appended. Index.

F299　日沼倫太郎　現代作家論
Hinuma Rintarō. *Gendai sakka ron.* Nanbokusha, 1966. 273p.

Studies of 11 writers including Takami Jun, Tamiya Torahiko, Kojima Nobuo, Shiba Shiro, Kita Morio and Dazai Osamu, etc.

F300　佐々木基一　現代作家論
Sasaki Kiichi. *Gendai sakka ron.* Miraisha, 1966. 250p.

Examines the significance of Showa literature through the works of Abe Tomoji, Kajii Motojirō, Nakano Shigeharu, Hori Tatsuo, Ishikawa Jun, Sakaguchi Ango, Itō Sei, Sata Ineko, and Kubo Sakae.

F301　島田昭男　昭和作家論
Shimada Akio. *Showa sakka ron: itan burai no keifu.* Shinbisha, 1977. 229p.

Genealogy of the libertines. The burai school of thought among Showa writers: Dazai Osamu, Tanaka Hidemitsu, Sakaguchi Ango, Isonokami Gen'ichirō.

F302　巖谷大四　瓦板　昭和文壇史
Iwaya Daishi. *Kawaraban Showa bundanshi.* Jiji Tsūshinsha, 1978. 346p.

Description of sensational events in the prewar and wartime literary world, including the suicide of Akutagawa Ryūnosuke, the murder of Kobayashi Takiji, etc.

F303　中村真一郎　昭和作家論
Nakamura Shin'ichirō. *Showa sakka ron.* Kōsōsha, 1979. 326p.

Studies of the prewar and wartime works of Muroo Saisei, Origuchi Shinobu, Yokomitsu Riichi, Kawabata Yasunari, Kajii Motojirō, Miyoshi Tatsuji, Hori Tatsuo, Funabashi Seiichi, Kanzaki Kiyoshi, Maruoka Akira, Sata Ineko, Takami Jun, Tachihara Michizō, and Katō Michio.

F304　小松伸六　美を見し人は・自殺作家の系譜
Komatsu Shinroku. *Bi o mishi hito wa: Jisatsu sakka no keifu*. Kōdansha, 1981. 330p.

A study of 18 men of letters who committed suicide: Akutagawa Ryūnosuke, Ikuta Shungetsu, Makino Shin'ichi, Eguchi Kichi, Hasuda Zenmei, Dazai Osamu, Tanaka Hidemitsu, Hara Tamiki, Kusaka Yōko, Katō Michio, Hattori Tatsu, Kubo Sakae, Hino Ashihei, Mishima Yukio, Kawabata Yasunari, Kobayashi Miyoko, Murakami Ichirō, and Arima Yoriyoshi.

Novels

F305　日本現代小説の世界　実方　清 編
Nihon gendai shōsetsu no sekai, cd. by Sanekata Kiyoshi. Shimizu Kōbundo, 1969. 386p.

Covers the period from the start of the Sino-Japanese War to the postwar period. The world of fiction is seen through the representative works of 10 writers: Kawabata Yasunari, Nakajima Ton, Dazai Osamu, Hori Tatsuo, Niwa Fumio, Ōoka Shōhei, Hotta Zen'ei, Shiina Rinzō, Shimao Toshio, and Endō Shūsaku.

Poetry

tanka

F306　中野嘉一　新短歌の歴史
Nakano Kaichi. *Shin tanka no rekishi*. Akimorisha, 1967. 393p.

Traces the development of the new tanka movement from the early Showa era to the postwar period through the works of Maeda Yūgure, Toki Zenmaro, Watanabe Junzō, Yashiro Toson, etc. and contributors to the tanka magazine, *Kokufū*. Chronology, 1926-65. Illustrations, Index.

F307　木俣　修　昭和短歌史
Kimata Osamu. *Showa tankashi*. Kōdansha, 1978. 4v. (Kōdansha gakujutsu bunko)

A critical study of tanka groups and their magazines from the first year of the Showa period to 1953. Chronology, 1926-53. Author and subject indexes.

F308　昭和万葉集
Showa Man'yōshū. Kōdansha, 1980. 21v.

The Man'yōshū of the Showa period. A collection of poems recording the political and economic development of the 50 years since 1926, with copious notes. Contains a biographical directory of the poets, an annotated bibliography of wartime collections of poetry, and a chronology of poems composed during 1976-80. Author index.

haiku

F309　松井利彦　近代俳句研究年表
Matsui Toshihiko. *Kindai haiku kenkyū nenpyō: Showa hen*. Ōfūsha, 1968. 678p.

An outline of modern haiku, consisting of a chronology of modern haiku studies, 1926-50. Indexes of titles, poetics, authors, subjects, and first words.

F310　松井利彦　昭和俳句の研究
Matsui Toshihiko. *Showa haiku no kenkyū*. Ōfūsha, 1970. 350p.

A collection of 21 essays first published in the haiku magazines *Hototogisu* and *Kyoshi*. Discusses the haiku movement in the Showa era. Contains a chronology, 1912-50. Illustrations. Index.

shi

F311　昭和詩論の研究　日本近代詩論研究会編
Showa shiron no kenkyū, ed. by Nihon Kindai Shiron Kenkyūkai. Nihon Gakujutsu Shinkōkai, 1974. 800p.

Continuation of "Nihon kindai shiron no kenkyū" (F148). compiled in 4 parts:

-1 Reproductions of poetics on modernism, realism, lyricism, proletarian and anarchist poetry, popular songs, folk songs, children's songs, etc.
-2 Studies of poets.
-3 Chronology of poetics, 1926-45.
-4 Chronology of modern anthologies, 1923-45.

F312　現代詩物語　分銅惇作 等編
Gendaishi monogatari, ed. by Bundō Junsaku and Yoshida Hiroo. Yūhikaku, 1978. 298p.

History of modern lyric poetry.

F313　大岡　信　昭和詩史
Ōoka Makoto. *Showa shishi*. Shichōsha, 1980. 277p.

Surveys the history of Showa poetry from 1921 to 1945, covering dadaism, anarchism, proletarianism, esprit nuveaux, lyricism, and the wartime .poetry of patriotism and resistance. Poets discussed include Miyazawa Kenji, Nishiwaki Junzaburō, Miyoshi Tatsuji, Maruyama Kaoru, Tanaka Fuyuji, Tachihara Michizō, Tanaka Katsumi, Kurahara Shinjirō, Hishiyama Shūzō.

Wartime Literature

F314　巖谷大四　非常時日本文壇史
Iwaya Daishi. *Hijōji Nihon bundanshi*. Chūō Kōronsha, 1958. 216p.

History of literary groups during the War. Under the wartime emergency act literary groups were organized as a unit with writers conscripted as reporters. A brief chronology, 1926-57.

F315　昭和戦争文学全集
Showa sensō bungaku zenshū, ed. by the Editorial committee. Shūeisha, 1964-65. 16v.

A complete collection of Showa war literature, 1928-45. Each volume contains an explanatory essay, a short chronology and a glossary.

V.1 The Manchurian Incident.

V.2 The Chinese offensive.

V.3 Deadlock in China.

V.4 Declaration of the Pacific War on Dec. 8, 1941.

V.5 Deployment of the fleet.

V.6 Battles in the South Seas.

V.7 Army life.

V.8 The naval offensive.

V.9 An army without weapons.

V.10 War diaries of young officers.

V.11 Adolescents in despair during the War.

V.12 A country in despair.

V.13 The atomic bomb.

V.14 Citizen's diaries.

V.15 Voices of the dead.

V.16 (Supplement) Secret documents.

F316　本多秋五　戦時戦後の先行者たち
Honda Shūgo. *Senji sengo no senkōsha tachi*. Enlarged ed. Keisō Shobō, 1971. 480p.

Wartime and postwar literary leaders. Contains critical studies of Miyamoto Yuriko, Nakano Shigeharu, Takami Jun, Kubo Sakae, and others.

F317　鶴岡善久　太平洋戦争下の詩と思想
Tsuruoka Yoshihisa. *Taiheiyō sensō-ka no shi to shisō*. Shorinsha, 1971. 375p.

Collection of essays on nationalistic poetry and the thinking behind it. A chronology of wartime poems, 1934-45.

F318　戦争文学全集　平野　謙　等編
Sensō bungaku zenshū, ed. by Hirano Ken, et al. Mainichi Shinbunsha, 1972. 7v.

A complete collection of war literature.

V.1 Meiji, Taisho.

V.2 Showa prewar and wartime literature.

V.3-6 Showa postwar literature, 1,2,3,4.

V.7 (Suppl.) Consists of war literature of many literary genres, including war songs and political cartoons.

F319　高崎隆治　戦時下の雑誌
Takasaki Ryūji. *Senji-ka no zasshi, sono hikari to kage*. Fūbaisha, 1976. 260p.

Survey of war coverage in 200 major periodicals. Includes reproductions of cover designs.

F320　都築久義　戦時体制下の文学者
Tsuzuki Hisayoshi. *Senji taisei-ka no bungakusha*. Kasama Shoin, 1976. 258p. (Kasama sensho)

Collection of previously published essays on the wartime activities of literary men: Ishikawa Tatsuzo, Dazai Osamu, Hino Ashihei, Kobayashi Hideo, Kubokawa Tsurujirō, Yasuda Yojūrō, Kamei Katsuichirō, and Ozaki Shirō.

F321　高崎隆治　戦争文学通信
Takasaki Ryūji. *Sensō bungaku tsūshin*. Fūbaisha, 1977. 352p.

Consists of critical essays, reminiscences and memoirs by writers from 1937-45. Contains a catalog of the author's collection of wartime literature chronologically arranged by date of publication.

F322　安田　武　定本戦争文学論
Yasuda Takeshi. *Teihon Sensō bungaku ron*. Daisan Bunmeisha, 1977. 349p.

A collection of previously published critical essays on war literature, with emphasis on Yamamoto Yūzō, Kishida Kokushi, Hino Ashihei, Ozaki Shirō, Takeda Taijun, Ueda Hiroshi, Hirotsu Kazuo, etc.

F323　高崎隆治　戦時下文学の周辺
Takasaki Ryūji. *Senjika bungaku no shūhen.*
Fūbaisha, 981. 208p.

A collection of essays on the literature written by
war correspondents during the second World War.

Postwar Period

F324　本多秋五　物語戦後文学史
Honda Shūgo. *Monogatari sengo bungakushi.* Shinchōsha, 1960-65. 3v. in 5 books.

This narrative history of postwar literature was first
serialized in *Shūkan dokushojin.*

V.1 was published in 2 separate formats.
V.2 was published in 2 separate formats under the
title "Zoku monogatari sengo bungakushi."
V.3 concludes the history, chronology and indexes.
Illustrations include portraits.

F325　中村真一郎　戦後文学の回想
Nakamura Shin'ichirō. *Sengo bungaku no kaisō.*
Chikuma Shobō, 1963. 256p. (Chikuma sōsho)

Recollections of postwar literature. Explains the
author's literary background and his postwar experi-
ences with the literary periodical *Kindai bungaku*
and others. Contains biographical explanations of
literary coterie magazines and a chronology,
1935-59, edited by Kokubo Minoru. Illustrations
include group photographs and cover designs of
magazines.

F326　われらの文学　大江健三郎　等編
Warera no bungaku, ed. by Ōe Kenzaburō and Etō
Jun. Kōdansha, 1964-67. 22v.

Our literature: a collection of works by young
writers of the 1960's.

F327　戦後文学展望と課題　小久保　実　編
Sengo bungaku, tenbō to kadai, ed. by Kokubo
Minoru. Kyoto, Shinkōsha, 1968. 478p.

Collection of critical essays on issues of postwar
literature, 1945-55. A bibliography of major works,
source materials, and a chronology, appended.
Portraits.

F328　磯田光一　戦後批評家論
Isoda Kōichi. *Sengo hihyōka ron.* Kawade Shobō
Shinsha, 1969. 276p.

Studies in postwar literary criticism by Fukuda
Tsuneari, Hirano Ken, Hanada Kiyoteru, Haniya
Odaka, Nakamura Mitsuo, Itō Sei, Yoshimoto

Takaaki, and Etō Jun. Contains a history of postwar
criticism.

F329　佐々木基一　戦後文学の内と外
Sasaki Kiichi. *Sengo bungaku no uchi to soto.*
Miraisha, 1970. 283p.

Collection of previously published essays on postwar literature, proletarian literature, comments
about writers, etc.

F330　本多秋五　戦後文学史論
Honda Shūgo. *Sengo bungakushi ron.* Shinchōsha,
1971. 234p.

A study of intellectual disputes concerning the history of postwar literature.

F331　戦後文学論争　大久保典夫　等編
Sengo bungaku ronsō, ed. by Ōkubo Tsuneo, et al.
Banchō Shobō, 1972. 2v.

Disputes over postwar literature. Consists of excerpts of review articles in periodicals grouped
under inclusive topics. Each topic is summarized by
a specialist. Reference bibliography in each volume.
Index.

V.1 -Disputes over subjectivity in literature.
-Men of letters and the War.
-Politics and literature in the postwar period.
-The art of short poems.
-Seikinha (Romantic group).
-Modernism.
-Intelligentsia.
-Genre novels.
-*Lady Chatterley's lover*, by D.H. Lawrence.

V.2 -Disputes over *The stranger* by Albert Camus.
-*Shinkū chitai* (Zone of emptiness) by Noma
Hiroshi.
-Kokumin bungaku (People's literature).
-Contemporary kana usage.
-Marxist literature.
-*Taiyō no kisetsu* (Season of the Sun) by Ishi-
hara Shintarō.
-History of the Showa era.
-*Fuefukigawa* (The River Fuefuki) by Fukuzawa
Shichirō.
-*Aoki ōkami* (Blue Wolf) by Inoue Yasushi.
-Purity of literature.
-Postwar literature.

F332　現代の文学
Gendai no bungaku. Kōdansha, 1972-78. 40v.

Contemporary literature, a collection of works by postwar writers, starting with *Shinkū chitai* (Zone of emptiness). V.38 and V.39 consist of masterpieces of postwar literature. Supplement volume contains a .history of postwar literature and a chronology, 1945-76.

F333　寺田　透　戦後の文学
Terada Tōru. *Sengo no bungaku.* Kawade Shobō Shinsha, 1973. 330p.

Collection of reviews of postwar novels by Noma Hiroshi, Ōoka Shōhei, Shiina Rinzō, Takeda Taijun, Mishima Yukio, Takahashi Kazumi, and others.

F334　武井昭夫批評集
Takei Teruo hihyōshū. Miraisha, 1975. 6v.

Collection of essays by the Marxist writer, Takei Teruo on literary criticism, drama, etc.

F335　谷沢永一　標識のある迷路
Tanizawa Eiichi. *Hyōshiki no aru meiro.* Kansai Daigaku Shuppan Kōhōbu, 1975. 460p.

Discusses literary thought from the Taisho to the postwar period. A list of special issues of periodicals published in the 20 years since the War, and a bibliography of postwar intellectual history, appended.

F336　佐藤静夫　戦後文学の三十年
Satō Shizuo. *Sengo bungaku no 30-nen.* Kōwadō, 1976. 422p.

The Marxist view of 30 years of postwar literature, 1945-75. A collection of serialized articles which first appeared in the Akahata (Red flag) newspaper.

F337　戦後日本文学史，年表　松原新一　等編
Sengo Nihon bungakushi, nenpyō. Revised and enlarged ed. Ed. by Matsubara Shin'ichi, et al. Kōdansha, 1978. 568p.

A history of postwar Japanese literature,
- from the surrender through the 1950's, by Matsubara Shin'ichi;
- from the Peace Treaty through the 1960's, by Isoda Kōichi with a supplementary section giving an outline history for the 1960-70's;
- from 1961-78, by Akiyama Shun.
Chronology, 1945-78, appended. Indexes for personal names, newspaper and periodical titles, and subjects.

F338　戦後の文学・現代文学史　古林　尚 等編
Sengo no bungaku: Gendai bungakushi, ed. by Furubayashi Takashi and Satō Masaru. Yūhikaku, 1978. 292p. (Yūhikaku sensho)

Describes changes in literary thought from the end of the War to the mid-1960's. Bibliographies for some 60 writers and critics, appended. Author index.

F339　中島健蔵　回想の戦後文学
Nakajima Kenzō. *Kaisō no sengo bungaku.* Heibonsha, 1979. 459p.

Recollections of postwar literature, from the surrender to the 'Anpo' (U.S.-Japan Security Treaty) of 1960. Contains an article on the author by Watanabe Kazutami and a bio-bibliography, 1903-79. Chronology, 1920-60. Index.

F340　江藤　淳　落葉の掃き寄せ
Etō Jun. *Ochiba no hakiyose.* Bungei Shunjūsha, 1981. 341p.

'Sweeping fallen leaves': a collection of 10 case studies of material censored during the Occupation period and their effects on postwar Japanese literature.

F341　紅野敏郎　昭和文学の水脈
Kōno Toshirō. *Showa bungaku no suimyaku.* Kōdansha, 1983. 459p.

Evaluates postwar literary coterie magazines, giving editors and group names as well as biographical data.

F342　篠田一士　日本の現代小説
Shinoda Hajime. *Nihon no gendai shōsetsu.* Shūeisha, 1960. 548p.

Continuation of "Nihon no kindai shōsetsu" (F130). A collection of essays on postwar and contemporary novels, serialized in the magazine *Subaru* between 1975-79.

F343　戦後詩大系　嶋岡　晨 等編
Sengoshi taikei, ed. by Shimaoka Shin, et al. San'ichi Shobō, 1970-71. 4v.

Collection of anthologies of 200 postwar poets, arranged in Japanese syllabic order. V.4 contains an outline history of postwar poetry by Ono Jun'ichi, a survey of schools of poets by Shimaoka Akira, and a chronology of anthologies, criticism and events, 1945-69, ed. by Ogawa Kazusuke.

F344　吉本隆明　戦 後 詩 史 論
Yoshimoto Takaaki. *Sengoshi shiron*. Daiwa Shobō, 1978. 275p.

Discusses poetry as an expression of the thought, experience and rhetoric of postwar literature. Index.

F345　戦後文学教育研究史　日本文学教育連盟 編
Sengo bungaku kyōiku kenkyūshi, ed. by Nihon Bungaku Kyōiku Renmei. Miraisha, 1962. 2v.

Discusses research and methodology in the literary education of children after the war. Appended are a chronology of the movement for the literary education of children, 1945-62, and a bibliography on the subject, 1959-62.

INDEX

G

H

Ikeda Genta, C152
Ikeda Kikan, C98,C151
Ikeda Kikan senshu, C59
Ikeda Yasaburo, B94
Ikeda Yasaburo chosakushu, B25
Imai Gen'e, C8,C100
Imai Takuji, C88,C139
Imao Tetsuya, A29,E126
Inja no bungaku, D32
Inja no fubo, D31
Ino Kenji, F19,F241
Inoue Kazuo, E170,E173
Inoue Muneo, C58,D49
Inoura Yoshinobu, A92
Inseiki gengo no kenkyu, D46
Inseiki no kadanshi kenkyu, E76,E92
Inui Katsumi, D75
Ippen to jishu kyodan, D126
Ise monogatari kohon to kenkyu, C129
Ise monogatari no seiritsu to denpon no kenkyu, C120
Ishida Mizumaro, D123
Ishida Yoshisada, D32,D34,D52
Ishikawa Matsutaro, E167
Ishikawa Teiji, F66
Ishikawa Toru, C78,C90
Ishiko Jun, F202
Ishimoda Sho, D85
Ishimura Yasuko, D54
Ishizu Jundo, D6
Isoda Koichi, F327
Isogai Hideo, F27,F297
Itagaki Naoko, F83
Ito Haku, B84
Ito Hiroshi, C143
Ito Hiroyuki, D37
Ito Kazuo, F38
Ito Sei, F56
Ito Shingo, C102
Ito Teiji, D153
Itoga Kimie, D57
Iwabuchi Etsutaro, A132
Iwahashi Koyata, A99
Iwai Yoshio, A122
Iwanami koza: Nihon bungakushi, A32
Iwanami koza: Nihongo, A130
Iwase Houn, C107
Iwaya Daishi, F82,F264,F301,F313
Izawa Motoyoshi, F168
Izumi Shikibu nikki ronko, C144
Izu Toshihiko, F22

J

Janru-betsu hikaku bungakuron, F115

Jikko to geijutsu, F261
Jinsai, Sorai, Norinaga, E42
Jishu bungei kenkyu, D125
Jishu to chusei bungaku, D127
Jodai bungaku kenkyushi no kenkyu, B85
Jodai bungaku: kenkyu to shiryo, B2
Jodai bungaku kokyu, B31
Jodai bungaku ronso, B27,B30
Jodai bungaku to gengo, B28
Jodai chokokushi no kenkyu, B100
Jodai gakusei no kenkyu, C167
Jodaigo chukogo no kenkyu, B93
Jodai Nihon bungaku gaisetsu, B5
Jodai Nihon bungakushi, B18
Jodai Nihon bungaku to Chugoku bungaku, B4
Jodai Nihon koten bungaku no kenkyu, B10
Jodai no kotoba, B91
Jodai shiika no ie to niwa, B101
Joruri ayatsuri shibai no kenkyu, E136
Jorurishi ronko, E139
Joryu bungei kenkyu, F80
Joryu sakkaron, F81
Josei to minkan densho, A113
Josetsu tenkanki no bungaku, F262
Juyo no kiseki, F117

K

Kabuki no jidai, E159
Kabuki no tanjo, E127
Kabuki seiritsu no kenkyu, E130
Kabukishi no gashoteki kenkyu, E128
Kabuki to ayatsuri joruri, E122
Kabuki: yoshiki to dento, E125
Kadokawa Gen'yoshi, A108
Kaga Otohiko, F131
Kageki Hideo, D131
Kagero nikki kenkyu josetsu, C143
Kaiso no sengo bungaku, F338
Kaitei Nihon kayoshi, A82
Kamakura chokokushi no kenkyu, D157
Kamakura chokokushi ronko, D158
Kamakura jidaigo kenkyu, D45
Kamakura jidai monogatari no kenkyu, D105
Kamakura jidai no shozoga, D156
Kameda Tsutomu, C160
Kamei Katsuichiro, F64
Kamei Shunsuke, F236
Kamigata manzai 800 nenshi, E151
Kamigata rakugo no rekishi, E148
Kamio Nobuko, C34
Kami to hito tono aida, F43
Kamo no Chomei no shuhen: Hojoki, D118
Kamo no Mabuchi ron, E109

Kanai Kiyomitsu, D125,D126,D127,D141,D146
Kan'ami to Zeami, D140
Kanashimi no bungaku, F48
Kanazoshi no kenkyu, E64
Kanazoshi shinko, E66
Kanda Hideo, F169
Kanpon Showa no bungaku, F283
Kansho gendaishi, F142
Kansho Nihon koten bungaku, A66
Karaki Junzo, A20,D1,D16,D28
Karonshu, A75
Kasai Sukeharu, E168
Katagiri Yoichi, C73
Katano Tatsuro, C158
Kataoka Yoshikazu, F234
Kataoka Tsutomu, F79
Katarimono bungei no hassei, A108
Katarimono no keifu, A110
(Zotei) Katarimono no kenkyu, D151
Katarimono no kenkyu, E137
Kato Hidetoshi, F196
Kato Shuichi, A14
Katsumoto Seiichiro, F77
Kawaguchi Hisao, C37,C39
Kawakami Mitsugu, D154
Kawakita Michiaki, F200
Kawakita Noboru, C128
Kawano Yorito, B78,B85
Kawaraban Showa bundanshi, F301
Kawatake Mokuami, E121
Kawatake Shigetoshi, A91,A93,A94,E121
Kawatake Toshio, F190
Kawazoe Kunimoto, F2,F69
Kazamaki Keijiro, A2
Kazamaki Keijiro zenshu, A38
Keene, Donald, A86
Keicho irai shoka shuran, E170
Keihan shosekishoshi, E178
Kenkyu shiryo gendai Nihon bungaku, F94
Ken'yusha no bungaku, F229
Kibyoshi kaidai, E60
Kido Saizo, D68
Kiki kayo, B70
Kiki shinwa ronko, B40
Kikkawa Eishi, A106
Kikuchi Ryoichi, D94,D95
Kikuchi Yasuhiko, C66
Kikuchi Yasuo, F144
Kimata Osamu, F159,F161,F306
Kimura Ki, F102,F111,F222,F223
Kinbara Tadashi, C42
Kindai bungaku, F91
Kindai bungaku hyoron taikei, F90
Kindai bungaku kansho koza, F98
Kindai bungaku kenkyu sosho, F85

Kindai bungaku: kenkyu to shiryo, F4
Kindai bungaku no hakkutsu, A29
Kindai bungaku no hyoron to sakuhin, F69
Kindai bungaku no itansha, F139
Kindai bungaku no meian, F39
Kindai bungaku no naka no Sei-O, F109
Kindai bungaku no senseiryoku, F24
Kindai bungaku no tanjo, F218
Kindai bungaku noto, F77
Kindai bungaku ronso, F18
Kindai bungakushi, F11
Kindai bungaku shichoshi, F44
Kindai bungaku soseiki no kenkyu, F238
Kindai bungaku to Kirisutokyo shiso, F37
Kindai bungaku to sono genryu, F32
Kindai bungei hyoronshi, F219
Kindai bungei hyoronshi, Taishohen, F28
Kindai bungei hyoronshu, F6
Kindai buntai hassei no shiteki kenkyu, F118
Kindai buntai keisei shiryo shusei, F120
Kindai engeki no tenkai, F190
Kindai gikyoku no sekai, F181
Kindaigo no seiritsu, F247
Kindai haiku, F169
Kindai haiku kenkyu nenpyo, F308
Kindai haironshi, F170
Kindai kokugo kyoikushi, F123
Kindai meisaku kansho, F58
Kindai Nihon bungaku, F30
Kindai Nihon bungaku hyoronshi, F7,F12
Kindai Nihon bungaku no bunsuirei, F259
Kindai Nihon bungaku no iso, F14
Kindai Nihon bungaku no kozo, F5 ·
Kindai Nihon bungakuron, F2
Kindai Nihon bungaku sakka kenkyu sosho, F78
Kindai Nihon bungakushi, F16
Kindai Nihon bungaku shichoshi josetsu, F38
Kindai Nihon bungakushi no koso, F21
Kindai Nihon bungei no kenkyu, F46
Kindai Nihon fuzokushi, F193
Kindai Nihon gikyokushi, F177
Kindai Nihon kaigashi, F200
Kindai Nihon no bijutsu to bungaku, F98
Kindai Nihon no bungaku kukan, F35
Kindai Nihon no bungaku to shukyo, F36
Kindai Nihon no bungo, F59
Kindai Nihon no jiden, F134
Kindai Nihon no kotoba to shi, F141
Kindai Nihon no sakka-tachi, F67
Kindai Nihon shokumotsushi, F195
Kindai Nihon yoga no tenkai, F199
Kindai no bungaku to bungakusha, F74
Kindai no kokugo, F122
Kindai sakka no kisoteki kenkyu, F66
Kindai sakka ronso, F79

Nihon kindai shiron no kenkyu, F148
Nihon kindaishi to Kirisutokyo, F146
Nihon kindai shosetsu, F125
Nihon kindai shosetsu gairon, F126
Nihon kindai shosetsu no sekai, F128
Nihon kinsei bun'en no kenkyu, E12
Nihon kinsei bungaku no seiritsu, E7
Nihon kinsei bungakushi, E1
Nihon kinsei shiso no kenkyu, E39
Nihon kodai bungakushi, B6
Nihon kodai no densho bungaku no kenkyu, C133
Nihon kodai ongakushiron, B97
Nihon koten bungakushi no kiso chishiki, A7
Nihon koten bungaku taikei, A62
Nihon koten bungaku zenshu, A64
Nihon mangashi, F202
Nihon minzokugaku bunken somokuroku, A147
Nihon minzokugaku taikei, A141
Nihon mojinshi, A109
Nihon mukashi banashi taisei, A117
Nihon ni okeru gaikoku bungaku, F112
Nihon no chohen shosetsu, F131
Nihon no eigaku hyakunenshi, F104
Nihon no geidan, A103
Nihon no gendai shosetsu, F341
Nihon no hanko, E166
Nihon no inja, D33
Nihon no kango, A134
Nihon no kindai bungaku, F34
Nihon no kindai bungaku, Asukai, F3
Nihon no kindai bungaku: hito to sakuhin, F57
Nihon no kindai bungaku: sakka to sakuhin, F73
Nihon no kindaishi, F143
Nihon no kindai shosetsu, F130
Nihon no kinsei jutaku, E158
Nihon no koten geino, A96
Nihon nomin shishi, F145
Nihon no minzoku geino, A95
Nihon no mukashi banashi hikaku kenkyu josetsu, A116
Nihon no ongaku, A107
Nihon no puroretaria bungaku, F49
Nihon no setsuwa, A84
Nihon no shiika, F153
Nihon no watakushi o motomete, F132
Nihon ongaku no rekishi, A106
Nihon puroretaria bungakushiron, F54
Nihon puroretaria bungaku taikei, F50
Nihon romanshugi bungaku kenkyu, A234
Nihon ryoiki no kenkyu, Moriya, C134
Nihon ryoiki no kenkyu, Yagi, C135
Nihon ryoiki no sekai, C136
Nihon ryukokashi, F189
Nihon seikatsu bunkashi, A145
Nihon seishinshi kenkyu, A19
Nihon shakaishugi engekishi, F182

Nihon shijinsen, A77
Nihon shingekishi, Akiba, F174
Nihon shingekishi, Matsumoto, F176
Nihon shinwa, B38
Nihon shinwa no hikaku kenkyu, B42
Nihon shinwa no keisei, B37
Nihon shinwa no kenkyu, B33
Nihon shinwa no kiban, B41
Nihon shinwa no kisoteki kenkyu, B36
Nihon shinwa no kozo, B43
Nihon shinwa no sekai, B34
Nihon shiso taikei, A24
Nihon shizenshugi saiko, F239
Nihon shoki kenkyu, B60
Nihon shoki no kenkyu, B59
Nihon shoki seiritsu no kenkyu, B61
Nihon shomin bunka shiryo shusei, A98
Nihon shuppan bunkashi, F204
Nihon suiri shosetsushi, F136
Nihon tantei sakkaron, F138
Nihonteki shizenkan no kenkyu, A23
Nihon wakashiron, D47
Nikki bungaku gaisetsu, C141
Nikki bungaku no kenkyu, C140
Ningyogeki no seiritsu ni kansuru kenkyu, E134
Ningyo joruri to bunraku, E133
Nippon minshu engekishi, F184
Nishida Masaru, A29,F24,F277
Nishida Masayoshi, F129
Nishida Sadamoto, C146
Nishida Taketoshi, F211
Nishida Tadakazu, C12
Nishio Koichi, D93
Nishio Minoru, A29,D5,D120
Nishioka Toranosuke, A139
Nishitsunoi Masayoshi, B47
Nishizawa Masaji, D113
Noda Hisao, E5,E56
Nogaku no kigen, D144
(Zoku) Nogaku no kigen, D145
Nogakuron kenkyu, D138
Nogaku zensho, D148
Nogeiron, D137
Noguchi Motohiro, C122
Noguchi Takehiko, E113
Noji Shusa, D155
No no keisei to Zeami, D139
No no kenkyu, D141
No: kami to kojiki no geijutsu, D142
Noma Koshin, E77
Nose Asaji chosakushu, A42
Nose Asaji. E93
Noson butai no sogoteki kenkyu, E123
No to kyogen, D146
Numoto Katsuaki, C36

Shinpojumu Nihon no shinwa, B39
Shinsen Nihon koten bunko, A65
Shinsoban Nihon bundanshi, F84
Shin tanka no rekishi, F305
Shintei haiku shiriizu, F172
Shintei kindai Nihon bungaku no keifu, F20
Shinto to bungaku, A21
Shinwa no genzo, B35
Shioda Ryohei, F213,F240
Shirai Tadanori, D119
Shiriizu kodai no bungaku, B15
Shiryo Nihon bungakushi, A11
Shi shosetsu sai-hakken, F129
Shi shosetsu sakkaron, F127
Shizenshugi bungaku, F232
Shizenshugi no kenkyu, F226
Shodaimyo no gakujutsu to bungei no kenkyu, E10
Shoheiko to hangaku, E164
Shohon Chikamatsu zenshu, E145
Shoki emakimono no fuzokushiteki kenkyu, C154
Shoki haikai no tenkai, E92
Shoki kayoron, B71
Shokumotsu sanken, E173
Shoku seikatsu kindaishi, E194
Showa bungaku e no shogen, F275
Showa bungaku 14-ko, F274
Showa bungaku no seiritsu, F273
Showa mondai no shomondai, F285
Showa bungaku no shukumei, F281
Showa bungaku no suimyaku, F340
Showa bungaku sakka kenkyu, F297
Showa bungaku seishinshi, F270
Showa bungakushi, Ara, F269
Showa bungakushi, Hirano, F272
Showa bungakushi, Yoshida, F271
Showa bungakushi no koso to bunseki, F278
Showa bungaku shiron, Aeba, F282
Showa bungaku shiron, Hirano, F284
Showa bungaku shiron, Ogasawara, F276
Showa haiku no kenkyu, F309
Showa hihyo taikei, F289
Showa 10 nendai bungaku no tachiba, F280
Showa Man'yoshu, F307
Showa no bungaku, F286
Showa no sakkatachi, F76
Showa sakkaron, F302
Showa sakkaron: itan burai no keifu, F300
Showa senso bungaku zenshu, F314
Showa shiron no kenkyu, F310
Showa shishi, F312
Showa tankashi, F306
Shui wakashu no kenkyu, C13
Shuppan koto hajime, E174
Shuzui Kenji chosakushu, E120
Soka no kenkyu, D72

Soma Tsuneo, F239
Soraigakuha: Jugaku kara bungaku e, E41
Sosho Nihon bungakushi kenkyu, A29
Suda Atsuo, A90
Sugae Masumi no tabi to nikki, E87
Sugano Masao, B55
Sugimoto Tsutomu, E52
Sugisaki Shigeto, C55
Suwa Haruo, E124,E128,E174
Suzuki Hiromichi, C87,C91,C117,C119
Suzuki Keizo, C154
Suzuki Tomotaro, C4
Suzuki Toshio, E175
Suzuki Tozo, E88

T

Tachikawa Kiyoshi, E67
Taguchi Kazuo, D147
Tahara Tsuguo, E38
Tai Shonosuke, D135,E117
Taiheiki no hikaku bungakuteki kenkyu, D91
Taiheiyo sensoka no shi to shiso, F316
Taikei monogatari bungakushi, C97
Taisho bungaku no hikaku bungakuteki kenkyu, F254
Taisho bungakuron, F257
Taisho bungakushi, F252
Taisho haidanshi, F267
Taishoki no bungei hyoron, F251
Taisho no bungaku, F258
Taisho sakkaron, F265
Taisho tankashi, F266
Taishu bungaku, F135
Taishu bungakuron, F137
Taishu geino shiryo shusei, A104
Tajima Ikudo, C72
Takada Mamoru, E81,E82
Takada Mizuho, F39,F47
Takagi Ichinosuke zenshu, A41
Takagi Takeo, F140
Takahashi Gen, C124
Takahashi Kazuo, C15
Takahashi Mitsugu, C132
Takahashi Seiichiro, E155
Takami Jun, F270
Takamori Kuniaki, F123
Takano Tatsuyuki, A82
Takasaki Masahide chosakushu, B24
Takasaki Masahide Hakushi kiju kinen ronbunshu, A59
Takasaki Ryuji, F318,F320,F322
Takata Mizuho, F260
Takeda Motoharu, D62
Takeda Yukichi chosakushu, B25
Takei Teruo hihyoshu, F333